Storm Passage

By the same author

A FIGHTING CHANCE (with Chay Blyth)
JOURNEY TO ARDMORE
AMAZON JOURNEY
COCKLESHELL JOURNEY
GINO WATKINS—A BIOGRAPHY

JOHN RIDGWAY

Storm Passage

HODDER AND STOUGHTON

LONDON SYDNEY AUCKLAND TORONTO

For Jamie, Krister and Staff
—A Grand Crew

Contents

Illustrations

Acknowledgment
* Gavin Young

Maps and Diagrams

1

The Pick-Up

"I want you to build me the strongest sailing boat ever built," said I.

Tony Taylor, chief executive of Camper and Nicholson, pulled his large frame just a little more upright in the strong chair behind his desk. "Who's going to pay for it?" he asked, dusting the lapels of his navy blazer with the back of his plump right hand. Behind him, I could see clear across the bustling Gosport ferry terminal, to where a fleet of sleek black submarines nestled in the lee of the Blockhouse Fort, at the mouth of Portsmouth harbour. It was 20th March 1973 and the sun beamed from a clear blue sky, spring was with us and it was a time for optimism.

"I'm going to pay for it!" I heard myself reply, full of boldness. "There will be no backers, so it'll have to be small—I've thought a lot about this, and your Nicholson 32 without a motor, and specially built to my requirements, is the boat I'm looking for."

"O.K., we can do that for you," he said, getting up without further ado, "let's go and take a look at one in the marina."

It was warm outside, and as we strolled along the smart wooden pontoons the air was filled with the clatter of halliards, slapping in the breeze against the tall masts of millions of pounds' worth of big luxury yachts. By the time we reached a small businesslike boat, Tony had already explained something of the extensive tests his company had made on the Nicholson 55 *Adventure*, which the Royal Navy were entering in the forthcoming Whitbread Round the World Race. Everything gained from these trials could of course be built straight into my boat. It

9

needed no more than ten minutes aboard the sturdy second-hand 32 to convince me this was indeed the boat I was looking for: the heavy-displacement long deep keel and the five hundred improvements made over the years, when more than 270 of these boats had been built, made it my ideal cruising boat.

Tony agreed to call a planning meeting for the project and I left the yard, with that slightly breathless feeling which always seems to go with the start of a risky venture.

The voyage I had in mind was a winter cruise in the North Atlantic with my wife Marie Christine, and our six-year-old daughter Rebecca, plus two or maybe three of the instructors from our School of Adventure at Ardmore in north-west Sutherland, Scotland. The idea was to show Rebecca something of the outside world before she had to leave Ardmore for her schooling somewhere on the 'mainland' of Britain; for until now she had led a pretty isolated life, going to school each day up through the wood to the small blue house where her teacher, Mrs. Ada Bell, lived. One of the national women's weekly magazines had thought Rebecca's life so unusual, that they had published an article on it entitled 'The Loneliest Little Girl in Britain'. Because of our work at Ardmore from March to the end of September each year, our family voyage would have to take place in winter—when the weather in the North Atlantic is probably as bad as anywhere on earth.

We planned to sail from Ardmore, which is just twelve miles south of Cape Wrath, in the last days of September 1974 and our first port of call was to be Madeira, where we hoped to walk across the 5,000-foot-high island before sailing on to one of the outlying Canary Islands. From then on it was unlikely that we would see any more yachts—the summer season would be well and truly finished. Our next destination was to be Villa Cisneros on the edge of the Sahara Desert, which Rebecca would find very different from the mountains and lochs of Ardmore, and then we hoped to head further south and visit some of the scattered Cape Verde Islands. By this time it would be nearing the end of November 1974, and we would have to beat 1,500 miles against the Trade Winds to reach the Azores in the early days of December.

The 1,700 mile voyage from the Azores back to Ardmore in December could be nothing but violent; sooner or later the boat would be tested to the limit—and with my wife and child aboard I was pretty keen that the boat should be strong enough to pass that test. To this end I was prepared to spend a lot of time during 1974 with Halmatic, who would build the hull and Camper and Nicholson who would fit out the finished boat.

It was exactly nine months after we had first talked to Tony Taylor of Camper and Nicholson, on 19th December 1973, that my wife Marie Christine and I stood on the bridge leading across to the marina pontoons looking down on *English Rose V*. The air was cold now, and the clatter from the forest of masts was much greater in a rising south-westerly gale. Smuts from factory chimneys and grit blown from the car park, had laid a dirty blanket on the white boat's new decks. Several men were still working on the rigging and electric wiring, and fitting the winches and self-steering gear, and this gave an impression of chaos. She looked much smaller than any of the other boats nearby, but this couldn't conceal the hunched power of her lines. The uncluttered foredeck, stout twin backstays, and the thicker than usual gold anodised mast which was now raked slightly aft to maximise her windward performance, all added to a general impression of strength. Her gleaming white hull set heavily in the water, almost submerging the coats of dark red antifouling paint which protected her from barnacles, and the lack of even portholes, let alone windows, lent a slightly sinister air which marked her out from the other boats.

I was quite satisfied with the boat, even before I first stepped aboard, and felt her comforting steadiness beneath my feet; to me she seemed a cross between a Dreadnought and an ocean racer. Marie Christine, perched on the food lockers amid all the muddle in the cabin, said she thought the boat had a happy friendly atmosphere.

All the same, there were problems: in seven days' time, on Boxing Day, I was to set sail for Ardmore in the north-west corner of Scotland, nearly a thousand miles away up the stormy west coast of Britain. As is usual with special projects, delivery dates had fallen sadly behind-hand and now there were only two more working days before the yard began its Christmas holidays. There was still much to be done and so many men were working on board that they tended to get in each other's way. Quite clearly we were not going to be able to carry out the promised sail trials in the comparatively sheltered waters of the Solent, and with no engine to fall back on I was feeling pretty worried about the trip home to Scotland.

Most of the boats in the marina were battened down for the winter, there was never a sight of another sail. The optimism of spring was long gone; paying for the boat had been difficult as it had cost a lot more than I had originally estimated, and to make things worse, the oil crisis was in full swing; fuel was now so hard to come by that the drive down from Scotland with the Land Rover full of essential equipment for the boat was an achievement in itself. The yard was also having trouble with power cuts and fuel shortages and alternative travel was complicated by rail strikes. People all about were talking of economic collapse and all in all the buying of a new boat seemed a bit daft.

Inflation was making everything I touched wildly more expensive than I could afford, so that evening I decided to drive to London and visit friends rather than get under the workmen's feet on the boat and be tempted to buy any more equipment. Marie Christine decided to brave the strike-troubled train journey back to her mother's home in Brighton, to get on with the Christmas shopping with our six-year-old daughter Rebecca.

It never takes long for London to give me something of a sinking feeling, and when I returned to Gosport only a day later, on the morning of Friday 21st, I felt as if all my colours were fast running dry. Laden with charts, pilots, sextant and other navigation paraphernalia, I bundled aboard to find that work was to more or less stop for Christmas around lunchtime. The Christmas spirit was already well under way, and the clank of empty beer cans accompanied by cheerful ribaldry, thrown down from the sail loft only served to heighten my own panic at the unfinished state of the boat. One scrap of good news was that *Adventure* had won the first leg, from Portsmouth to Cape-town, of the Whitbread Round the World Race. The afternoon dissolved in merrymaking, so I decided to sleep on board to make sure that the essential jobs there were finished early next day, as the yard had kindly agreed to put some men on over-time on the Saturday morning.

Nestling into my sleeping bag that night, my nose was filled with the exotic scent of freshly sawn teak mixed with the harsher smells of new fibre glass and synthetic glues. It was quite dark because the marina lights were all switched off to save electricity.

There were three reasons why I had to risk sailing the boat up the west coast of Britain in the middle of winter: first of all the boat and I needed a good trial before going firm on the voyage planned with Marie Christine and Rebecca for the following winter. The second reason was simple economics. I could not afford the cost of hiring a low-loader lorry for the 1,500 mile round trip, and thirdly the bridges north of Perth were too low for the boat to be carried on a fish lorry.

Lying there, alone in the dark, I wondered how the trip would differ from my other experiences at sea . . . we would have a roof over our heads so at least it should be better than the ninety-two-day rowing trip Chay Blyth and I had made from Cape Cod, U.S.A., across to the Aran Isles off Galway in 1966, but then that had been in summer. My abortive fifty-day solo sail from the Aran Isles to Brazil in the 1968 single-handed Round the World Race had also been in the summer, and six years of living and teaching offshore sailing on the west coast of Scotland had taught me that the North Atlantic in summer is a vastly different place in the winter.

"What are you worrying about?" I asked myself. "It's paid for, and it's all so simple—just hoist the sails and push off!"

But another small voice argued "Only a fool would set off on a trip like this at this time of year—and with no sea trials either —you're asking for trouble, and there'll be plenty of it where you're going!" I dozed off, ambivalent as ever, only to wake in the small hours with a sore throat and the beginnings of a cold, caused no doubt by the fumes from the fibre glass and glues. Before it got light on Saturday morning, I stalked off to the café just outside the main gate to the yard, for a feed of egg and chips and a couple of cups of hot tea, which put a better face on things.

Although all the vital things were done by noon, there was no doubt it was going to be a rough trip: only one bunk and no heating except for a couple of gas rings. I was more than pleased when Jim McEwen and his father arrived in mid-morning to spend the day helping with the stowage. Jim is sales manager for my publishers, Hodder and Stoughton, and his encouragement has been a welcome support at the start of most of my journeys—never more so than on that grittily cold December morning, when the sky came over rather black and storm cones were hoisted over the Navy H.Q. buildings across the harbour I realised this was it, I had the boat, I just had to sail her home.

Half way through the afternoon the tall bearded figure of Jamie Young emerged from the dank mist. The first to arrive of a total crew of three and myself, he was dressed in jeans and a yellow oilskin top, and he carried only a small ditty bag slung over his shoulder. Slim and yet unusually strong at twenty-two, his short bouncing gait always makes him look as if he'd be more comfortable trotting.

"Aye Aye," he muttered, gruff as ever, as he swung through the shrouds to land like a cat on the deck. "I see they haven't been changing their shoes to come on here, then," he laughed, remembering the fierce rules applied to *English Rose IV* at home at Ardmore.

"You needn't worry, boy, it'll all change when we leave here!" I retorted, and his only reply was a grin as he set about making a cup of tea for everyone. Jamie seemed pleased with the boat and quickly settled into my bunk for a lonely Christmas on board, not at all put out by the miserable rail journey down from Ardmore. After six years with us in Scotland I knew him pretty well. He was unusually hardy and very keen on boats and the sea and I felt we'd manage on our own if we had to. All the same, I felt a bit guilty at leaving him alone on board at Christmas, as I drove along the coast towards Brighton that evening to be with my family.

My cold reached its peak on Christmas Day, and the outlook was thoroughly miserable. I even stopped running along the beach in the mornings, and no amount of visits with Rebecca to see the dolphins performing at the Aquarium could cheer me up. The weather charts on T.V. looked grim and I wanted to get on and get it over and done with.

Francis Ash, twenty-one, a dinghy sailing instructor for three years at Ardmore and currently reading law at York University, phoned in to say he would be at the boat by eleven o'clock on Boxing Day morning. The fourth crew member was to be

Chris Brasher, who won an Olympic gold medal for the steeple-chase at Melbourne in 1956 and who had since worked extensively on newspapers and in T.V. I had greatly enjoyed his visits to Ardmore and I was really looking forward to his own special brand of enthusiasm on the coming voyage. However, it was not to be, for at ten thirty in the evening of Christmas Day the phone rang: it was Brasher to say that he couldn't come owing to pressure of work.

Now we were three.

Boxing Day dawned grey and damp along the Brighton sea front. After a sad farewell to her mother, Marie Christine, Rebecca and I drove our heavily laden Land Rover towards Gosport. Fine drizzle kept the windscreen wipers busy, but there was little traffic. I could tell from the long silences that Marie Christine was as worried as I, and arriving at the yard in Gosport came as something of a relief, because it gave us an excuse to be too busy to talk as we loaded the boat up with food. Quite soon it was done, however, and even though Francis had not yet arrived Marie Christine decided to set off with Rebecca on the long drive to Ardmore—as far distant from Gosport as the Pyrenees or Munich. It would take three or four days, driving alone and running the gauntlet of the diesel oil shortage; also there was a diversion along the way, to pick up a quarter ton of lead ingots for ballast in one of the Shetland-type boats at home.

Jamie was full of chat; he had had a lively Christmas, after all, with the Bathgate brothers, who had just spent nearly a month bringing a powerful motor cruiser down the east coast from the Firth of Forth. The recounting of their escapades helped me to get over the sadness of Marie Christine and Rebecca's departure.

"Hallo," called Francis Ash, as he came gliding down the pontoon towards the boat. Jamie and I were both delighted to see him again; he looked as cool as ever with an open intelligent face and crinkly brown hair. He was accompanied by a slight fair-haired girl who turned out to be a fellow student at York, but she only stayed long enough to see him safely aboard.

Within ten minutes we were away. High spring tide was at 1100, and we wanted to get well on our way on the ebb. The wind dropped to nearly nothing for a while and we just seemed to hang in the narrows between Portsmouth and Gosport until quite suddenly, the falling tide really got going and sucked us out into the Solent. A fresh westerly breeze sprang up and we headed for Bembridge Ledge at the eastern end of the Isle of Wight, under full sail. There was no swell and although everything was coloured in shades of grey, we made good progress past the grim round forts which guard the approaches to Portsmouth. The three of us were good friends and we quickly settled down to the idea of a routine of two hours on watch and four off. Our own jokes and laughs were supported by plenty of good cheer from the Boxing Day radio, and even the shipping forecasts seemed keen to help with light north-westerly winds which would allow us to make south-west down and out of the English Channel.

Once round Bembridge Ledge buoy we headed south-west along the misty southern shores of the Isle of Wight towards St. Catherine's Point lighthouse, which shines for seventeen miles from a point over a hundred feet above the island's southern tip. Jamie and I were already impressed with the improved steadiness and performance to windward of this new boat when compared with the boat in which I sailed in the single-handed Round the World Race in 1968, and which we had used continuously ever since, at Ardmore. The long deep keel of the new boat allowed us much closer to the wind than the bilge keels of the other one, and there was no leeway.

It was cold at night. We had duvet jackets to wear under our oilskins and plenty of clothes besides, but two hours on watch was long enough. Unfortunately the wind fell more or less calm in the long dark hours, and everything began to drip with condensation inside the cabin, and misty drizzle on the sails outside. Cold and miserable we were each in turn seasick on our night watches, as a long swell rolling up the Channel from the North Atlantic outside, reached us when we cleared the Isle of Wight. Of course we hadn't yet got used to the change of conditions from Christmas ashore and Francis Ash complained of stomach pains which we unsympathetically put down to over-eating. It wasn't until the evening of 28th December, two days later, that we found ourselves fifteen miles south of Eddystone Lighthouse, which stands on a rock about twelve miles south of Plymouth. The wind had backed to the south and

at last it looked as if we might round Land's End without having
to tack south again. We were feeling well enough recovered
from the seasickness to choke down hot soup and curry, and
Francis made no mention of his stomach ache. The one black
spot was the shipping forecast, which always told of gales raging
in those northern sea areas we were bound for.

"Thames. Dover. Wight. Portland. Plymouth: South-
westerly 4 to 5. Increasing 5 to 7 to gale 8. Rain. Moderate."
It was half past midnight in the early hours of Saturday,
29th December. The shipping forecaster's voice sounded distant
and clinical, and we all felt a bit warmer when the B.B.C.
resumed its Night Ride programme.

By two o'clock we had tacked far enough south to give the
Lizard a good clearance, so I was able to lay a course to the
west, free enough of the wind, to have us romping along at
more than five knots. When I crawled out into the cockpit for
my next watch at eight in the morning the wind had dropped
off a bit but the glass was falling too; up ahead the baleful light
of Wolf Rock blinked through another raw drizzling December
morning.

The Wolf is a Godforsaken sort of spot, the light rears 110 feet
out of the sea some eight miles south-west of Land's End. I had
passed it several times before on different ships and boats, twice
when sailing from Plymouth to Fastnet Rock, off south-west
Ireland and back; it's not the sort of place you forget. Once
round it, however, we could turn north for the first time, easing
the sheets on a broad reach before a stiff breeze from the south-
west. It was like rounding the corner, the gales were most likely
to come out of the south or south-west, and from now on we
should be running for home. By the time we had finished a good
breakfast of hot porridge it was ten o'clock and fully light, and
five miles away to our right lay the hunched brown shape of
Land's End.

The long expected gale came all right in the early afternoon
and as we bowled along under only a scrap of a storm jib we
began to feel sick again, and the seas started to build up beneath
a ragged grey sky. Morale sagged and we had a rotten night of
it when the wind veered into the north-west and we had to bash
along close hauled towards the Irish Sea. The only compensa-
tion was that it was the first day the Walker log, with its trailing

spinner, had clocked up more than a hundred miles for the new boat's passage through the water.

When the wind veered still further into the north we tacked to and fro for a bit, but the dawn found us lying below decks feeling too sorry for ourselves to move. A cup of tea put a bit of life back into us, and the glass which had dropped to 1014 at midnight was now rising rapidly; but before going on watch at noon, Francis admitted his stomach was not getting any better. When I relieved him in the cockpit at two, he paused for a minute before going below.

"You know John, I've always been afraid of the sea . . . that's one of the reasons I came with you on this trip—to see if I could conquer the fear," he said rather earnestly.

"Huh! Now you tell me!" I laughed, trying to make light of it. What else could I say? It all sounded like a rotten weak plot for some lousy movie. I was feeling far from confident myself, and having a lot of difficulty holding down a couple of dry biscuits which served for breakfast and lunch combined. What I needed now on this gale-torn trip with hundreds of miles of rocky lee shore stretching ahead of our motorless boat, was reassurance—not a weakening crew. And yet the moment I'd said it I knew I'd done wrong, but I've learnt there are few things which can be unsaid: and I was left alone in the cockpit with the memory of the hurt look on his long nervous face. No one said much after that, we just got on with what had to be done and kept quiet, keeping to ourselves the thoughts of how far it was, how much stormier it must get and how close the hostile coast would be all the while.

And so we came to the last day of 1973, and, as with all things, the bad weather came to an end. Oh! the sun came out and a light breeze from the south-east wafted us along at a steady four knots in calm, calm water. Out came all the damp sleeping bags and clothes to dry in the sun on deck. As the grey skies disappeared so did the seasickness, and in its place great appetites which called for the sausages so carefully bought for us by Marie Christine—where was she now, I wondered—she was expected in Inverness for the New Year with Rebecca who was to stay with her friend Shona. . . .

"Bad news," growled Jamie, while I was shaving. "They're bad!" And with that he lobbed the soggy bundle out of the hatch and into the sea. "Still the boat's going well, isn't it?" I replied, knowing what Marie Christine would say when she heard of the waste.

"Porridge and fried eggs, then," Jamie grinned, ruefully.

It was a glorious day, never to be forgotten. Soft sunlight ricocheted into every part of the boat lighting the inside in a way I had forgotten was possible during the nine long months since Tony Taylor and I had sat inside that other Nicholson 32 back in March. At once everything seemed possible again, we began to notice the fulmars and kittiwakes together with the great black back gulls once more; they had been playing around us all the time since we had left Portsmouth, but we had ignored them, preferring to look inward in self pity, at our misery. We waved gaily at a fishing boat, which altered course to inspect such a small sailing boat so far from port in mid-winter: oh yes, it was as if we felt really at home.

Perhaps it was the comforting sound of the little Honda generator which cheered us up as it recharged our two big 102 amp/hour 12 volt batteries, because as soon as it was turned off the glass, which had held all day at a new high of 1027, began to fall once more. The shipping forecast at 1755 hours offered southerly winds increasing to gale force 8. At least it was behind us and visibility was expected to be good to moderate with a little rain at times.

"We'll run up the east coast of Ireland, that'll give us a bit of shelter if the wind veers to the west at all—which is what you'd expect, isn't it?" I asked Jamie, and he nodded thought-fully.

So began a great run: at half-past eight in the evening of New Year's Eve we had Tuskar Rock lighthouse abeam two miles off on our port side as we rushed north. At this sentimental time I thought of all those countless thousands of Irish emigrants for whom, in the great days of sail, 'the dropping of Tuskar light' on the south-east corner of Eire, was often the last they ever saw of their beloved homeland. And again I remembered the wonderful welcome the Aran islands and the people of Galway had given Chay Blyth and me when we landed after rowing across the Atlantic in '66, and all the sad songs they had sung for Marie Christine and me when I went back to start on the Round the World Race in '68. 'Danny Boy', a crowded table in a low-ceilinged smoky room, a blind pianist . . . no I couldn't forget.

The New Year was only twenty minutes old and by that time we had the Arklow light vessel close abeam on our port side and giving two big flashes of the season's greetings every twenty seconds. It was a 'grand New Year' as they say at home, we were tearing along under the storm jib again but the seasickness had not come back—there was all the interest of the lights along the coastline, and there was the New Year with all its hopes too. Jamie and I felt exhilarated, only Francis was quiet, and secretly I feared there might be more wrong than just the stomach ache. I was trying hard not to think about the grumbling appendix he had once had trouble with at Ardmore. He looked pale and it seemed to me that he was making a big effort not to complain.

Although it was blowing a good gale the visibility was pretty clear next morning and I could see the distant lights of Belfast to the south-east: to get in there meant a long uncomfortable bash to windward. No, the best thing would be to run on north for another thirty miles or so; this would bring us to the north-east of Ireland. If Francis decided to call a halt there, we could make for somewhere along the north coast. Personally, at this time I thought he would get no worse and once home it would all look no more than a storm in a teacup. That damned optimism again!

Grim daylight found us not far offshore near Cushendall and Cushendun, it was comforting to watch the house lights coming on one by one and the first vehicles stabbing the dark with their headlights as the drivers moved off to work on that first Wednesday morning of the New Year. Brooding high above these coastal villages lay the cloud shrouded mountains of the north-east.

"I know this area pretty well," remarked Jamie as we looked at the chart when I handed over the watch to him at ten o'clock. "You see," he said, munching a fried egg sandwich, "I lived here—at Ballycastle for fifteen years when I was young; we had a farm."

"What about all these overfalls around Rathlin Island?" I asked, surprised and pleased at this bonus information.

"Well I wouldn't cut off the corner and try to get through the

Sound, I remember they used to tell terrible tales about the tide-race in there," he grinned mischievously.

We were looking at the very north-east corner of Ireland. The North Channel, as it is called, between Ireland and the southern end of the Mull of Kintyre in Scotland, is scarcely a dozen miles across. On the chart the whole area is liberally marked for overfalls and tide rips, and eddies; a southerly blow like this would kick up ugly confused seas against a strong tide running down through the area in daylight.

Francis told us now that he had a lump on his lower right abdomen. I gave him four tablets of tetracyclene, a powerful antibiotic which in military use had proved capable of keeping most infections at bay. Ten minutes later he vomited. Much of the drug must have come up again.

"This is the situation, Francis old top," I said. "You came off watch at eight this morning, and you're due on again at noon."

"Yes," he replied weakly, from under the sleeping bags and blankets on top of the food bins.

"Well clearly you can't do it—you just aren't well enough. It looks definitely like your appendix to Jamie and me. What do you think?" I paused, trying to think what to say next.

"Yes, I'm sure it's the appendix," our friend groaned, in between spasms of pain which caused him to jack-knife his knees as he lay on his side. The rolling boat wasn't helping.

"Well, in less than an hour we will be abeam of Rathlin Island—if we don't turn west and land on the north coast of Ireland somewhere. . . . The next place will be on one of the Hebrides, and that's not so good. Shall we put in now?" I said, my mind pretty well made up.

"I'm sorry, yes, I think we should," Francis replied slowly. I gave him four more tetracyclene and reassured him as best I could, before poking my head over into the cockpit to discuss the next move with Jamie, who was adamant that the nearest possible place we could put in was Portrush a good fifteen miles to the west along the north coast.

"We must read the Pilot over and over again," I said, as we gobbled down the remains of Marie Christine's Christmas cake.

"What will you do when you get there?" he asked.

"Nip ashore and dial 999 I suppose—what do you think?" I replied, thumbing the index of the Pilot for the name Portrush.

"Well that seems quickest—I've never done it before," he chuckled, then suddenly—"Look there's the Giant's Causeway!" and so it was; four hundred foot high columns of basalt, what the Pilot described as 'an iron-bound coast fringed by heavy surf'. Grand though the sight was, we were too busy to look for long. The entry to Portrush was not going to be easy, and it was almost certainly going to be dark by the time we reached the port.

It was the usual grey windswept afternoon, but the coast was close and it looked cold too; the one good point was the flat sea as we rushed along, close under the lee of the land. At over six knots in smooth water we left a foaming white wake and it was also comfortable for Francis. The coast was now trending towards the south-west, and we were now coming quite close to the wind.

In order to avoid too much tacking at the harbour mouth we decided to pass inside the Skerries, a chain of rocky islets some two miles long, with a channel of only about two hundred yards in width between them and the mainland. At the western end of the channel is Ramore Head, on which part of Portrush is built, in order to keep in the middle of this channel it was necessary to keep the Storks beacon astern of us bearing 083°. In the failing light and poor weather prevailing, and with a chart entitled 'Scotland West Coast—Approaches to the Firth of Clyde', this was really the sort of caper best kept for emergencies, but then this was an emergency so we did it—at least we didn't have to wonder whether or not the engine would start!

Once round Ramore Head we could see the light at the entrance to the harbour. It looked pretty narrow.

"We'll nip in—have a quick look round and nip out again. Then think about it outside, nip in again and drop the anchor," I laughed at Jamie; if it wasn't so serious it would be good fun.

"O.K." he nodded, and I could tell this was just his style. "I'll go up and clear the anchor for dropping." And with that he plunged off through the chilly spray on his way to the anchor hatch where it was set into the foredeck.

It was getting hard to see now. We fairly crashed through the narrow gap between the big walls, which enclose the little harbour, and we found ourselves in a small patch of inky water which glinted with the reflected lights from the shops, street lights, and wharves around.

"Ready about," I roared to the yellow figure wedged up in the bows.

"Lee ho!" I shoved the helm hard away from me. Nine tons of boat made a tight turn, first facing up into the wind which howled off the mainland, then as the headsail thundered, on round until the bows were facing the harbour entrance once more. I tightened the jib sheets and we shot out into the open sea again.

"What d'you reckon?" I said, as Jamie joined me in the cockpit.

"Best plan seems where we went about, astern of those fishing boats on the southern side of the harbour—I'll have the anchor ready to go."

"Yeah, that seems best, I'll try and stop her, so wait till I shout before lobbing the anchor over," I said, getting ready to go about once more.

The next run in went well again, except I wondered how many times I could shoot through at such speed without something going wrong—like a collision, either with another boat or the wall.

In retrospect I think this made me lose my concentration.

Half way from the entrance to the main street which lined the back wall of the harbour I put the boat about again, I could see Jamie's figure now stooped over the anchor, ready to let it go.

Instead of stopping, as she came up into the wind with both sails flying, the heavy boat (fifty per cent heavier than my other boat *English Rose IV*) continued to make way—alarmingly—towards the squat shapes of the fishing boats where they lay at their moorings.

"Now!" I squealed in panic, above the thundering sails.

The rattle of fifteen fathoms of $\frac{5}{16}$ inch chain cable came back in reply.

"Oh well, at least we're alive," I thought, as the fishing boats came nearer and nearer. A collision was inevitable. There was a sudden jolt, which threw me forward, but I hung onto the tiller. The anchor had taken hold. The boat was now being pulled backwards from the bow, it swung broadside against the chain and then the relentless wind took control and pushed her steadily back.

Within a minute we were lying comfortably at our anchor, a long way astern of the fishing boats—more or less in the centre of the harbour. Jamie had already dropped both sails, and while I secured them with sail ties, he was busy dragging out one of the faithful Avon inflatables which we had last used in the Magellan Straits the year before, and assuring Francis that "it won't be much longer".

It took a little over half an hour to get ourselves into a professional-looking, but empty, waterfront bar. In view of the troubled times, I thought the barman commendably calm in his directions to the call box at the back of the pub "to make a 999 call".

2

Rolling Home

"YES, THE PATIENT is under observation and as comfortable as can be expected," the metallic voice informed me through the telephone. We'd had a lot of bags of fish and chips in a brilliantly lit but deserted Portrush fish bar. A crackly T.V. set in the empty lounge of a semi-closed, not many starred, hotel had shown us the black and white misery of the Battle for Stalingrad. There was no reply from the phone at home in Ardmore, but Marie Christine's mother (in a phone conversation which was definitely from another world) assured me that her daughter and grand-daughter were well and staying their first night back in Ardmore with Lance and Ada, and so couldn't be reached. It was time to go back to the boat.

Next morning, life seemed much more friendly although the grey town buildings around the harbour still didn't look their best in the wind and rain. Jamie was up with the ghost of the lark, and paddled ashore to get stores and a bath and also to check with the hospital on Francis. I got the generator going and returned to my bunk for a bit more sleep, and by the time the wandering shopper returned in the late morning I'd had a nice steady hot wash and shave, and cooked a hot meal.

"It'll be a bit harder—just the two of us," Jamie said.

"Yes, and darker and rougher too; but I suppose the Minch should be more sheltered than out in the Atlantic," I replied.

"Very narrow though, isn't it—not much space if it's really windy. What's the forecast?" Jamie asked.

"Well we are in sea area Malin now and going to Hebrides. We've recorded twenty-nine forecasts here since we left Gosport. Malin and Hebrides have offered the possibility of

gale force 8 or more on twenty-eight of those occasions—it was
6–7 on the other one! It's presently forecast south-east force 7
to severe gale 9," I said as clinically as I could.

Jamie shrugged and heaved the generator into the cabin to
lash it away in the stout wooden box built for it, where the
engine would be if we'd had one. I continued to pore over the
west coast of Scotland chart—searching in vain for a sheltered
route without a rocky coastline on the downwind side. It was
a bit of a puzzle.

"I think there's someone outside," said Jamie suddenly,
standing upright, and then clambering up the steps leading
from the cabin to the cockpit.

"It's a fellow in a rowing boat. He wants to come aboard,"
he called down to me.

"Oh, all right—bring him in," I sighed, far from keen to
start an airy-fairy conversation about boats at this stage of the
voyage.

"Hello, I'm Brian Cunningham—are you John Ridgway?"
It was a slim fit-looking fellow in his early thirties. Darkish hair,
firm handshake, steady gaze. "Plenty of push," I thought.

"And this is Jamie—we're on a trip home to the north of
Scotland," I explained, then waited for him to go on and tell us
why he had come to see us.

"I saw you coming along the coast yesterday—through my
binoculars. Recognised the name of the boat. You must be mad
sailing round here in January," he said, quickly. "I've been
trying to get on one of your courses—so I thought I'd come
down to see if you were here this morning—my father is waiting
on the quay."

"Do you like sailing?" Jamie sounded really gruff now.

"It's my reason for living!" Brian replied. "I work for
I.B.M. in Greenock but I'm over here for Christmas with my
wife and child, to see my family—you see I'm from here,
really."

"We're short of a man—why don't you come on with us?"
Jamie's voice made it clear we had no time for idle chatter.

"It's one o'clock now, we're sailing at four," I added quickly.

"Oh! I'd love to—I used to own a twenty-four foot 'Venture'
called *Icebird* and we sailed her up to Iceland a couple of
summers back . . . but I'd have to ask my wife about this

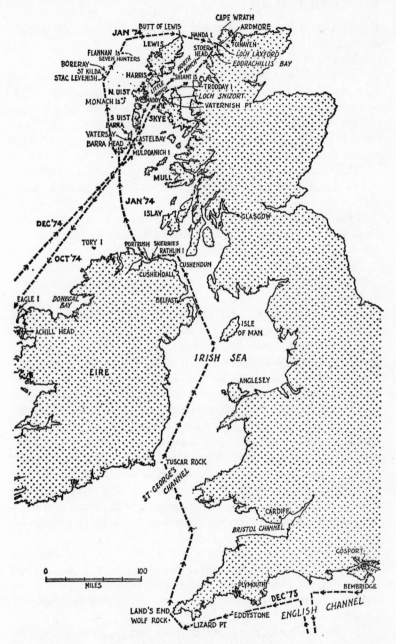

Winter voyages around Britain

though, she'd have to make her own way back to Greenock,"
he laughed, half-heartedly.

"You're on," was Jamie's uncompromising reply.

"If you're here at three thirty we'll pick you up from the
quay in the Avon dinghy—if not, well we'll understand," I
smiled, getting up from the chart table to start things moving.

"We can find you some oilskins!" I shouted as an after-
thought, as he paddled the heavy rowing boat back to the inner
end of the quay.

"His wife'll kill him—he won't turn up," I said to Jamie.

We sailed at ten past four, shooting out as fast as we'd come
in.

Brian waved cheerfully from the bows. His wife and tiny
child waved back from the harbour wall. "Bloody 'ell Scouse!"
I thought, "do we know what we're doing?"

The glass was reading 995 and falling, 1027 was long ago.

"It's smaller than I remember it," mused Jamie, gazing back
at Portrush.

"That's life, isn't it?" replied Brian; we were going to get to
know each other pretty well in the coming days.

In the eight hours to midnight we covered forty of the
hundred mile distance to Barra Head on the southern tip of the
Outer Hebrides. Even so, we could have sailed harder, but we
were going easy on the sails now, because the No. 2, storm and
spitfire jibs had all got broken piston hanks already. On Brian's
father's advice we were making a big curve out to the west in
case the wind should veer to the west and push us towards the
rather inhospitable coast. The midnight forecast was: 'South
force 7 to severe gale 9. Rain', and the glass had fallen to 991.
Poor Brian was being violently sick every few minutes in the
most cheerful manner I have ever seen, but of course it was an
unexpected change for his stomach from the holiday eating and
drinking.

Apart from the eerie lights of a few trawlers out on Stanton
Banks we saw no shipping, and in the early hours, in spite of the
high wind, the visibility was good in between showers, but when
daylight came it brought rain and low cloud and the visibility
became bad.

It was because of the curve that we went wrong. It complicated the navigation, when really I should have kept it as

simple as possible. The gale and the cold and the dark didn't help.

Anyway, at ten minutes to two on the afternoon of Friday, 4th January, Brian was doing what would have been Francis's watch.

"Oh my God!—look at THIS!" Brian moaned.

Jamie and I crashed into each other as we rushed for the main hatch to look out. Had he cut his leg off, or something?

Dead ahead and less than two miles away lay an island mountain, it just soared up from the sea into the cloud. To the right of it and well out on our starboard bow, perhaps two and a half miles away, there was another smaller island with a white lighthouse just barely visible in the cloud base. BARRA!

The unlit light atop the white stone tower was 683 feet above us, give or take a few feet as we rode up and down on the storm waves.

As a result of the curving course, we had been steering north-east for four hours—coming back in from the Atlantic, to pass south of Barra Head and on up north in the comparatively sheltered waters of the Minch. We had simply come too far to the north. Barra Head now lay to our south-east and we would have to beat into the full majesty of the gale, if we were to get round the headland and into the Minch.

On the radio we heard that the island ferry steamer had been cancelled owing to bad weather. This didn't cheer us up.

Events now became rather confused. The glass which had fallen to 990 in the early hours of the morning, had nevertheless held quite steady at that level for the past twelve hours: now it began to drop again. The afternoon dragged on, until the clock told us that the very dark day was now officially night and the barometer mounted next to it above the chart table read 985. The wind was blowing force 10 from the south, or as Brian announced, when invited to comment on it during his 1800–2000 hours watch "it's blowing like there's going to be no tomorrow".

There was some risk of this last remark coming true—for us— if the wind should veer suddenly to the west and drive us onto the exposed west coast of the Hebrides. Accordingly we steered north-north-east, with no sails up at all and trailing 720 feet of two-inch rope in a large loop fastened to either side of the boat on the stern. The idea of this was to slow us down, because about seventy miles away from Barra on our present course lay the unlit island of St. Kilda. Admittedly it presented a frontage of only a couple of miles, and it was most unlikely we would hit such a pinprick in the Atlantic, even if we did drift that far. But there was just a chance of trouble—and the cliffs were the highest in the British Isles, up to twelve hundred feet.

That night Brian's seasickness continued and Jamie and I were worried about his dehydrating. The loss of fluid in vomit is quite considerable and poor Brian could keep down neither food nor drink.

Towards midnight the wind began to ease off a bit and the glass which had fallen to 983 in mid-afternoon began a small rally to 985. The forecast was still south force 7–9, but by three in the morning we were becalmed on a huge swell; we could only estimate our position as some three-quarters of the way from Barra towards St. Kilda, that would be about twenty-four miles short of St. Kilda. We had had to take in the Walker log when we laid out the warp.

My main concern now, was that if the wind really came up again from the south-west or west, we might be blown twenty miles onto the Monach Islands off the coast of North Uist. But by the time we got the 0630 forecast of 'south 6–8 locally storm 10 to cyclonic'—the wind was rapidly rising to force 10 from the south-east, and we were all feeling a bit tatty.

Brian was on watch from six to eight o'clock that morning. In spite of my urging him to lash the helm and leave the boat to drift down wind trailing the warp, he insisted on staying outside at least until daylight.

How lucky he did.

At 0730 he emitted a terrible cry of alarm which had the effect of terrifying me almost as completely as the sight I saw when I emerged to join him. There, ahead in the beginning of dawn was Stac Levenish, a six-acre, 185-foot-high, pyramid-shaped rock. We were approaching St. Kilda. Apart from an all consuming sinking, sick kind of feeling, I thought "this is the best sea scene I've ever seen since *Ryan's Daughter*" only of course we didn't have the music.

For me the most frightening thing, and I was in a rather jumpy state, was the power of the wind and the way the sea was climbing so far up the Stac. It was like magnetism, if this thing had attracted us all the way from Barra Head how could we possibly draw clear of it with only a few hundred yards left? My impression was that we were being drawn towards it by some invisible means, that which ever way we headed—be it forwards, sideways or even backwards—we were going to hit it.

Then I made another mistake.

"Get the spitfire up," I shouted, and Jamie seemed to be there already with Brian close behind, hauling up the tiny scrap of foresail. It was up by the time I had let go one end of the warp and started to hand it in: the 720-foot length of rope seemed to weigh a ton, we were now moving forward with such power that I could scarcely pull it in at all, never mind 240 yards. I couldn't use the winch because the rope was all tangled up in kinks because it was brand new polypropylene.

The next thing I remember is the wind veering—we weren't going to hit Stac Levenish after all—no it was going to be Boreray, another island three and a half miles north-east of St. Kilda of 189 acres and 1,245 feet high. It looked quite impressive as it drew nearer, even though I was flapping about like a landed fish, trying to hand in the warp: the black cliffs were 300–1,000 feet high.

I don't think Brian or I were thinking straight by this stage—I can't answer for Jamie—we seemed to be like a matchstick on a puddle blowing hither and thither. Exposure in a storm at eight o'clock on a January morning where we were was a fairly likely occurrence. We were saved by the wind easing to a milder south-westerly.

We had been lucky; first, Brian spotting Stac Levenish and second, the wind change; I think the latter may have saved our lives. Either way it had been too close for comfort, a pretty poor effort on my part, all things considered. There must be no more mistakes. The wind was falling away fast now and Jamie wanted to put up more sail and be on our way. Instead, I insisted we all have something hot to eat and drink followed by three or four hours' sleep, with one man checking that we were well clear of Boreray. To me it seemed most important that we shouldn't get too tired, we must be able to think and act straight—no more muddles like putting the sail up before getting the warp in!

At noon we decided to make sail again, this time heading for the Flannan Isles which lie some thirty-seven miles north-east from Boreray and about sixteen miles clear of the west of Lewis. Although there was just a hint of sun and a gentle south-west force 5 wind the glass was still steady at 983. I knew it was only a lull.

Sadly, the Flannan Isles have no hospitable reputation, either; this close group of low rocky islets is also known as the Seven Hunters, and they are remarkable for the way they rise sheer from the sea and so make landing difficult at all times. In spite of this they do have a lighthouse, one of the remotest in the world, built by Robert Louis Stevenson's father in 1885–9. The seventy-five-foot white stone tower shows its light of two flashes every thirty seconds at a height of 330 feet above the sea, and it is visible for twenty-four miles in good weather. It was from here that three lighthouse keepers disappeared without trace, in one of the great unsolved mysteries of the sea.

Homeward bound from America on the night of 15th December 1900, the steamship *Archer* passed close enough to the Flannan Islands to be certain there was no light. Bad weather prevented the lighthouse relief ship *Hesperus* from investigating the *Archer*'s report until after Christmas, but when a party was eventually landed, they found nobody—alive or dead. The light was in perfect operational order, except it hadn't been lit for some time; in the living quarters everything was ship-shape and Bristol fashion except for an overturned chair, there was even an uneaten meal on the table. The last written record, on a slate was for nine o'clock on the morning of 15th December. The official log book told of a week of heavy gales (I could well believe that!). The western landing place was badly damaged high above the high tide level. One hundred and forty feet above the sea a concrete rope box had been completely demolished, even turf along the cliff top, 200 feet up had been torn by the seas.

The only clue appears to be that one set of oilskins was found hanging in its place behind the door—the other two lots were missing. On this slender evidence, the official enquiry based its report: "It is to be assumed that the three men, for some reason, left their post, were caught by an unexpected heavy sea and drowned."

We will never know.

Loading *English Rose V* at Ardmore.

The crew. Back row: Marie Christine, Staff, Jamie;
in front: John, Rebecca, Krister.

Sailing out past the croft, heading for Madeira.

Breakfast in bed.

I must confess that as we approached the Flannans in the late afternoon of Saturday, 5th January 1974, it was not the mystery but the deteriorating visibility which occupied my thoughts. Breaking seas could be expected on a two and a half mile front somewhere up ahead of us, and the south-west wind was already whining its fierce song in the rigging again. I was in a hurry to get north, in case the wind should veer west and start pushing us towards the Hebrides.

Perhaps it was this ever present fear of being driven onto the lee shore, that caused me to steer three miles to the west of our planned course in a distance of thirty-five miles between Boreray and Flannan Isles; or perhaps the flood tide carried us further north than I had expected. Either way there was no mistaking the flashing white light which came up on our starboard bow in thick weather, when it should have appeared on our port bow!

This further jolt to my confidence, only served to emphasise the need to get out of this murderous weather. I was simply not thinking or acting in a safe manner.

It was not to be. The wind swiftly ran back up to gale force and beyond, by the grace of God still from a southerly direction. At seven o'clock that evening we were able to fix our position fairly satisfactorily with the radio direction finder. The Butt of Lewis, which lay almost thirty-three miles east of us, was now in a clear line across the sea, and this meant the Radio Beacon should be quite reliable.

From seven thirty that night, until three o'clock in the morning, we just lay with the helm lashed amidships and the warp trailed in a loop over the stern as the storm blew force 8–10 from the south, and we drifted safely further to the north.

"Looks like you'll be seeing Iceland again then, Brian," chuckled Jamie.

We all had confidence in the boat; once or twice she suffered a really big knock, from a wave breaking all over us, but with all the drop boards in place to seal off the entrance to the cockpit, the windowless cabin gave the impression of being in a tunnel—the sea seemed a long way away on the outside. This effect was increased by the sound deadened mast, as I remembered only too clearly the dreadful noise of the halliards on the mast of *English Rose IV* during my lonely fifty-day trip from Eire to Brazil in '68.

We estimated that we'd drifted some twenty-two miles a bit east of north in the eight hours up until 0300 Sunday, 6th January and Ardmore was now only sixty-four miles away in a straight line.

Next morning, far away to the east and dotted along the horizon to the south we began to see what appeared to be little pointed snow-covered islands, which were really isolated peaks on the mainland. I didn't know it, of course, but not far from the most northerly of these, Foinavon, Marie Christine and Rebecca were scrambling out to Ardmore Point to look for any signs of us. My wife was half fearing the worst, but Rebecca, with all the genius of a six-year-old was quite sure all was well. "Don't worry, Mummy, they'll soon be here," she kept saying.

At quarter past eleven, that night we took a sharp turn through a narrow entrance on the north side of Loch Laxford and entered Loch à Chadh-fi, gybing the mainsail as we did so. Then we were hit by a squall; during the day you can see them coming, black across the water from the hills around the loch, by night . . . you can't. This was the first time I'd ever come in in the dark before, and it was black, and I hadn't thought of the squalls.

We had up the full mainsail and No. 2 Genoa at the time; and there was nothing for it but to keep on at full speed. We must trust to memory that we could manage the 90° turn to the left through the seventy-five-yard-wide channel, between the headland at the bottom of our croft and Chadh-fi Island. I was at the helm, with Jamie anxiously watching for the mooring, boathook in hand up in the bow. Brian waited in the cockpit with me, alarmed at the speed and narrowness of it, yet ready to act with the jib winches at an instant's notice.

High up on the hillside, tucked out of the wind, I could see the white sides and black unlit windows of the two old croft houses.

"All asleep, the bleeders!" I thought, uncharitably.

Past Heckie's lambing pen, and the potato patch, just a black square on the steep grassy slope. Then the peat shed, the Anaidh headland itself. Dead ahead lay the island.

" 'Ere we go!" I called to Jamie, pushing the help away and pulling in the mainsheet at the same time.

"Tighten the jib sheet, Brian," and he was away, racing the

handle back and forth, adding the sound of the clickety winch to those of the wind and rushing water in the night.

Then we were under the dark wood, searching for the mooring buoy.

"I see it," shouted Jamie, above the wind.

So did I. "Ready about! Let the jib fly now, Brian."

"Leeho!" The sail really thundered. We were moving too fast, it was Portrush all over again. Up we came and rushed past the buoy.

"Have to do it again, old top!" I shouted to Jamie, and I heard him laugh into the wind. Round we went again and next time we got it. "Must remember she carries her way," I muttered, stumbling up the deck to help smother the sails, as Jamie let them down.

"Look, there's a light." It was Brian who noticed the paraffin lamp in the bedroom nearly two hundred feet up on the hill. The noise of the sails had woken Marie Christine even though the stone walls of the house are four feet thick. She saw the deck light come on as soon as we picked up the buoy and then dragging on some warm clothes she called to Becca to stay in bed while she went to pick up Daddy in the Dipper. Next thing she was trying not to slip on the nearly vertical wet grass of the hill and waving her torch in welcome. The old sixteen-foot timber rowing boat moved easily downwind to the yacht. We three crew were delighted at not having to inflate the Avon dinghy in the dark.

"Hello," squeaked my wife. "How did you get on?"

"Some trip!" I replied, catching the painter.

"Some boat!" added Brian.

3

The Boat that will sail in October, will sail the World over

THE IDEA WAS for Marie Christine and me to make a voyage with, but not specifically for our seven-year-old daughter Rebecca, before it became necessary for her to leave Ardmore for school somewhere else. Although we were more than pleased with her progress at the three Rs during her first two years of schooling, which had been spent alone under the careful tuition of Mrs. Ada Bell. Ada lives with her husband Lance at the blue house, on a croft just the other side of the wood about a half a mile from our home. We are the only two families now living permanently out at Ardmore, an isolated peninsula more than three miles by narrow hilly footpath from the lonely single track coast road. Our main communication with the mainland is by boat, up Loch à Chadh-fi, but in winter this is unreliable owing to storm or ice. During the summer from March to the end of September, we run the John Ridgway School of Adventure. We have lived permanently at Ardmore since 1968, and the School is the mainspring of my life, an attempt to live as nearly independently as I can. We have no outside commitments.

The summer of 1974 was as busy as any. Whether the courses were for eighteen businessmen or women, or for fifty young people; whether the instructing team was ten or twenty, there was little time for organising a three month expedition/voyage. Such things are always more easily talked about than actually put into operation. Two things were certain: the new thirty-three-foot boat, and the time, 28th September to 31st December

1974. We wanted to be back at Ardmore to prepare for the 1975 season by 1st January.

Once we had the new boat at Ardmore in early January 1974 we knew we would be able to go ahead with the idea of the voyage, and by early summer we had the project pretty well set up. The logistical side was easier than usual: there would be none of the frustrations of the Chile trip when stores had to be shipped/flown half way round the world and back. On this voyage we could carry our house and food with us.

"Please let's get some sun!" implored Marie Christine, knowing my dislike of loafing about on beaches and fearful of some exotic winter cruise to Iceland.

"Well it may just be the tiniest bit windy as we ghost along from the Azores to Ardmore in December but here's the plan," I announced one dark February night as we basked in front of the peat fire in the croft.

"Leave Ardmore at the end of September and sail direct to Madeira—maybe walk across the island, it goes up to about 6,000 feet doesn't it? Then sail on down to one of the remoter Canaries and then maybe on, to visit the Sahara Desert. After that we could explore the Cape Verde Islands—nobody ever seems to go there, it should be good for the underwater swimming. From there we would have to sail about 1,500 miles into the trade winds and beyond, to the Azores—who knows what they'll be like? Then we could grit the teeth a little and head off for the 1,700 mile winter north Atlantic sail home." I paused, gauging the atmosphere of the two-lady audience in the firelight.

"It'll be pretty uncomfortable, won't it?" asked my wife, remembering her last summer hol—to the Gran Campo Nevado Icecap in Chile.

"Ah!" I snorted, "you can get used to anything—what do you want—JAM? Think of it . . . there you'll be, the pair of you, sunnin' your 'asses' at my expense." Rebecca was looking at her father as if she wasn't absolutely sure I was right in the head, but too shy to say.

"Think of the cold and the seasickness," murmured Marie Christine.

"Well, you'll have to try the football pools," I said hastily.

"What do you think, Rebecca?" I asked. "Would you like to

go on a sailing boat down to Madeira with Mummy and Daddy—or stay at school?" I asked.

The trump card—for Rebecca it was Hobson's choice—staying at school was out, she had missed going to the Amazon and Chile—she definitely didn't want to be left at home again, so she nodded in silent doubtful assent.

"I suppose I could teach her on the boat," was all Marie Christine said.

The trip was on.

Saturday, 28th September, came along far too soon, we were all tired at the end of the season, and things didn't get done as quickly as they might. I confirmed the beginning of a northerly airstream with the weather people at Wick and I didn't need the October routing chart to tell me this was our chance to slip south.

"We'll sail at two this afternoon," I said shortly, at breakfast, and the crew looked as if they felt it was an impossibility.

Stafford Morse, known as Staff, had the most difficult problem: as the water man he had to move seventy gallons of sweet spring water from Heckie's well on the hillside, to the tanks and jerrycans on the boat, some hundreds of yards away where she lay heavily down to her marks at her mooring under the wood. A short cheerful Australian of twenty-one, with a heavily bearded face that reminded me of a fair-haired Ned Kelly, Staff soon had the reluctant Krister Nylund enlisted to help and promised he could make the deadline. Krister, on the other hand was not so sure, never exactly famous for high-speed packing, the tall twenty-four-year-old Swede with the white 'afro' hairstyle and beard was rather mazed by the intricacies of disentangling his local social commitments with a certain young lady not a million miles from Durness.

Jamie, on the other hand, was raring to be gone. The piles of food, rope and other vital equipment which now littered every inch of space inside the boat were of no consequence. He would be ready to sail straight away if necessary; as long as the bits were checked off and everything was down below, Jamie would be quite happy to do the actual stowage as we went along.

And get away we did, although it was nearer five o'clock than two, and Rebecca was still protesting she must bring her dressing gown. It was quite a windy afternoon but the racing clouds were out of the north and the sky was shot with blue. When the sun made one of its fleeting visits, the steep crofts looked incredibly green, and the wood, the most northerly on the west coast of Britain, was ringed with reddening bracken, but autumn frosts had still to take much green from the leaves of the trees. After the last trip down from our little white house, Lance and Ada took us out to the waiting yacht. The 25,000 bees were safely asleep in their hive, Boy Blue, the grey Connemara pony was across Loch Laxford in a field for the winter; and last but not least, Rebecca's Pussy Ridgway was dozing contentedly in front of the peat burning range at Mrs. Shaw's croft in Scourie.

The sails rattled and drummed, impatient as Jamie.

"Let go!"

The red buoy plopped down into the black peaty water. Slowly at first, then gathering momentum the heavy white bows swung across and then downwind. The working jib was eased, and the mainsheet payed out until the main boom pointed a gold finger at the crofts at right angles to the hull. *English Rose V* was running on her way—chasing the sun south. The water clinked and gurgled against the hull, who could want for more?

Once out in Laxford we turned north-west, coming fairly close to the wind as we began nodding to the Atlantic swell. Down below things began to crash about as the boat heeled sharply and piles of gear turned to a heap of milling odds and ends. Behind us now, framed by the twin peaks of Ben Stack and Arkle, Lance turned the long blue boat for home, nursing a thumb recently broken in his workshop over at the school. Ada waved bravely, trying not to worry too much about Rebecca.

Within quarter of an hour we were out of Laxford and heading south down the Minch in quite a big sea, and we began to roll heavily. Becca, quite unused to the motion fell and hurt herself in the cabin, her shrieks were not so much from pain as from shock at the new cold and hostile world she had suddenly entered—what price now Ada's warm schoolroom? She clambered up the few steps out of the cabin and flung herself sobbing in her mother's arms. Her mother had just crawled up the same steps, green with sickness after a brave attempt to still the restless pots and pans which clanked to and fro with every roll of the boat. Each clad in a red duvet jacket, they clung to each other for consolation, while Krister swung himself across to the leeward rail and was violently and noisily sick. Rebecca looked on with saucer eyes, quite unknowing about the miseries of seasickness. Staff quickly followed Krister's example, then I followed him and then Marie Christine—all in quick succession.

We ran south at speed, taking the seas a little on our starboard quarter as we raced past Handa Island's craggy cliffs and headed on for Stoer Head, eight miles away across Eddrachillis Bay. It was cold on deck, in spite of duvets and the following wind so Marie Christine and Rebecca went below to lie in the single bunk in the cabin; Krister and Staff struggled across the tangled heap of gear in the cabin, on through the combined loo and washing compartment into the forepeak or bows of the boat where we had rigged two long narrow pipe-cot bunks, like sagging stretchers, on either side of the boat. Once in their bunks, they collapsed like broken reeds, moving only occasionally to cough up more food into the black plastic bucket they had taken forward with them.

Jamie and I left the boat on self-steering, and then we crawled out on deck to change the foresail down to the No. 2 jib, before reefing the main right down to the top row of reefing eyelets. The afternoon programme on Radio 2 was interrupted at 1615 to give a warning of severe gale force 9 imminent from the north for sea area Hebrides. That was us!

As I took off my oilskins and heaved my way across the tiny chart table to wedge myself in the curved bunk on the port side with Marie Christine and Becca, I had the feeling that things had got off to a pretty poor start. Becca was feeling miserable and complaining of a 'tummy ache' and imploring her mother to rub it to such an extent that Marie Christine soon had worn the blue woollen pullover into little bobbles of tangled material over her daughter's stomach. Quite suddenly Becca sat up and was violently sick into a plastic bowl which had luckily not yet been stowed away. After tidying up a bit we just lay down to sleep in our clothes, consoling Becca with the thought that at least she had won the seasickness competition by being the last of all to be ill—except for Jamie, who wasn't sick anyway so didn't count—and this cheered her up a good bit.

Suddenly there was a sharp 'crack' from the porthole above our feet and directly over the chart table. The glass had cracked and immediately it began to drip water steadily. Cursing my luck, I groped around for a tea cloth and jammed it into the gully formed by the teak hand rail which runs beneath the ports on either side of the cabin. "That should soak it up a bit," I said, and collapsed in the bunk again, feeling just awful.

So we rolled on into the night; no one even suggested food. All four portholes were leaking, not where they opened but round the washer which was supposed to seal the round glass against its circular brass frame. The suppliers of these expensive fittings, were pretty unpopular with us that night.

Up on deck I could see the reassuring bulk of Jamie, where his wet oilskins glinted yellow in the reflected glow of the stern light. His watch went on and on; feeling sympathy with the 'sickies' he didn't disturb them, and whenever I awoke from my cramped and fitful sleep he was always there. Marie Christine made two journeys out of the bunk: once to find the apples for Jamie, and again to stop three Gaz bottles from banging about beneath our bunk. On both occasions she was sick.

Mercifully the weather got no worse, because we were nearing the three-mile-wide bottleneck between the uninhabited Shiant Isles and the rocky coast of Lewis. Jamie took us through the channel at half-past midnight in a rain squall, my orange oilskin jacket stretched tight between the main hatch and the perspex drop board to keep the rain out of the cabin. Once through into the Little Minch the wind began to die away and the glass began a steady rise from 991. At three in the morning Marie Christine struggled out of the bunk and called Staff to take over on watch; then she set about making food for Jamie who had been above on deck for about ten hours and had had neither lunch, tea nor supper. While he choked down great quantities of delicious cold chicken between thick slices of fresh, home-baked bread, Staff, Marie Christine and I managed only a few nibbles of Ada's fresh ginger biscuits and some hot tea.

Becca awoke full of beans at seven and remarked, "I've never been to sleep before with my coat on and the door open"—she had a lot of it coming!

It was a clear beautiful Sunday morning. The autumn light

heightening the atmosphere of a John Buchan adventure as we slipped on south between South Harris and the great island of Skye.

At 0800 Krister emerged from his place in the forepeak.

"Is it still only evening?" he asked, in his sing-song Swedish accent, rubbing his eyes.

"No, we slept right through," grinned Staff. "Jamie did the night."

"Well, I better eat something," replied the Swede stroking his beard with his left hand. And away he went, tucking into great bowls of Alpen followed by a boiled egg and plenty of bread—with maybe a bit of chicken if it got in his way. We were all pleased he was well again.

We all felt pretty fragile but we had a calm sea and the steady northerly breeze pushed us quietly along, past dark distant mountainous coasts splashed here and there with the white fingers of lonely lighthouses which enabled us to keep fixing our position using the hand bearing compass. A couple of ships passed, one the *Hebe* from Helsinki, overtook us close on the starboard side to the great excitement of Krister who is really a pugnacious Finn pretending to be a calm Swede— "They're really turnips you know, Dad!" as Becca would say. With all our warm clothing on we were able to sit up on the foredeck in the pale wintry sun, and watch the black roofed white houses of Loch Maddy on North Uist, slide out to our right.

"Look at that black house in the sea—over there—it's moving!" Becca cried, squeaky voice full of excitement.

Sure enough, it was moving, and at quite a speed too. What from our distance appeared as a black house, was in fact the sinister conning tower of a very large submarine travelling rapidly down the Skye side of the Little Minch above five miles away from us.

It was an exciting day, particularly for Becca who was reluctant to unclip her safety line and come down into the cabin even towards late afternoon when the air became distinctly cold.

"Never mind how cold this north wind is," I said tuning in for the 1755 shipping forecast. "Just pray it continues—it's much much better than a warm gale in our teeth from the south-west."

We were lucky again; "north-north-west force 5–7 showers. Good visibility," said the voice from far away, and I could have cheered. I had a good wash and shave and finished in time to have a look at the gannets diving into a blood red sunset while we were still in the shelter of Barra Head which is at the southern tip of the chain of Hebridean Islands. There were delicate kittiwakes all around the boat and high over head we could hear the distinctive 'honking' of a V-flight of wild geese homing south-east from their summer grounds in the far north.

"Looks a bit different from when we were up here in January —eh, Jamie," I said, watching him tucking into another beef sandwich.

"What'll it look like next January?" he laughed in reply.

Staff was on watch 1600–2000 that night, and he was glad to be coming off soon after we came out into the North Atlantic proper because we hit a big swell and he was soon feeling very sick indeed.

"I suppose that may be the last land we'll see beforeMadeira comes up out of the sea in front of us in two weeks' time," mused Krister, as he looked back at Barra Head while lighting the red and green oil lamps for the bows.

"That's right," Jamie laughed so much the crumbs made him cough. "If John gets the navigation right," he gasped, and I patted him ever so gently on the back.

It was a rough night, the boat seemed to be falling into holes in the ocean. Staff was sick all night, but we were making over six knots in the early hours in the right direction and Krister saw his first ever moon rainbow. Marie Christine and Rebecca moved down to the chart table end of the bunk and I stayed with my head at the forward end, and by this means we passed another night in our clothes. I kept muttering to myself that we could get used to anything.

As a result of the bumpy speed, and in return for our continuous feeling of fragility, we were at a position some sixty miles to the west of Tory Island off the north coast of Ireland by 1400 on Monday, 30th September. Another good thing was that the glass had risen twenty points to 1015 since the start of the trip forty-eight hours previously. It was so cold that not only did we not sit for long on deck, but we all wondered what on earth a long trip in the North Atlantic would be like in

December; and although I wracked my brains I couldn't think of any other such trip to look up in any of the several sailing books I had on board, and neither could Jamie.

Towards evening the wind fell away and we began to feel a bit better. Jamie, Krister and Staff were sharing the watches; doing four hours on and eight off, I was holding myself in reserve in case of an emergency or bad weather. Watches are the best way to avoid boredom on a long trip. I decided to cook the evening meal of dehydrated food; as we would be eating a great deal of this type of easily stored food for the next three months, I thought it important that we start with a good positive attitude towards it. The secret really does lie in the cooking; I had eaten a lot of dehydrated food, sometimes for long periods over the past fifteen years and much of it had tasted pretty grim, through not being soaked before cooking and therefore not properly re-constituted. Loafing about on a boat all day gave no excuse for not soaking the evening meal well in advance.

We had minced beef and rice. The beef poured into a sauce-pan of cold water out of one yellow two-gallon jerrycan, in a stream of little grey-brown pellets; the rice flowed from another, into a pressure cooker ready for harsher treatment in boiling water later. As with any staple diet, a good bit of variety in presentation helps tremendously, and on that day I called heavily on the tabasco and garlic, and kept the tomato ketchup and Lea and Perrins handy for individual tastes. And I added a sprinkling of mixed herbs to the rice. The store cupboards contained plenty of little jars of spices and herbs for use on other occasions: coriander, cumin, cardoman, turmeric, cinnamon, bay, hot sweet pepper, paprika and others.

It was the first hot meal of the trip, and luckily it turned out all right.

"The best meal I've had for seven months! Better than macaroni cheese—and that's my favourite," said Becca, as she finished a good plateful. It was the first food she had eaten for two and a half days, so really it was only a case of hunger being the best ingredient. Everyone knew I was no sort of cook at all, and each person felt sure they could do it much better, but at least we all realised there should be no shortage of good grub— whatever else might befall us.

September went out like a lamb. Everyone slept well that night as the northerly airstream weakened to force 2 but still persisted. One of two brass bolts used to secure a pair of brass plates, which prevented the tiller from riding up and allowing the self-steering lines to slacken, sheared during the night. Luckily we carried a few long stainless steel bolts and they enabled us to get the self-steering going again first thing in the morning.

"Land ho!" Staff's unexpected cry had me up on deck like a shot while Marie Christine prepared the lunch. "I don't think you'll be able to see it from down there," he called from the top of the mast, "it's way out to the east; must be Achille Head on the west coast of Ireland."

I was surprised: surely he couldn't see a 2,182 foot mountain from forty miles? I riffled the pages of my trusty *Burton's Nautical Tables*, saved from inattentive schooldays at Pangbourne long ago. Sure enough, there in the Distance of Sea Horizon table it gave 2,000:52.3 miles, and at the bottom it gave 10,000:117.0 miles. I could hear Jamie mumbling into his mug of hot tomato soup, something about ". . . last bit of land we'll see before Madeira."

"Well," I announced, "it is a remarkably clear day."

"Jamie has played that Melanie tape so much it's flattened the battery—we'd better get the Honda going this afternoon to re-charge it," I added, changing the subject, and there was a light bump on deck as Staff jumped the last few feet down the mast.

Perhaps it was a dividend for our efforts in January, but the weather was astonishingly good to us. While unfavourable gales raged in other sea areas about us, we led a charmed life in a northerly airstream that was most unusual for the time of the year. The wind swung between north-west and north-east and we logged daily distances of between 110 and 147 miles. It was a fairly uncomfortable ride in some ways but nothing like as bad as I had feared from the expected south-west gales. Inevitably Ireland soon slipped astern, and the weather began to grow a little warmer as our course was not much to the west of south.

Six is a large number for a three-month cruise aboard a Nicholson 32 which is normally laid out to accommodate four in comparative comfort. It was our experiences between Gosport and Ardmore in January which had persuaded me to go for a powerful crew of four hands—and my belief that people will get used to any conditions in time, quickly too if the attitude is right, and they are able to get on well together in an atmosphere leaning more towards the common good than the individual.

With these thoughts in mind I had altered the lay-out of the interior of the boat during the summer.* The large forward cabin was kept as bare as possible: the whole thing painted out with white cork anti-condensation paint and a tiny area of wooden floor was fitted just big enough for one person to stand on at a time. Then we put in four long narrow bunks, two on each side. These were each made up of a seven-foot length of one and a half inch alloy tube inboard fitted with eight ounce terylene sailcloth bunks laced to heavy stowage battens on the outside of the cabin. A net was fitted forward centre of the cabin to add to the space afforded by the spare bunks for storing clothes and other personal items. In practice, there should only be two fellows asleep in the forward cabin at any time while we were at sea. The only ventilation if it was at all wet on deck, came through the square hole left by the removal of the water-tight door. Of course, whenever possible the blue plexiglass forehatch would be opened and this allowed a good drying current of air at most times if we were running before the wind.

The forward cabin was not much—but it was home—that is perhaps the best that can be said of it. Krister and Jamie coped well enough on the two upper bunks except that as this trip progressed they grew plump and buckled their poles a bit; they learned to live with the condensation. Poor Staff's stomach was never really happy with his heaving berth on the lower port side, but we all admired his capacity for suffering in silence.

Immediately astern of the forward cabin lay the toilet compartment with its magnificent Blake loo sited, conveniently in rough weather, at the foot of the mast on the port side. The Honda generator and much clothing was stowed in the wardrobe locker fitted in the outboard port side of the compartment. A little more than half a leg's distance across the boat from the front of the loo lay the washbasin with further cupboards above

* See Appendix I and II for a fuller specification of *English Rose V*.

and below it. We used a bowl in this basin to wash in, because of my paranoia about the possibility of leaks from skin fittings I had made sure the basin was fitted with neither taps nor drain pipe.

The only other room in our small home was the saloon or main cabin. To make most use of the space we used gaily coloured curtains in place of doors between the forward cabin and the loo, and the saloon and the loo. The lay-out of the saloon was again unusual; still really designed for only one person it was functional rather than homely. Coming down the steps from the cockpit, the sink, food cupboards and two-ring Gaz cooker were on the immediate right or starboard side, and forward on the same side was all one large food bin, divided into three sections internally. Entrance to this bin was only through three hinged lids set in the top, which also served as a bunk big enough for two people to sleep on, head to toe. This was normally to be Becca's bunk and she wedged in between various boxes and pieces of gear in general use, and a terylene lee-cloth which prevented her from falling off and down onto the cabin floor.

On the port side of the saloon from aft, there was first of all a narrow vertical slot entrance to a rather too small oilskin locker for such a large crew. The forward wall of this slot was formed by the board on which were affixed various navigation instruments directly above the chart table: radio direction finder, radio receiver and short wave converter, these were all powered by small $1\frac{1}{2}$ v pen-torch batteries. Also on the board was the hand-bearing compass, a perspex holder for pencils and dividers, and the radio loudspeaker. The chart table faced aft, and to sit at it meant sitting on the foot end of the main bunk occupied by Marie Christine and myself; it had a hinged lid like a school desk and all the charts were stowed in the compartment beneath this lid. One long bookshelf ran some nine feet all along the port side of the saloon, above the chart table and the bunk; we carried as many books as we could and they certainly got read.

The bunk was specially designed and built for me by Camper and Nicholson, and it was hard to adapt it for use by more than one—but then you can get used to anything . . . at least we had a roof over our heads. Built in a curve, following the shape of the hull, the bunk was made of plywood; running down from the bookshelf to flat-topped lockers set on the cabin floor. There was an air-space between the fibre glass of the hull for insulation, and a stout terylene lee-cloth hung from a horizontal alloy pole on the inboard side of the bunk down onto the top of the same lockers. The bunk was lined by a warm orange four-inch vinyl-covered foam mattress. The whole contraption could be converted into a long seat by removing the pole and jamming the edge of this mattress inside a teak flange which ran along the top of the lockers beneath.

At meal times there would be one person on watch but the other five would have to perch themselves somewhere. We usually ate out of plastic bowls and didn't really feel the lack of a table. If the pole was down it was just possible to get four adults and Becca shoulder to shoulder on the seat, but more often than not someone would sit on top of the food bins. We soon got used to this style of things, and Marie Christine's food was always so delicious that the way we were eating it was far from our minds. It was only in port that we missed a more conventional table and chair sort of arrangement.

Because of the stormy time of year and the fearful reputation of the Bay of Biscay, I kept about 360 miles to the west of Ushant, out in sea areas Sole and then Finisterre, and never entering Biscay at all. The clear moonlit nights were a great joy to the watch keepers, each in turn living out his own little world up there in the night; sometimes standing on the sail lockers running down either side of the cockpit, and peering forward past the mast and on over the navigation lamps where they glowed red and green in Lance's beautifully made wooden brackets right up in the bows. Sometimes, standing there swaying with the movement of the boat, with fingers lightly holding the after edge of the sprayhood at chest level, it was like riding in some splendid chariot. Each man saw it differently, and was alone with the sheer star-studded grandeur of it—of such things are the great memories of a lifetime made.

By three o'clock on the morning of Monday, 7th October we were only 150 miles due west of Cape Finisterre, the northwest corner of Spain, and a 1,000 miles from Ardmore.

In spite of the increasing warmth of the days most of our time was still spent below deck, usually reading, and here again each

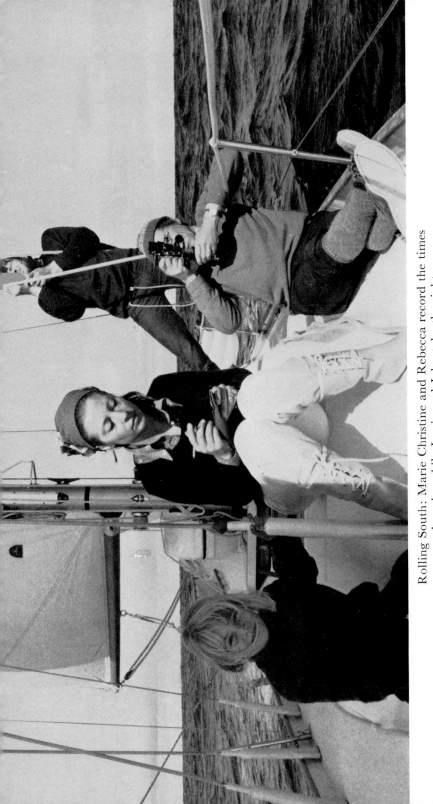

Rolling South: Marie Christine and Rebecca record the times and angles while Jamie and John take the sights.

Time for a reading lesson, above, and for washing up, below, with Jamie wiping.

person's choice was subtly different. Krister would only read text books and official manuals, like *The Sextant Simplified*, *Reed's Nautical Almanac 1974* or any of the technical leaflets I kept in a special plastic envelope in the chart table concerning the electronic equipment. No sooner had he exhausted this dust-dry material than he absorbed signalling manuals and he even tackled *Galleywise—not just a cook book*. Sitting hunched over the chart table between watches, with dark green earphones half hidden among the great pile of his curly fair hair, he listened to Radio Sweden or searched the wave bands for his new lan-guage—the musical Spanish he had learned in Patagonia with us in 1972, and during the subsequent year he had spent alone in South America, after we had left to come home. He never chose to share any part of this wealth of data, being far too involved in the concentration of absorbing it, but there were to be many times when he could fill empty gaps in my own knowledge in potentially awkward situations at difficult times. For example it took him only an hour or two to grapple with and master a radio navigational aid system called Consol, which I had never had the time to study myself. So from then we could rely on Krister to double check any position we obtained, by R.D.F. or astronomical means, with his own Consol position; of course this was only possible if we had the special Consol charts for the area, but this was for just about anywhere north of the Canary Islands and as far west as the Azores.

Jamie on the other hand, read anything from *Anna Karenina* to *The Blake Lavatory Owner's Handbook* and from *Heavy Weather Sailing* to *The Naïve and Sentimental Lover*; his problem was the devastating speed with which he consumed the stuff—here again I was happy to find that many of the practical problems which faced us could be solved by something Jamie had found in his wide reading, which was usually carried out during con-centrated bursts in his bunk. As the self-appointed bo'sun on the boat he was always busy with some job or other, the neat result of which I'd find here and there all over the boat, it was surpris-ing that he could pack so much into his time.

Marie Christine divided her time between the cooking and general preparation of meals and teaching Rebecca how to read. In between times she read as much as possible, always scorning the long stretch of factual sailing or expedition books on the shelf. This scorn applied without relief unless her imagination was caught by some particular situation we found ourselves in, or even a hypothetical situation in the future. Then, in the general effort to marshal as many facts as possible, she would devour a relevant book to come up hours or days later with some completely uncharacteristic remark like "I see Thor Heyerdahl says he found oil all across the Atlantic. Do you think these tankers really are clearing their tanks out here?" Most times, though, Marie Christine was far happier deep in H. E. Bates's *Seven by Five* short stories or intrigued by the machinations of Le Carré's *Tinker, Tailor, Soldier, Spy*.

Staff was the mathematician among us, any problem of calculation or something needing a touch of physics would usually find his rather earnest approach too much of a siege to remain unsolved for long. He was also Becca's favourite story-reader, and Staff's rendition from the cockpit before supper one night, of Paddington Bear's triumphant tussle with Mr. Playfair on the T.V. quiz, remains one of my prized memories of the trip, even though it took place in the very early days of the voyage. Staff's reading was strictly limited by rules laid down by the sea state: it only needed the slightest wobble to be on, and all thought of reading had to be off. He brought along three epics of his own which he'd recently bought in Edinburgh: Bonington's *Annapurna*, a grizzly account of the cannibalism involved in the Andean air crash *Alive*, and thirdly one of the most controversial books of the trip, Sylvain Mangeot's *Travel of a Manchurian*, which opened up a new world for each of us in turn. The size and wonder of China, Tibet and also the mystery of the Himalayan state of Bhutan, provoked in each of us different ideas of China and the part it will play in the future; needless to say Staff, as a young Australian, was the most sensitive to the possibilities.

For myself, I found it quite impossible to read any of the voyages of others, those fat books that seem so attractive when my feet are resting in front of the soft peat fire of a winter's evening, while the wind rattles the slates on the roof outside. I've never had the ability to retain factual information of any kind, so really that left only fiction, and I became deeply involved in Le Carré's books. I read Graham Green's *A Sort of*

Life and only wished I had remembered to bring a few other autobiographies along with me.

For Becca reading or just looking at pictures became a central part of her new life. From the educational point of view she had a goal: to finish the series of thirty-six Peter and Jane reading books. She had read some twenty-five of these illustrated primers before the start of the voyage, and whenever I asked her at what age she was meant to have them done by the answer was always the same enigmatic "Well I know a girl who was eleven and still hadn't finished the last book," but I'm sure seven would be pretty close to the target age. Although she struggled a bit with the holiday camp mystery, which was more interesting for boys, she couldn't get enough of the more factual books about the production of coal, paper, cocoa and the like. The result of this sort of learning was always the same, when school was finished for the day: on would go the little brown duffle coat, safety harness and gloves, then after a quick scramble up the vertical steps to the cockpit the innocent watch keeper would have to endure a barrage of technical questioning, "I say, Krister—d'you know that cocoa grows in Africa . . .?" As well as Staff, Jamie would also read books to Becca if asked, either in the bunk or up in the cockpit. Krister preferred to teach skills like tying rolling hitches and bowlines with a sort of armour plated patience. If badgered sufficiently, both Marie Christine and I would read a chapter of some favourite from Becca's library, but her solitary upbringing at Ardmore has encouraged a remarkable self-sufficiency, and although surrounded by adults reading or discussing subjects of little or no interest to herself, she was quite capable of sitting quietly for hours engaged in some simple pastime of her own invention.

4

Warmer Seas

"THERE'S A BIG PLANE—flying straight towards us," Jamie shouted down excitedly from up on deck, late in the afternoon of 7th October when we were about one hundred and fifty miles west and a little south of Cape Finisterre. Everyone crowded into the cockpit, to get a good look at the visitor, which I recognised as an R.A.F. Nimrod, a long range search and rescue version of the Comet.

As it came in, low over the smooth grey sea, my first thought was that there must be something wrong at home, but it simply swept past close over our stern in a thunder of jet exhaust and then turned in a graceful curve to come over once more before quickly disappearing back the way it had come. We stood about waving all the while but there wasn't the slightest sign of any signal from the huge silver plane.

"He won't have had any trouble reading *English Rose V* on the dodgers—it can't be us he's looking for," I said as we climbed back down into the cabin to wait for Marie Christine's supper; the dodgers are long strips of terylene cloth which are fastened outside the guardrails on both sides of the cockpit to keep spray off the men on watch. For just such easy identification the name of the boat was painted in huge blue lettering on the white cloth.

Marie Christine's sprig of white heather, stuck in the porthole handle above the cooker had certainly brought us good luck with the weather. The shipping forecasts from home told of savage gales in all sea areas around Britain, but we were now all but south of Finisterre at the extreme limit of the B.B.C. coverage. Whenever the sun shone now, the sea took on that

52

warm pale milky blue look it never seems to have at home. School lessons were most often done sitting on cushions up in the bows, although duffle coats or duvets were still the order of the day.

Krister saw a yellow finch-like bird one morning, which circled the boat several times looking for a landing place, before it flew off again; this meant we were probably not too far off the coast of Portugal. An immature gannet, goose-sized and boldly pied blackish-brown and white took a foolish interest in the black spinner on the end of our log line. Time and again it reared up to thirty feet or more before swirling its wings into the characteristic bomb-burst dive after its racing mechanical prey. Foiled on each occasion the silly creature appeared from beneath the surface holding its beak slightly to one side in a quizzical expression.

"Push off," Krister shouted, clapping his hands and fearing for the spinner on its thin line. But the big bird took a lot of persuading that there was no fishy reward for all its efforts, before it finally gave up and flapped heavily away with only brief periods of gliding as it flew low over the sea in search of an alternative meal.

As the warm sun rose majestically from the Atlantic, over the rim of our eastern horizon, at dawn on Wednesday, 9th October it found us becalmed on the twelfth day of our voyage. The sea was gently flexing its muscles beneath a smooth skin of silvery blue. A dozen little black storm petrels with white rumps were flitting bat-like to and fro across the calm waters trying to raise a breeze. I climbed the mast, moving easily up the stainless steel steps, the sun warm on my face. I paused for a while at the top, to look round the horizon for any sign of life; but within our small world, a circle of some fourteen miles in diameter, there existed nothing else except a few restless sea birds. Floating 17,000 feet above the seabed of yellow mud, the crew's main preoccupation was the delicious smell of pancakes for breakfast which wafted up from the main hatch.

"Lovely 'daiy'," called Staff's Australian voice, as he fiddled with the self-steering gear in an effort to keep us heading south.

"Yeah—this is the style," I replied, starting the climb down for breakfast and hoping there would be plenty of lemons to squeeze on the sugary pancakes.

By lunchtime Becca had struggled through four pages of reading on the foredeck, and a zephyr of wind had sprung up from the west. With full mainsail and our big No. 1 Genoa headsail pulling gently we were making south at about two knots. Krister and Jamie went for the first dip of the voyage, plunging off the bow and swimming at full speed, while the white hull moved inexorably past their threshing arms. We pulled them back up to the stern on the hundred-foot length of floating blue safety rope they'd trailed over the stern before going in, they made sure to grab the rope well before its end which was marked by a small red and white cork buoy. Scorning the folding alloy steps I put over the side, they heaved themselves back up and over the side of the boat. "You never know when we might have to do this," laughed Krister, "so it's good practice."

Before supper Becca and I took our customary spin round the deck. This involved Becca carefully fitting her blue safety harness and clipping the karabiner on the end of her safety line to one of the safety lines, which ran uninterrupted from the bow down either side of the deck to the cockpit. Staff had thoughtfully added the heavy climbing karabiner to the existing safety clip at the end of Becca's line because it had a larger opening which made it easier for her to 'clip on' round the translucent polythene piping we had fitted to the safety wires in order to save wear on the deck from chafe.

Once up on deck, I would follow her as she scuttled for the bow, hands reaching forward along the guardrail wires, knees bent and bottom sticking firmly out behind her. At this early stage of the trip she was still very aware of the possibility of falling over the side. At the bow she could hold on to the solid stainless steel frame of the pulpit with both hands and peer forward and down at the water. If the boat was moving at speed we'd ride up and down and there would be a lot of giggling about how it was like riding a rocking horse. Each time the bow dropped down on a wave, a great cloud of white spray flew up and back on either side, sometimes throwing a delicate rainbow across the gap between the smooth racing surface of the oncoming sea and the roll of foam against the bow. We'd stay for a while, the fine spray mist wetting the tips of our noses, to play at counting whatever might be living there on the surface of the water just a few feet beneath us. In those early days off the coast of Portugal we saw mostly a strange sort of jellyfish, only a couple of inches in length which looked to be a flattish oval disc of clear jelly with three parallel thin lines of purple matter running across the middle, and a few scattered dots.

Towards dark on that particular day, 9th October, when we were a couple of hundred miles west of Lisbon and some 420 miles north-east of Madeira, Becca and I returned to the cabin for "a delectable supper of chicken supreme and fried yellow rice followed by bread and butter pudding"—as Staff recorded in the log.

Close-hauled on a fair breeze which came out of the west-south-west soon after midnight, we sped through the night on a smooth sea beneath a clear sky and a fair number of shooting stars were seen by the watch keepers.

"Mummy, Mummy!" came the persistent cry, which always heralded another day, from above the food bins. "My tooth's come out." Becca was brandishing the tiny bit of ivory over the lee-cloth as if on a crusade.

"Well, I'm sure the fairies would find this boat a long way to fly out to from the land," replied her mother, thinking quickly. "I think we'll just have to save it until we get to Maderia and put it under the pillow there."

"Yes—I think that's right," said Becca gravely, never one to drown a fairy.

Staff was soon off watch at eight o'clock and then he made a valiant attempt at scrambled eggs for breakfast from the quantity of catering dried egg powder which Marie Christine had brought along for cake making. While it was quite edible there was no demand for a repeat the following morning; this sort of dish calls for a long hard trip and a lot of hunger to make it appreciated . . . but the time would surely come!

We now had a couple of days of light variable winds and the warmth brought on a welcome spate of hair cutting, beard clipping and sunbathing; but we weren't used to hanging about and the excitement at the thought of arriving at Madeira was mounting. Jamie had never been out of the British Isles, except for a brief weekend stop at Rotterdam while serving as voluntary bo'sun's mate on a winter fitting-out cruise aboard the sail training ship *Winston Churchill*. We all kept telling him how it would be so warm and sunny compared with his beloved north-west Scotland. Staff and Krister too, endured the calm with ill-concealed excitement, while Marie Christine and Becca were impatient to get ashore and into the small flat we had owned for the past few years on the outskirts of Funchal.

A great bank of black cloud climbed steadily over the northern horizon all through the afternoon of Friday the 11th, it glowered above us as we tucked into a curry supper I'd cooked with extra sultanas added for sweetness. The Caber-lunzie were booming out their sea shanty 'It's not the leavin' of Liverpool that grieves me . . .' on the stereo cassette player when the first gusts hit us shortly after seven o'clock. In the remaining five hours to midnight we covered twenty-five miles and really bit into the distance separating us from Madeira.

When Jamie took over the watch from Krister at midnight the wind was still rising, but it had veered to the south-east and we were doing six knots in a sea now far from calm, so at one in the morning I reluctantly crawled from my bunk, pulled on my oilskins and safety harness to join Jamie on deck in the business of reducing sail. All sleepiness was soon gone, we were roaring along through the night with the lee rail dipped well in the rushing sea. It was hard to hang on up on the foredeck, and as the boat crashed from wave to wave, so the bows sprouted wings of white phosphorescent fire. Although I was wearing little or nothing under my stout yellow oilskin suit the water wasn't cold. Jamie was loving it. "Soon be there now!" he shouted, face streaming with spray, as he sat fastening the jib sheets with bowlines to the clew of the working jib we were putting up in place of the No. 1 Genoa.

And so we crashed on, the wind continued to rise a bit more, but it backed to the north-east which eased the motion of the boat a little—but not enough for most of us—all except Jamie and Krister began to feel the old familiar queasiness stealing over us once more.

"There's a ship out to port," called Jamie, from in the cock-pit. This was not unusual, we had seen several both by day and night in the past few days. Automatically I paused for a moment from my task at the mast, where I was just about to lower the working jib and replace it with the No. 2 jib, to match the by-now heavily reefed mainsail. Far out on the horizon more or less on our beam I could make out what looked like a pale blue-green island.

"Heading west for South America maybe—out of the Mediterranean," I called back, "she'll pass way ahead of us." There was no reason to be concerned, so I just got on with the business of changing the headsail.

Far away, high up on that duck egg blue island, the officer of the watch was looking at us through powerful binoculars. Perhaps he saw the headsail drop, or maybe he was just inquisitive as to why such a small sailing boat should be out in these waters so late in the year. Whatever it was, he decided to alter course, not a decision lightly taken in days of quick turn-rounds and booked berths. The huge empty black hull shuddered into a tight curve to starboard, and churning propellers carved a pale bow of eddying wake across the deep blue of the ocean.

"She's altered course—coming right at us," called Jamie excitedly, and both Krister and Staff came up to see what was going on.

"Oh Lord! I wonder what's up now," I replied, fearful of some sort of incident when things were going so well to plan. And I hurried the business of hoisting the No. 2 jib to ensure we would have plenty of manoeuvrability when the tanker closed with us.

Once back in the cockpit I gave a quick briefing to cover every possibility I could think of. Jamie disengaged from self-steering and took the tiller himself; Krister manned the binoculars watching for any clue as to the tanker's possible tactics—they do take an awful long time to stop. Marie Christine sat close to the companionway with the eraser pad at the ready to jot down any signal or other communication, and Becca sat close to her mother clutching the morse card which listed the major morse signal letter groupings of the international code. Staff stood ready to dart up to the mast and drop the sails if there was any question of stopping.

"She's coming pretty close!" Jamie's usually very relaxed voice showed a trace of alarm. I said nothing. Collisions had played quite a part in my life already. The Atlantic rowing boat was damaged by an Army escort in '66, shortly before the voyage was due to start, and my other sailing boat *English Rose IV* had been effectively put out of the race to be the first single-hander to sail non-stop round the world in '68. On that occasion I had a week's start on the next competitor, Chay Blyth, and a fortnight on the eventual winner Robin Knox-Johnson; the resultant limping into Recife in Brazil after a crash with a T.V. trawler off Galway, Eire, at the start had signalled the end of the sort of chance which doesn't come often in a life time. The chart spread out in use on the chart table in the cabin below was still covered with my daily positions on that race—oh, yes I knew about collisions all right. It needed just one slight roll of the hull if we were anywhere near the ship and the spreaders high on our mast would almost certainly crash against the high deck line of the tanker.

Nearer and nearer it came—with Becca hopping up and down with excitement at the biggest thing she had ever seen in her life. High up on the port wing of the bridge were crowded a number of people, in fact most of the ship's crew must have been out with cameras and binoculars. They were all waving and there was even a girl in a yellow shirt. We were passing in opposite directions port to port not fifty yards apart. Suddenly the great black bows loomed over us and we read *Mobil Explorer* in big white letters, then we were whirling along the towering black sides of the ship while the engines throbbed in our ears.

"Are you O.K.?" the officer's voice echoed mechanically from the loudhailer as he held it to his lips. We all waved like mad and Staff called, "How far to Madeira?" and we saw the white-shirted figure walk back into the wheelhouse as the rest of the tanker passed us. Then we saw the tips of the big slow-turning propellers chopping the water as the engines ran slow astern. Suddenly it was past us and we were bucking about in the turmoil created where the big seas stood up short and then fell over themselves as they ran into the ship's wake.

"He's swinging away to the west again—maybe he'll come back and answer my question," laughed Staff.

"I doubt it, time's money with those fellows—they don't hang about," I replied. Only that morning I'd got a bit cross because another ship had altered course drastically to investigate us in the dark and I had felt that if we'd put on the brilliant deck floodlight earlier we might have saved the other ship wasted time.

Anyway I was wrong, the *Mobil Explorer* turned completely round and came back to overtake us, again on our port or windward side—a manoeuvre which took nearly half an hour to complete.

"You are 149 miles from Madeira," the officer's voice came again as they rumbled past, and even more people were out on deck waving this time, many of them pointing at Becca's deliriously excited figure.

As she drew ahead of us she let out a farewell series of great hoots in clouds of white steam from the forward side of her funnel, and we replied with blasts from our own little gas foghorn which sounded squeaky by comparison. There was one little girl who would never forget the meeting.

It was just after noon on the following day, as I was standing on the stern hanging onto the twin backstay wires which run down from the top of the mast to either side of the stern, and wondering whether to chance putting up the spinnaker for the first time on the trip—when I saw land.

"I have won the Penguin!" I shouted the famous cry, and people crowded out on deck through both the main and the forehatch.

We were sixteen days out from chilly Ardmore and there, already high above the horizon were the sharp peaks of Porto Santo island jutting nearly 1,700 feet into the cloudless brassy sky. As first to sight land I was winner of a bonus Penguin or Golf biscuit—I would always choose a Penguin—from the fast diminishing ship's supply of chocolate biscuits left over from last season at Ardmore. The mountains must have been obscured by the haze for they really were a long way above the horizon. Needless to say my triumph was greeted with some derision by a number of other plump chocolate biscuit fanciers.

"Let's put up the spinnaker to celebrate," I cried, for the wind was still blowing fairly strongly dead over our stern. Jamie was delighted, and immediately set about rigging the special sheets that are needed to fly the big balloon sail forward of the mast.

Soon we had everything ready, with all five adults on deck and Becca watching from inside the cabin steps.

"All right?" I called out from my place at the foot of the mast, and everyone nodded their heads. "O.K.—up she goes!"

I had three turns of the galvanised wire halliard round the drum of the winch, and I started pulling like mad. Behind me the sail bellied out over the bow. Then the wire turns rode over each other on the drum and for a few seconds the sail hung in the air suspended over the racing water away forward of bow. Too late I freed the wire and tried to heave the head of the sail to the top of the mast: with a slow roll it collapsed, spun anti-clockwise, and wrapped itself tightly around the forestay. This is a wire running from the top of the mast to the bow of the boat, which serves both to keep the mast up and also as something up which to slide the leading edge of all the foresails except the spinnaker.

Our pride and joy now looked like a string of sausages hung from a washing line. Nobody said anything. Letting the halliard go again achieved nothing, the sail was held up by the friction of the ultra fine terylene sailcloth around the smooth stainless steel of the forestay. For half a minute or more we just looked at it; and then, all on its own it began to unwind itself. I got set to winch up the head of the sail the remaining few feet to the top of the mast.

"Crack!" We had a huge red, white and blue balloon blossoming forward and above our bow. Jamie pulled back the rope or sheet which was controlling the long gold-coloured alloy pole which now stuck out from a point nearly a quarter of the way up the leading side of the mast to the windward bottom corner or clew of the sail. Immediately we could feel an improvement in the speed, and the rolling deck steadied beneath our feet at the same time.

We were approaching land at last, after covering some 1,700 miles in sixteen days. Nobody quarrelled at the need for two men on watch while the spinnaker was up, in fact everyone was up on deck now, either reading, sunbathing or helping with the handling of the boat as we travelled along in the sun towards the mountains ahead. Staff the helmsman, was steering by hand now, with the self-steering disconnected, and Krister was playing the spinnaker sheet from the cockpit to ensure we got maximum forward lift from the sail. While Jamie was up the mast fastening short lines across the gap between the mast and the forestay, to prevent another twist occurring in the spinnaker, I was thumbing through *Crewing for Offshore Racing* for any other tips I could find on the subject.

Marie Christine and Rebecca lay out in the sun on the fore-deck occasionally peering through the binoculars at the land, as it slowly changed from a silhouette into what looked like a desert island about four miles across. Perhaps it was the end of a long dry summer, but such grass and vegetation as there was appeared to be burned brown, and the mountains were an arid sandy colour. Although there were a few white houses dotted here and there we saw little sign of life as we sailed by, some five miles off the coast on that glorious afternoon.

"I can see Madeira," cried Becca suddenly, full of excitement as the light began to fail at six that evening. Away down to the south-east we could see our goal, where it lay like a purple bruise on the horizon some twenty-five miles from Porto Santo.

"Have a beer," grinned Jamie. We had dropped the spinnaker and the boat was moving easily under the full mainsail and working jib for the night. The sea had calmed down a bit and above us millions of stars lit a velvet sky, while on either side lighthouses blinked their welcome.

"Cheers," I said, tilting the can of lager to my lips in celebration, as we all sat in the cockpit eating Marie Christine's special supper of minced beef and macaroni cheese liberally dosed with tomato purée.

We had just finished the pleasant meal when we saw the bright lights of a liner up ahead. She was crossing the horizon more or less from west to east.

"There'll be plenty of shipping tonight," I said, remembering my visit to meet a London newspaper reporter off the island during the 1968 single-handed race. On a still June night I had ghosted round Barlavento lighthouse, which was now a dozen miles ahead of us on the eastern tip of Madeira, and then I had sailed slowly along the southern shore of the island planning to make for a point just off the capital Funchal, some seventeen miles west of Barlavento by dawn. A passing freighter had come too close for comfort, so I'd flashed my torch on the sails in warning, but this only attracted the ship still nearer. I became rather worried that not only might the ship collide (that awful word again) with me, but she might run onto the nearby shore.

At the last minute, in a torrent of megaphonic abuse in some foreign language, the officer of the watch altered course and sheered away in alarm. I could only think that he had mistaken me for the Funchal pilot, even though we were still about fourteen miles from the point.

To minimise the dangers this time, we decided to heave-to for the night off the south coast of the island, about ten miles from Funchal, and set sail again at first light to make our engineless entry to the harbour some time in the morning. This all went without a hitch, in spite of much activity by small fishing boats; we lay with the full mainsail up and the boom sheeted hard in over the centre of the boat and with the No. 1 or working jib aback and also sheeted in hard. This meant the boat lay more or less stationary across the wind; and the lights of the village outlined the coastline for the watch keeper's convenience, although the mountains which run up steeply to 6,000 feet on the thirty-five-mile-long island were covered by a thick layer of local cloud.

We were all up at six in the morning for a quick breakfast of tea and a bowl of Alpen each, then everyone fell to the business of making ready for port after our long spell at sea. It was a dull cool day, the clouds hung in a long pall over the mountains and Jamie kept muttering about how it was no warmer than Scotland.

We carefully piled the anchor chain into buckets, keeping a complete anchor set ready for emergency use at either end of the boat; and the various mooring ropes or warps as they are called, were also lashed handily to the guardrails at various points of the boat. Then we inflated the Avon dinghy, only to find that the six holes in the rubber floor had not been repaired since our return from Chile, where they had been used to secure long wooden runners beneath the dinghy to take the rub of the shore, and also to help us to steer straight.

"Now I can see why there seemed to be so much water in the boat that night when we took Francis ashore to the ambulance in Portrush," said Jamie, as he helped Staff to stick black masking tape across the holes. Krister had the small Seagull outboard motor out from the back of the engine space and soon we had the dinghy over the rail and the Seagull mounted on its wooden stern bracket. In the practice run Jamie got the engine started easily enough, so we took it off again and stowed it on the yacht and hauled the dinghy tighter up to the stern rail to stop it from shipping water. We were ready to enter port.

We were now much nearer in to the coast and we were close-hauled under mainsail and working jib. The sharp squalls off the mountains made sure we kept up a fast clip towards Funchal. A Caravelle jet plane screamed low overhead in a tight right-hand turn on its approach to the island's short run-way, which is cut into the steep side of the mountains not far above sea level. We could now see quite clearly the white houses on the nearly vertical terraces of the small holdings; trees and even patches of flowers were easily identifiable above and below the winding coast road. Primitive cave houses by the sea contrasted strangely with grand houses of the properties higher up the slopes above Funchal. We even saw a thing like a pink pagoda in among the modern blocks of the tourist hotels which clustered close to the sea on the outskirts of the town.

Between them the islands of Madeira and Porto Santo have a population of something around 300,000 and a fully third of all these people live in Funchal. The houses with their terra cotta roofs are stacked up tightly one behind another all the way into the clouds which most days seem to settle at around 3,000 feet up on the mountains; but so luxuriant is the vegetation that the buildings appear only to be scattered among the green. And so it was at ten thirty on that morning of Monday, 14th October as we sailed carefully through the 400-yard entrance to the harbour; between the 150-yard-long pier jut-ting from the shore at the end of the town's main street and the head of the massive breakwater or mole which runs for three-quarters of a mile in a crooked elbow from the shore at the western end of town.

A big white German liner and a couple of freighters were alongside the busy mole, and tall spidery cranes swung back and forth laden with cargo. Our destination was the cluster of twenty or so foreign yachts nestling on the sheltered side of the pier. We moved slowly into the centre of the harbour with our small Portuguese courtesy flag flying cheerfully from a signal pennant below one spreader, and Marie Christine's bright yellow sou'wester hanging from the other to signify that we needed medical clearance on entering a foreign port. The breeze was now so light that we lowered the sails and Jamie lashed the Avon to the starboard side of the yacht, then fitted the Seagull motor and set about driving us into a suitable berth to drop anchor which Staff and Krister manned on either end of the boat.

At first things went well, and it looked as if Marie Christine and Becca were unnecessarily nervous in hiding below in the cabin, reading Paddington Bear books. We slipped neatly enough between a pair of expensive looking ketches and began the smooth 180° turn that would take us away from the shore, now only forty yards ahead, and into a gap I had chosen between two twenty-five-foot fibre glass sloops, the left-hand one from Switzerland and the other from Sweden. It could be argued that we should have dropped the light anchor off the stern as we turned—but we didn't. Jamie cut the engine and in a silence mounting with embarrassment we approached a convenient red metal buoy lying between the Swiss and Swedish boats. It seemed as if everyone was out on deck to watch the new arrivals, and they had all come from Europe by the same way as us—sail. Up on the pier hundreds of tourists craned their idle necks, and old bent harbour boatmen paused from polishing fine old brasswork on their ferries to be in on the result of this particular round in the never ending pastime of visiting yachtsmen's antics.

With my hand trembling on the helm and my voice squeaking in my throat, I delivered the perfect 'collision á la Portrush' learned in stormier northern waters. Only this time there was no anchor dropped off the bow to bring us up short just in time.

"Fend it off, Krister!" I squealed. There are very few Swedes in this world so I reckoned that one less wouldn't be missed.

Always keen on a bit of balletics, he leapt off the bow and onto the small can-shaped buoy—showing us that his repertoire included log rolling as well as simply jumping over barbed-wire fences with both legs together from the standing position. I can't say I remember hearing much thunderous applause, but I remember the dull clunk as the red buoy hit our shiny white bow. I think I felt stabbing pains from the irate Swiss and Swedish owners on the flanks, and my attempts at friendly nodding were sharply interrupted by the booming megaphone

"It's all gone wrong again!" Struggling with the spinnaker.

Teeth cleaning above, and beard trimming with Staff, opposite. Below, Staff does some running repairs.

from the pilot boat which had somehow appeared off our bow.

"No hay motore," I called, palms raised in supplication. "Agh! Britannico," he cursed, forgetting to take the loudhailer from his lips.

"We're snookered now!" I thought, glaring at Jamie who was chuckling something about, "We're not very good at coming into port."

So we sort of hung there, our stern swinging perilously close to the Swiss, until the pilot boat, fast and low, suddenly rushed at us.

"I take your stern anchor," the pilot called, as his bulging black rubbing strip swished along, all too close to our hull, and I reached over and passed the anchor to a cowed subordinate who was darting nervously about the clean white decks in a pair of old gym shoes. I formed the opinion that the swarthy mani-cured pilot manoeuvred his brass-covered launch more for the benefit of rubber-necked young Scandinavian ladies on the pier than through any main concern for my own well-being. However, it was all soon finished without further dents to boat or ego; and when it was done and we lay neatly between two neighbours, to an anchor off either end of the boat and a stern rope off one quarter to the red buoy, the pilot landed a chubby white-shirted customs man complete with officer's hat aboard us. Then with a final elegant wave and a growl from his engines he was gone in a surge of power, back to his station under the sheer black rock wall of the pier and to the serious business of watching the young lady visitors.

Down in our small cabin the friendly customs man breathed garlic fumes over me while I filled in the various forms for health and immigration as well as those concerning his own depart-ment. Then Staff put the pair of us ashore at the slippery oil-stained pier steps, and we made our tour of the various govern-ment offices. The sun had come out now, and in the still midday air my legs felt a bit wobbly as I followed the plodding steps of my guide, the back of whose neck I noticed was sweating freely. Past grey-uniformed guards packing pistols in their belts, up beautifully tiled corridors he went, pausing now and then in air-conditioned offices while scraps of paper were signed by busy but obliging officials.

At last it was over, and shaking the hand of my new friend I left him in an office near the power station, resting in a straight-backed chair, with his hairy arms crossed patiently in his lap. As I walked unsteadily back to the pier I felt a free man, as if I had just been acquitted of some dishonourable offence.

In no time at all we were all ashore, some money changed into Portuguese escudos and a few items of grub purchased. Marie Christine, Becca and I said goodbye to the others and caught a taxi to our flat outside the town, to set the place up for a celebration supper that evening.

5

Madeira—The High Walk

WE UNLOCKED THE DOOR and walked in. Our footsteps echoed in the corridor, the place was cool and quiet, and there was a feeling of space after the confines of the boat. Out on the balcony 1,000 feet above the sea, it was the restful green of the banana plantations which first caught my attention—so easy on the eye after the glare of the sea—and the pale red roofs of the one-storey houses submerged in an ocean of broad green leaves. Further down the valley near the coast road there were spiky patches of sugar cane coloured in a green more blue than the bananas. Away to the west, tumbling 1,920 feet down into the Atlantic with a fringe of sparse eucalyptus trees on its crown, stood Cabo Girão, which the Madeirans claimed to be the highest cliff in Europe. Inland, the proud white walls of São Martinho church, stood atop a pointy hill of red volcanic dust which sported a poor growth of coarse brown grass and dried-up looking cactus plants. Behind the tall spire a great craggy gorge marched deep into the heart of the island amid bald mountains over 5,000 feet in height. Below us the hillside fell sharply away to the tranquil waters of the ocean, it was strange to think that if the water disappeared I'd be standing three-quarters of the way up a 20,000-foot mountain.

Far below I could see the tiny figures of Krister, Jamie and Staff as they started the long walk up the hill from the bus stop, and I smiled to myself as I remembered Ada, back at Ardmore after a holiday here in Madeira saying, "Why do you always have to live right up on a hill wherever you go?"

It was getting dark now, and over the hill in another valley further along the coast towards Cabo Girão the locals were firing their evening rockets, puffs of grey smoke and tiny flashes preceding the sound of their explosions by many seconds. They came in fact from the little fishing village, Camara Do Lobos, made famous in the '50s by a fleeting visit from Sir Winston Churchill while on a painting foray from Reid's Hotel on the outskirts of Funchal. The village had much more recently, only a few weeks ago in fact, suffered an outbreak of cholera—and I thought of the thin grey rats I'd seen scuttling between the naked children in the waterfront slums of the village a few years before.

When the fellows finally arrived for an evening meal with us they were quick to take a swig of the local wine, but they all preferred to wait for their supper while they relaxed in the first bath any of us had had for seventeen days. A kilo of potatoes boiled in their skins soon disappeared, along with endless slices of red tomato and mortadella, many glasses of wine and a large number of bananas. The fruit was kindly brought along by Lucy Da Silva who looks after the place for us while we are away. It was from her own trees.

The sun touched the top of Cabo Girão across from the sliding glass doors at the foot of our bed, at shortly after seven next morning. The predominant sound was the crowing of cockerels up and down the valley, but we could see half a dozen piebald pigeons strutting up and down along the low red-tiled wall on the edge of the balcony. Mixed with their soothing cooing we could hear the plaintive miaouing of a scraggy tabby cat which prowled the mounds of debris around the buildings in search of the same fieldmice as a pair of small hawks wheeling and hovering above.

A piercing shriek from Rebecca in the kitchen, shattered this peaceful start to the day. There was a clatter of pots followed by a patter of small bare feet, the bedroom door burst open and a sobbing figure threw itself onto our low bed and into its mothers' arms.

"There's a lizard in the jug, Mummy," wailed our daughter, and I marvelled again at the great range of feelings experienced by a child. In five minutes this same pitiful figure would be squealing with pleasure as we played football out on the balcony. I've heard it said that it takes a child to really understand the way another child sees an experience; adults have lost

the naïve intensity of life in a process called 'growing up'. And
I fell to wondering again about the lasting effects on a seven-
year-old girl's mind of all the dramatic as well as beautiful
experiences which this voyage held in store for Rebecca. We'd
never really know if it was worthwhile, but selfishly, like so
much of parenthood, it was a great joy to have her with us
every day.

"Come on—we must get up!" said my wife. "We've so much
to do," she added jumping out of bed.

The central feature of our visit to Madeira was to be an
attempt to walk from the south to north coast of the island.
Marie Christine loved Madeira for the warmth, sub-tropical
fruits and flowers, the bathing, the different outlook of the
islanders, and above all for the quiet privacy away from the
telephone after the busy summers at Ardmore. We had been to
the island several times before, but I had always rather endured
than enjoyed these visits. This time I meant for us both to enjoy
our brief stay; Marie Christine and Becca could spend their
time at the small Club Naval a mile away along the coast where
Becca could renew her friendship with the manager's children
and Marie Christine could lie in the sun. Meanwhile Krister,
Staff and I would do this walk across the island, which although
it meant only covering about ten miles as the crow flies, really
involved climbing a 5,000-foot mountain range crossing a
volcanic plateau, and dropping to the sea on the north side.

On its 308 square miles Madeira has three different climates,
up to 1,000 feet above sea level it is sub-tropical, between
1,000–2,500 feet Mediterranean, and above 2,500 feet the
climate is definitely temperate. The cloud formations rolling
down the Atlantic on the Trade Winds from the north-east pile
up against the mountain barrier of the island's upper northern
slopes and this results in an annual rainfall of up to a hundred
inches in those parts. This natural phenomena sometimes means
it might be raining heavily on this part of Madeira but sunny
both above and below it, and in fact droughts of up to six
months are not uncommon on the southern side of the island.
This same heavy rain sinks through the various volcanic strata
into a permanent subterranean reservoir containing up to
7,000 million cubic feet of fresh water, which runs off from sweet
springs 3,000–5,000 feet up on the northern slopes. Over the

centuries these springs have been channelled into a gigantic artificial network of narrow fast flowing waterways to irrigate the greater part of the entire island, with dramatic effect upon the agriculture and natural vegetation.

Because of the heavy rain and high winds we might encounter up in the mountains our walk took a little organising. Our rucksacks would need to contain sufficient food for the two or three days, sleeping bags, warm dry clothing, waterproofs, cooking gear and spare fuel and first-aid packs; all in all the loads would seem heavy enough after a few thousand feet of climbing on legs still weak from the confines of the boat. The likelihood of mist obscuring visibility meant trying to find a local guide to ensure we did in fact get across. Marie Christine was right there was much to do—and lazing in bed wouldn't get it done.

We were eating a hurried breakfast of toast and marmalade when Lucy arrived, bearing quantities of beautiful flowers, avocado pears, tomatoes and yet more bananas—all from her own small plantation among the bananas on the hillside below. Lucy is typically Madeiran, short and strongly built with jet black hair, she has an excitable nature and a talent for turning daily life into high drama. She and Marie Christine were clearly delighted to meet again; within a few minutes plans were being laid for a shopping expedition that morning to the exotic market in Funchal.

Waving goodbye to the shoppers on the seafront, I had a quick look at the yacht, where she nodded quietly at her moorings in the harbour: all was still, the fellows were having a bit of a lie-in. Then I made my way up a narrow alleyway off the waterfront to the offices of Antonio Giorgi. Here I was welcomed by the slim dapper figure of Michael Zino, twenty-five, whose neat moustache and dark hair reminded me strongly of Jack Nicholson. We moved through a spacious air-conditioned main office which exuded an atmosphere of calm security, amid massive old safes and an oil painting of a schooner which had somehow bent in its frame, and passed into an elegant private office with a non-ringing phone, overlooking the harbour. Through a convenient telescope I could see in startling close up that there was still no move aboard *English Rose V*, and I made a mental note to warn Marie Christine to be careful in her sunbathing if she was on the yacht.

Calculations of all the other telescopes and binoculars likely near windows all along the sea front reminded me of my short stay in Recife in north-east Brazil at the end of my single-handed sail in 1968. I was much helped by a minor consular official to whom I arranged to sell a pair of binoculars from the yacht. He lived with his mother and owned to a penchant for voyeurism. At tea in the flat one day high above the city, among a cluster of other sky-scrapers, I noticed he always had a pair of binoculars lying by the window and I asked him why he wanted another pair.

"Oh, they're for Mother," he said. "We both like to watch at the same time!"

Michael Zino's family owned the only house on the lonely Selvagem Islands which lie about a hundred and fifty miles south of Madeira and roughly ninety miles north of the Canary Islands, which was the next place we were heading for after Madeira. I was so attracted by his tales of the great colonies of shearwaters, and petrels and the abundance of fish to be seen by the casual snorkeller, that I decided there and then to try and make a landing there if at all possible.

"The bigger island is less than a mile across and the whole place is surrounded by reefs," said Michael. "There's always a swell and, of course, there are no lights at all—a big tanker was wrecked there just a few years back, it's still there. . . . Why don't you go and see Juan Borges who runs the Tourismo, he's a great family friend and he knows more about the Selvagem than I, also he could help you with the guide for your walk."

Ten minutes later I was seated in the graciously appointed office of the man himself, Juan Borges, a handsome immensely urbane man, perfectly dressed in a pale fawn suit, cream shirt and exquisite hand-knitted chocolate tie; the complete ensemble highlighting the scruffiness of my own appearance. With tremendous charm he regaled me with a string of anecdotes ranging from a visit to Inverness one Easter to visit distant relatives and his parting remark, "Well I'm glad I have seen it —for I shall never return," to tales of terror aboard the stranded tanker down on the Selvagem Islands. This latter yarn was beautifully acted to demonstrate the tricky business of negotiating the corridors below deck when the whole structure was still rolling from side to side in the surf.

Each time I tried to ask about the guide for my own pedestrian trip across Madeira, I was stayed by a raised hand, and while his own voice laughed on unimpeded the other hand sought a handy packet of big fennel-flavoured sweets.

"Gob stoppers," he said, "for tourists who come in here to complain about the weather!" and he went into a lengthy discourse about how these yellow-flowered umbelliferous plants, allied to dill, but distinguished by the cylindrical, strongly ribbed fruit had given their name Funchal to the capital of Madeira, because Zarco had found so much of it on the site of the city when he'd first landed on the island in 1419. Then, without a pause, we were onto the small matter of Captain Kidd's treasure, supposedly buried on the Selvagems, and how a previous owner of the uninhabited islands had consulted a clairvoyant in Switzerland, who had told him the treasure was buried close to dripping water, but when the dripping water was eventually found it turned out to be in an empty sea cave.

When I finally reeled from the Tourismo office, out into the bright noonday sun, I was full of knowledge and smelling strongly of the cough sweets, but just a little doubtful about the guide being fixed up for the walk across the island—which had to be arranged in a hurry.

Krister and I tried the Agrario Department next.

We were having little or no luck with busy officials who spoke neither English nor Spanish, when suddenly another visitor came into the office and made the most of the opportunity to practise his night-school English. A short smiling man with characteristic black hair he appeared to enjoy talking of the mountains which he himself visited every week for the purpose of the 'multiplication of strawberries', which we took to mean that he had a piece of high ground which was suitable for strawberry seedlings which were later transplanted at one of the warmer climates lower down towards the sea, for ease of ripening the fruit. He knew all the government lodges, which he explained were maintained either by the Agriculture Department, where we presently were, or the Forestry Department which was based in another building in the town. Then he opened a heavy cloth-bound record book which lay on the dark wooden counter before us; running a broad work-worn finger down the column for the coming week he shrugged his shoulders and told us the lodges were all full with hunters, as the rabbit shooting season was in full swing.

"It'll have to be the Forestry Department," I said to Krister, "we'll just have to leave it until tomorrow—they'll be closed now."

And after thanking our friend for his help, we left the building with the familiar feeling of frustration that goes with expeditions in Latin countries where tomorrow is always another day. If you want results 'you gotta keep the feet moving'.

Two days later it was on. Juan Borges made a rendezvous for us with a forestry worker at Prazeres, a little village on the south coast near the western end of the island. I was up before dawn and after a quick breakfast I made my way down the long hill to the bus stop with the familiar weight of the pack on my back. There were several others on the lane, and their numbers increased as we neared the winding coast road, commuters emerging from their houses which were hidden among the banana trees, they had the same worried gait you'll find any morning near a London underground station. When we reached the T-junction they darted across the main road to wait beneath the plane trees for the Funchal bus, and I stood alone under a wall waiting for No. 107, the seven thirty bus bound for the western end of the island. Judging by the looks I got from the commuters on the other side of the road, dressed in old jungle-green combat kit my transport might have been 'the three ten from Yuma'.

I could see Krister's white Afro, half a mile away, as he stood in the middle of the approaching rattle trap.

"Well, you woke up then," I called, hauling myself onto the crowded bus.

"No—it was Staff," Krister laughed. "We nearly missed the bus, we had to run all the way from the pier!"

The bus emptied rapidly as we drew further away from Funchal, and soon our fellow passengers were all country folk; the men short and chunky, with dark flashing eyes and bright white teeth set in smiling open faces, their muscled arms bulging beneath tanned skin like hungry lightweight professional boxers. The women by contrast were generally broader in the beam, there was a lot of black in their clothing and the fire of alcohol was not in their eyes, instead a look of resigned patience matched the crucifix each seemed to be wearing at her bosom. Large families, low incomes, cheap wine and the endless toil in tiny fields too small for machine ever to replace man, summed it up; but there was more gaiety than you'd find on many a London bus.

Until quite recent years the communication was only by boat, around the precipitous coast from village to village. The road is narrow, winding round every valley, crossing every garbage-strewn stream, climbing thousands of feet up every spur and down the other side. The citadels of tourism are left far behind in Funchal; the Madeirans' houses are low, white walled, and the windows green shuttered beneath terra cotta roofs. At halts, lizards dart on steep roadside walls of chiselled lava blocks, while the laughing conductor hands down wicker baskets of fruit from the rack on top of the bus. Grubby children laugh and play in the dust and the sun soaks into the island. Outside a run-down store, much stickered with Portuguese Communist Party posters, an ex-soldier lounges lean and hard, his jungle hat peaked fore and aft; in the window a few buckets, brushes and dirty china cups surround a light transistor radio wrapped in ripped polythene. Life goes on as usual.

It was already midday when the bus dropped us off at the minor road which ran sharply up hill to the Forestry Post. We had hardly fitted our packs on to our backs when the noisy old bus was gone, and we were left standing by the roadside. It was hot and quiet, as we began the long climb, and we weren't at all sure where we would meet the guide; in fact I was resigned to not meeting him at all.

"There it is—that house," said Staff, nodding towards a low place standing back from the road.

"Well it's a good advert," I said, "you can hardly see it, it's completely submerged in forestry."

There were some doves on the pale red tiles of the roof and a few chickens scratched about in the dense foliage covering the ground. *Posto Florestal* said a small sign by the door. We were about to go through the gate when an intelligent-looking girl of about twenty opened the door and came towards us.

"Are you looking for the guide," she called in good English. "I'm afraid my father is away in Funchal today, he got the message yesterday and sent word for a man to come down from the mountain to be here for eleven o'clock, but he hasn't come. . . ." I smiled bravely. These were just the sort of words I'd expected.

"Well perhaps we'll walk on up the road and then we'll either meet him at the top or half way down," I suggested. And we waited while the girl spoke, in Portuguese, with her mother.

"We'll come with you, as far as the man's house, maybe his wife will know something, it's only a few hundred yards," she said, turning again towards us.

As we walked slowly up the hill, for the mother was a stout heavy woman, the girl told us she had learnt her English at Lisbon University where she had studied economics.

"This will be the man," cried Krister, and appearing round the bend in the road through the tall pine trees came our guide. He was short and slim, with grizzled hair and an old man's face, worn and tanned by a lifetime spent in the open air. He wore a battered trilby and an old jacket torn at the pockets, his trousers were held up by broad braces and at his waist was slung a well-used leather belt of cartridges for the shotgun he carried on his shoulder. Not a word of English or Spanish could he speak, but he smiled a welcome through tobacco-stained teeth and turned to go straight back up the hill with us, leaving the gun and ammunition belt with the girl.

He walked easily, with a short even stride which never varied with the angle of the slope, his face wore the patient expression of a man who had been up this hill many times before, and was now simply waiting for the climb to be over once again. For us, with heavy packs, the road seemed steep indeed, after the days cooped up in the boat, and we were glad of the shade afforded by the trees. There were mottled eucalyptus and maritime pines in plenty, and here and there we passed chestnut trees which were already dropping their harvest of nuts wrapped in prickly green cocoons. The nuts were still too small to eat, so we passed them by. Occasionally we saw a solitary oak or plane tree but little else.

It was later in the day than we had hoped, so we never stopped, lunch would be taken at the top of the road at Fonte Do Bisfo about 3,500 feet above sea level. Soon we climbed above the tree line and emerged into rough heathland which Staff said was typical of large parts of his native Australia; the road dwindled to next to nothing as we left the trees, it became a rough muddy track much pocked by the rain, which had carved deep runnels through the greasy red clay. Overhead flew a few larks and some swifts soaring recklessly about in pursuit of insects. We came upon a group of women energetically clearing bracken and making the air ring with their cackling laughter.

We were all three sweating heavily now, and it felt good to be on the move again after the enforced inactivity of the trip down from Scotland. We felt pretty thirsty, but through a pantomime of gesticulations we gathered from the old man, who strode effortlessly along beside us, that there was plenty of drinking water at Fonte Do Bisfo.

In spite of the poor condition of the track there were still fresh tyre marks in the mud, and rounding the shoulder of a spur we heard dogs barking and much shouting and the occasional sound of a shot in the distance. Then we saw a battered green Peugeot pick-up standing empty on the track, and beside it stood a great barrel of a man, far too fat to have come up the hill by any means other than the vehicle. It was a rabbit shoot and men and dogs had been hard at it among the contorted tree heaths since dawn, but the going was so wet that the dogs couldn't get to grips with the scent, the fat man told us, cradling a loaded shotgun in his arms, and speaking in poor English with a strong South African accent. He had all the friendliness of a big fat man, and we welcomed the break from the climb, but the thought of lunch drove us on, through the shooters, all hoarse with their encouragement to the unfortunate dogs.

At last we were nearing the ridge of the mountains, and up on the yellow-brown grass of the slope we could plainly see cattle grazing, and above them a number of sheep and goats were sometimes silhouetted against the deep blue of the sky. Before we reached the grassland ourselves we passed through an area of what Staff called furze, and in the middle of this we came across a big truck onto which half a dozen men were loading armfuls of the furze while a solitary woman crouched over a small open fire in a clearing; she was the cook, and the smell of stew from her black pot urged us on our way to the summit for our lunch. However, because some cloud had appeared and it looked as if it might obscure everything, we paused a while to look at the view back over the south coast now more than 3,000 feet below us. The most impressive feature was the gigantic sweep of the blue sea which brought home to me the distance of 1,700 miles of open sea we had sailed to reach this little island. By comparison the steep fall of the land only occupied a fraction of the distance to the horizon which I half expected to show the earth's curvature. Down below, in the direction of Prazeres, we could see a thin spiral of grey wood-smoke rising vertically in the still air, over a vivid carpet of greens and browns of every hue. The houses were now too distant to distinguish as anything more than tiny squares of white.

Pushing on we reached Fonte Do Bisfo shortly before two o'clock, as the mist rolled thinly about the small hollow in which stood the stark grey stone house. We could see vague outlines of experimental plots of ground turned over to various seedlings, and there were some hutches or sheds for chickens which strutted about among the bushes. Once inside we found the place was fitted out like a miniature barracks, with cold stone floors still wet from scrubbing and coarse grey blankets neatly made up, complete with hospital tucks, on iron beds.

Lunch was tomorrow's breakfast. In the dash for the bus Krister and Staff had forgotten the honey, and our appetites, delayed in order to reach the summit, were too fierce to be satisfied with just a few biscuits: we ate all the breakfast Alpen as well, pouring iron-tasting water from the tap over the ready mixed Alpen, sugar and milk powder to make an irresistible, thin cold gruel. Our host was a young forester in his mid-twenties who wore a thin gold chevron on the epaulette of his pale grey uniform jacket; we couldn't help but notice the look of annoyance which spread across his aquiline features when the old man told him he was to take over as guide for the rest of our journey. Shrugging his shoulders in resignation he pointed to the watch on Krister's wrist, and although he couldn't speak a word of English or Spanish we got the message: there was no time to delay if we were to reach the next post, along the top of the island watershed, before dark.

We knocked back a small glass of strong wine each, provided by the 'guarda' as we called him between ourselves. We never knew his name because we didn't ask it, and we were never really sure if he was taking us on for one hour or twenty-four. With a smile and a wave we said goodbye to the old man who had brought us up the mountain, and then we were on our way. The ridge was shrouded in cloud and we kept on our hats and waterproof jackets over polar sweaters. It was as cold and misty as a summer's day on the coastal route we use for expeditions in the Cape Wrath area at home. But the going was fairly level along the gentle undulations of the broad grassy ridge-walk, and wiry sheep scuttled away ahead of us whenever we surprised them in the mist.

We had been going for about half an hour when the cloud cleared quite suddenly, and we were treated to a grand view of the north and south coasts and all along the mountain range. To our left we saw the tree-covered wilderness of the Janela valley which ran away to the north-western corner of the island, on the other side of the valley marched the 4,000-foot-high ridge of Fanal, running parallel with our own, towards the high plain of the Paul Da Serra which we hoped to reach in about three hours' time.

We climbed a round fifteen-foot-high triangulation tower some six feet in diameter and built of white-washed stone, by means of a spiral set of stones projecting from its side, and I could see Krister was already regretting his trial walk in Jamie's boots. Jamie, after a rush of blood to the head in far below Funchal Harbour, had decided that sailing was the thing for him, and mountaineering was strictly for landlubbers. Krister, with an eye for a bargain, had straight away offered to relieve him of his fine climbing boots, but now the shrewd Swedish pre-purchase precaution had misfired and he had sore feet with a long way still to go.

At four o'clock the sky was still clear but the heat was going out of the day as we approached a lonely cottage. The guarda greatly enjoyed stalking up unnoticed on his comrade who was busily digging a tiny garden close to the front door. The man was clearly pleased to have some visitors but the guarda wouldn't stop for a minute, insisting we press on before darkness came, after we'd walked just a few hundred yards further on we realised how the man in the cottage was employed. Far below we could see the smart functional building of a hydro-electric power station, and we found ourselves standing at the head of a mighty pipe which dropped perhaps 3,000 feet almost sheer to the power station. The water for the pipe came from a concrete canal set incongruously on top of the ridge. There was trouble: the guarda noticed a dead goat stuck up against the grating of the outflow pipe. It had only been dead a few minutes and it must have slipped off the concrete edge of the twenty-foot-deep canal and once in, there was no way up the sheer walls—it had struggled about but couldn't keep swimming for ever, and so it had drowned. The guarda reached down, grasped the dead animal's horns and pulled the soggy corpse out onto the narrow sidewalk, then he called to the solitary gardener and told him to phone down the depth of the water in the canal to the power station. Then, without further ado, we were off on our way again.

"*Trutta Grande*," he said, pointing at the canal and measuring an eighteen-inch gap between his hands to show us the size of the fish. Presently we came to the other end of the canal where the water gurgled in from a fast flowing *levada*, part of the network of artificial channels which cover most of the island. This one was of U-shaped concrete roughly two feet across and eighteen inches deep. "That's where the trout will be," I said as we passed the junction of the *levada* with the canal, "where the water is aerated as it falls into the canal."

We followed the *levada* for a while and I was disappointed that we didn't reach the spring, more than 4,000 feet up on the ridge which must be its source, but we veered away to the north of the *levada* in the urgent footsteps of the guarda. "Rabacal!" said the guarda presently, pointing down into the head of the Janela valley. A long way below we could see the neat red roof and white walls of the Agriculture Department's lodge. It was the place where we had expected to spend the night. None of us was keen to start the long descent to the lodge, because struggling back up through the dense laurel bushes wouldn't be much fun with our packs early next morning, and besides Krister reminded me that we had seen the place was booked for the night by rabbit hunters when we'd been in the Agriculture Department's office only a couple of days previously.

"Estanquinhos?" asked the guarda, and we hastily consulted our sketchy maps to look for the next lodge.

"Its almost as far again as we've come from Fonte do Bisfo," murmered Staff, "that'll mean another couple of hours across fairly level ground."

"Well we'd better get going then—or it'll be dark," I added. Krister just grimaced, but he said his feet were all right really.

The guarda walked quickly without a pack. We passed a nearly empty stream, whose pools contained a number of fingerling trout with white tips to their fins, and then we were onto the volcanic plain of Paul Da Serra, a desolate boulder-strewn place with a smart white statue of Senhora Da Serra, standing all alone on a plinth in the middle of nowhere. We were surprised to find a road gang laying a strip of tarmac with almost prehistoric machinery way out in the middle of the plain. Presumably this was a new road to cross the island but it was going to be a long job by the look of it, but then, of course, we were in a place where time meant very little.

It was just about dark by the time we arrived at the Forestry Post of Estanquinhos, on the far side of the plain. A damp mist was swirling around the smart white building, which with its red roof and green shuttered windows looked just like the typical home of a rich, middle-class Madeiran, except that it stood all alone in the clouds. There were differences inside too, thére was no sign of a woman's touch about the house, which was as bare as Fonte Do Bisfo. We had heard the last few shots of the rabbit hunters' day as we drew near to the house, and outside in the dusk a smart yellow Ford Capri was parked. Estanquinhos stood at the end of a road which winds all the way up from the south coast almost 5,000 feet below, and we now found that the road squad which we had passed were engaged in making this up into a road from what had been little more than a track. And it was because of the road that there was room for us in the lodge, for the red tiled floor of the kitchen at the back of the house rang with the hoots of the rabbit hunters. They cleaned their shotguns and swallowed slugs of strong local rum called *aguadiente* (firewater), and while they clearly enjoyed the return to the army days of their youth, for they all wore the camouflage kit of the Portuguese Army which made them look tough and cruel, they also welcomed their imminent return to the hotels and restaurants they owned down on the coast.

"Surely it can't be that far?" Crossing Madeira's central plateau.

Krister and John being shown the blow hole thousands of feet above the sea.

The top and bottom of sailing:
Staff untwisting the spinnaker
. . .

. . . Krister trying to get back
on board the hard way.

We dumped our gear in a bedroom which contained only one iron bed, and then keeping on our polar pullovers and woolly hats, we returned to the smoky warmth of the kitchen where hot coffee was now on the go, along with the *aguadiente*. The place was full of that coarse masculine atmosphere of comradeship, which you find in quasi-military posts in any remote place. Man welcomed man as brother, and the more the woodsmoke belched from the missing ring on the top of the range to yellow the walls, the stronger the bond became. The inefficient paraffin lamp and stacks of undried dishes standing on the draining board by a clutter of fire-blackened pots all proclaimed a masculine domain.

After the shooters had left, bearing a dozen rabbits to show for all their efforts, the place seemed rather quiet, and so a battered transistor was turned on, its tone matching the amateur glue marks which held together its cracked plastic casing. Our host was a short plump-faced fellow with a ready smile; he wore a slightly dirtier version of the same uniform as our own guarda who had made it quite clear that he would be staying at the lodge for the night as well as us. We cooked up a crude curry thickening with biscuit fragments over our trusty primus, which we had set up on the loose planks of the kitchen table. The guarda looked at us in a quizzical way when the crackly Portuguese newsreader gave what was obviously the latest developments in Northern Ireland, but his attention was soon diverted to the voice of Costa Gomes the new Portuguese supremo, who was giving President Ford a dose of liberty and fraternity in Washington. We were tired and soon excused ourselves to get an early night.

Next morning we awoke to find everything shrouded in mist, the resident guarda was muttering '*Frio*' through a thick brown balaclava helmet as he struggled to make French toast in the clouds of smoke issuing from the range. For us, it was reheated curry and biscuits for breakfast, before we began the long descent to the north coast. We wore our orange waterproof jackets again because the mist had drenched the laurel bushes through which we scrambled on our way down to the empty cottage of Caramujo. The path was overgrown and the visibility nil; we wouldn't have been able to find our way alone, but the guarda moved so rapidly down the slippery rock that it came as no surprise when he explained that he had spent five years at Estanquinhos before moving to Fonte Do Bisfo where he had been for the past three years. He seemed very cheerful as we went along, because his wife and family lived somewhere down below, along our route to the north coast and so he would be able to pay them an unexpected visit. He went out of his way to show us things of interest: suddenly leaving the path and beckoning us to follow, we staggered after him, dodging around and under the clinging laurel bushes and through clumps of ferns until we arrived at a narrow cleft in the rock at the foot of an overgrown cliff face. Our friend cleared some debris from the entrance and signalled us to put an ear to the hole.

"It sounds like the sea," said Staff, bent down in front of the tiny cave, "there's quite a wind coming up from somewhere!"

"We're about 4,000 feet above the sea here—I wonder if this is some sort of blow hole," I said, and the guarda squeezed water from the soggy moss which was growing right in the over-hung entrance of the place, this showed the wind coming up the hole must be very wet indeed.

After making our way back to the path we continued our steep descent, arriving shortly at the deserted cottage of Caramujo. This was a curiously English-looking place, not unlike a white croft house. The glass was broken in several of the windows and peeling paint added to the general air of desolation.

"Look! There are some apple trees," cried Staff in surprise, and we dropped our packs and ran across an overgrown lawn and threw sticks to shake the fruit from the upper boughs. But the apples were small and very bitter in that well-planned, but deserted garden, the chestnuts were no better either; perhaps the trees were just too high above the sea. In spite of its ram-shackle appearance, the sight of that little white cottage with its grey layers of mist rolling gently about it like fragments of lace, set against the sombre green of the steep mountain forest, that dejected small oasis remains one of my stronger memories of the whole voyage.

Just down from the cottage we came upon some blackberry bushes and Krister and I ate quite a few of the sweet berries to ease our growing thirst, in spite of Staff's warning about the worms. The fronts of our shins were beginning to hurt, but the guarda who was almost running now, had no pack to carry, and the path was really like going down 5,000 steps, each one foot high. The jarring weight of the packs gradually built up as the hours went on, and so we were more than relieved when we suddenly came to a fast flowing *levada* and were able to take the opportunity of a rest as well as a drink. We were down below the cloud now and the sun shone strongly once more, in sharp contrast with the cold damp forest of laurel woods down through which we had just come. Before us the slope dropped as steep as ever, still clothed with a mantle of dark green forest for another thousand feet or more; beyond that lay the green and yellow quiltwork of terraced fields, neat and small like overlapping dishes, where it ran down either bank of the tumbling river towards the village of São Vicente, which we could see quite clearly on the Atlantic coast at the mouth of the sheer-sided valley.

As we continued on down we noticed the trees were much taller now and the forest had something of the atmosphere of South America, I felt as if I were back again on the tropical slopes of the Peruvian Andes, happily following once more the course of the Apurimac which is the furthest tributary of the Amazon. Perhaps this was not such a far-fetched thought as it seems, for on this luxuriant island a total of 1,100 higher plants have been recorded, that is excluding mosses and lichens, and of these only some 120 are thought to be native to the island and nearly 400 are known to have been introduced by man. The Persea laurel, the most common tree in the area we had come through for example, is a wholly American species. Five kilometres away to the south-east the lodge was called after the Persea, by the local name of Vinhaticos. The taller trees were also a type of laurel closely related to the South African Stinkwood, and they were once much used for furniture making, being nearly as tough as teak, in spite of the nasty smell coming from the wood when freshly cut.

Soon we were down among familiar maritime pines and eucalyptus trees again, and we moved easily through an enchanted land of bright sunbeams and slanting shadows. We paused for a while near another blow hole, down which the guarda rolled stones, and Krister had a chat in Spanish with a woodman on his way uphill to cut trees with the mighty axe he carried across his shoulder. The path was changed now, from rock to greasy red clay, and breaking suddenly through the trees we came upon some A-shaped thatched huts on a new plantation which were being used for the storage of both the harvest and farm implements.

There was maize and apples aplenty, and the ground was strewn with the trunks of eucalyptus recently felled. After that, we passed through an area of deserted overgrown terraces, and I fell to thinking of how fewer acres worked meant less food produced at a time when the world cried out for more and more food. The woodcutter had told us the life was hard, and that many of the girls who used to work in the fields now left the island for the comparatively high wages offered in Europe for easier work as servants.

So deeply was I engrossed in this line of thought, about the impossibility of machine farming on terraces and the effects of education in removing people from fields to offices, that it came as a surprise when we suddenly arrived at the guarda's home. We left the path and passed between two small white walled houses, set close together. A glass was thrust in my hand and it was already brimming with rough red wine from the guarda's own vines. Behind us stood a massive wooden grape press. Suddenly the wife appeared, all dressed and shining faced to please her husband; and the sun shone on us and everything seemed grand. On the roof of the house neat lines of maize lay drying in the sun, and around our feet a glamorous cockerel pecked. Yes, we would have another glass of wine.

All too soon the time came to bid goodbye to the friendly guarda and we pressed on down to the metalled road for the remaining couple of miles to a small restaurant in São Vicente. Our 'shin splits' hurt even more on the hard road surface, and Krister decided firmly against buying Jamie's boots, but nothing prevented us from treating ourselves to a large lunch of stew at the restaurant while we waited for the daily bus which would take us back to Funchal.

It had been an unforgettable two days, and when we reached the flat in the early evening the hot baths were most welcome. Marie Christine also had a tale to tell: she had taken Rebecca to a small restaurant for lunch and had immediately noticed a solitary Lothario who sat preening himself at the table in front of her, hoping to make the acquaintance of the lonely young lady with the little girl. Acting like the true professional he was, he waited to discern the language before playing his hand. Once English was established with the waiter, our hero swiftly drew a matchbox and biro from his pocket and boldly scratched his message. Then he placed the inscribed matchbox on his table in such a way that my wife could clearly see the words: 'My name is Anthony. What is yours?' Still a lady likes to be noticed. Not all the charms of Madeira are mentioned in the travel brochures.

We were up early next morning, busy packing up the flat for the off. At nine thirty I met Lucy at the yacht club pier with the Avon dinghy to take delivery of three large green stalks of bananas, each four foot in length, from her plantation. As well as this she had three round bottles of local wine, each sheathed with wicker, and there were tears in her eyes as we waved her goodbye.

Rebecca said nothing, but we could tell she wasn't looking forward to the seasickness; her silences clearly meant that she would rather stay on the island to play with the other children at the Club Naval. It was brave of her not to say.

Our departure from Funchal was somewhat delayed by the non-appearance of Michael Zino aboard his scarlet tuna fishing boat the *Marlin*. The immediate result of this was that we ate too much mortadella at lunch and Marie Christine, Staff and I felt fearfully seasick as the boat heaved up and down in the choppy harbour water. We couldn't stay on deck because we were already pink with sunburn and it was uncomfortably hot with clothes on. Below decks the seasickness only grew worse. By the time the *Marlin* came alongside with Michael and his friend Miguel Vidal, we were pretty far through and it was getting on for nightfall. An avalanche fell into the sea from the cliffs at the eastern end of town, leaving a cloud of red dust hanging above the sea.

"Why not wait until the morning?" asked Krister, feeling quite all right, like Jamie. But I was feeling far too ill to want to do anything except get out and get on with it.

6

Rough Passage to the Canaries

WE SAILED just as it got dark; there was hardly any breeze
but we had no difficulty in gliding silently out of the harbour.
At first everything went well, our lights were on and the heavy
boat moved easily away from the harbour wall on a big swell
and a strangely airless atmosphere. By now it was pitch dark
with only a quarter moon and some of us were already thinking
of bed; then, as we ghosted clear of the tall headland which
shelters the harbour from the east, we suddenly felt the power
of the north-east wind billowing down from Europe through the
gap between Porto Santo and Madeira. Immediately, we had
to change the sails, we were hard pressed over and the higher
lights of Funchal were far away in the black of the night.
Krister and I braced ourselves in the bow, our oilskins pouring
water as each dip of the bow cascaded a breaker over us. It was
a bit of a struggle but we put up the No. 2 jib and left the main
down because we were running with, but a bit across, the wind
which was blowing a steady force 5–6 Trade Wind. While we
were crawling back along the deck in the glow of the stern light
I could see poor Staff already being wretchedly sick over the lee
rail. The boat was being thrown about a bit, and it was difficult
to keep my balance with three of us in the cockpit. A bigger than
usual roll threw me from one side of the boat to the other and I
crashed down on top of the crouched figure of Staff. When I
pulled myself clear he just lay there like a broken doll, with one
hand to his neck and a worried expression on his face.

"O.K., Staff?" I asked anxiously.

"Yeah, I'm all right—I just thought you'd broken my neck
again, that's all," he said, and pulling himself back to the rail

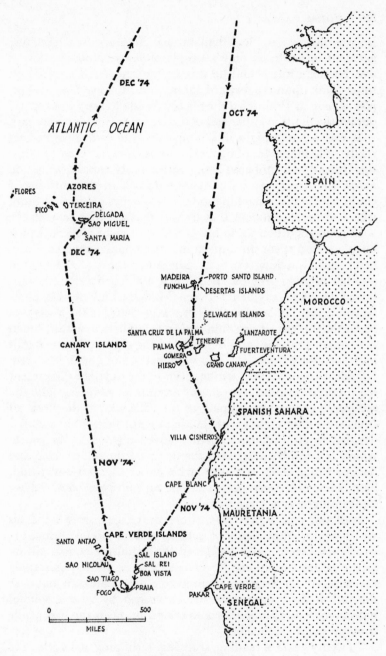

Islands of North Atlantic

he was sick again. Staff had broken his neck in a climbing accident in Australia only a couple of years before. Luckily it was Krister's watch and he was feeling fine. Staff crawled off to his bunk up in the forward cabin; and I followed him below, just as soon as I'd briefed the cheery Swede to keep a sharp eye out for the lights at either end of the Desertas Islands to our east.

It was a rotten night in a lumpy sea, the course we had set really called for a bit of mainsail, but no one felt keen to put it up. Instead, we lumbered along with a nasty corkscrew motion across the breaking crests. At four o'clock in the morning, I could tell from the retching sounds in the fore cabin that Staff, who had been confident that he was finished with seasickness, was in no condition to do his watch until eight o'clock. I took his place and spent an unpleasant four hours feeling cold and being sick, watching the stars pale and vanish at the start of another heaving grey day which was nothing like the pleasant cruise we had imagined between Madeira and the Canaries. Apart from Jamie and Krister, who were both towers of strength, the rest of us could stomach neither breakfast, lunch nor supper that day, and by nightfall the regular Trade Winds had not altered one jot. The visit to the unlighted Selvagem Islands was out of the question, even in the daylight the present sea conditions would rule out any attempt at a landing, also the self-steering gear was slipping as the rollers lifted the stern off course. So after a chat with Jamie at eight thirty that night, I decided to alter course a further fifteen degrees to the south, which at south by west eased the strain on the self-steering and had us riding more smoothly a bit closer to dead downwind. The Selvagerns were now well out on our port bow and we cleared them by a good margin.

Staff was still under the weather next morning so I did his watch again. After plenty of sickness and no food or drink, the two hours before dawn produced the definitive end to all my future sailing ambitions; it was cold and exquisitely miserable and much of the time was spent gazing not at the stars but over the rail at dirty grey water which rushed by with a spiteful indifference to all my efforts to cough up even the green bile from an empty stomach.

"Twenty years of reading, studying, scrimping and saving . . . and what do you get? Total misery in an expensive cold floating torture chamber," I thought dejectedly, waves of self-pity washing about in my skull.

"Positive thinking," I muttered gritting the teeth. "What an opportunity—a fresh start, some completely new all consuming interest—how lucky you are. . . ."

"I'll take over till eight." I turned and saw Marie Christine's wan face peering out of the cabin.

"O.K., thanks a lot," I answered weakly, unclipping my safety harness and making one last vain effort to be sick over the side. I even got down into the cabin and had my oilskins off before my wife could get up the steps and into the cockpit.

"Life's too short for this kind of suffering," she called down to me later, in a voice full of reproach. "Look at that row of books—they are all written by tormented people—what's the point?"

With heavy eyes I looked up at the shelf above my head, *Fearful Void, Impossible Voyage, Quest for Timbucktoo, Everest South West Face*, the titles read like a masochists' catalogue. "It'll have to be golf," I muttered and fell asleep.

At ten thirty that morning, Krister and Jamie hoisted a heavily reefed mainsail and we headed directly for the small island of Palma seventy-five miles away at the western end of the Canary archipelago. The boat was immediately steadier, and our condition began to improve by the minute. After a cup of tea and some biscuits, Becca and I sat outside in the cockpit and started a competition spotting shearwaters and petrels which most likely came from the Selvagern Islands somewhere behind us. We were particularly impressed with the pale green colour of the water in the waves just before they broke, the sun was out now and it lit up our lives once more.

"Land ho!" came Staff's hoarse cry at five o'clock that evening. He was up on deck and he couldn't wait to get ashore, after his ordeal of the past couple of days. What he had seen was the cloud-covered bulk of Tenerife away to the south; we were forty miles from our destination of Santa Cruz de la Palma and the wind was fair.

Jamie cooked a welcome supper of curry followed by fruit salad. Both dishes were heavily sprinkled with sliced bananas from Lucy's stalks on deck, which were ripening in spite of being almost continuously wet with spray. They tasted fine but we had to cut off the ends where sea water had got in and blackened the fruit. Everyone managed to keep their meal down and morale began to rise higher as the lighthouses at either end of the twenty-five-mile-long island came into sight.

Rather than chance entering a new harbour in the dark, with the onshore wind and heavy swell prevailing, we lay hove-to for the night, twenty miles off the port. When dawn came we could plainly see the spectacular peak of Roque de los Muchachos which at nearly 8,000 feet above the sea needs practically the entire twenty-five by fifteen miles of the island for its base. And as we sailed closer so we began to see the deep green of the banana terraces, which are the main source of the island's exports. Clouds rapidly shrouded the peaks but the pine-covered slopes directly above the banana plantations remained in sight. The port of Santa Cruz is the main town of the island, and with a population of only 15,000 it is much smaller than the 80,000 of Funchal, now 280 miles behind us. Built in the crater of a volcano La Caldereta, midway down the east coast of the island, it is a charming old town with plenty of atmosphere remaining from the sixteenth century when it was the third busiest port in the Spanish Empire, after Seville and Antwerp. From the sea it appears to be taken over by modern tall white blocks, but once ashore it is the narrow cobbled streets and grand old Spanish buildings with their hanging balconies of wood that impress.

The surf was breaking heavily as we approached the long stone mole, and tall cranes were extending it still further with huge concrete blocks. With no large-scale chart and no engine we relied upon the *Admiralty Pilot* for information, but we were disappointed for it was a long way out of date and the later supplement made no reference to such little matters as the fact that the tower had been removed from the end of the mole during the extension, and the yacht club was no longer painted green, and the two prominent rocks El Roque and El Calafate had been 'filled in'.

"Can I take your stern anchor?" came an American voice from a tiny pram dinghy waiting for us in the harbour. Our helper was a fair-haired, thirteen-year-old girl with a piece of string round the back of her head to hold her glasses on. The wind had fallen away to nothing in the harbour and we were relieved to find only half a dozen yachts anchored in a line abreast off the rocky shore. The girl and Staff soon had our Danforth anchor and bucket full of chain aboard her dinghy, then she flicked the outboard into life and set off for a convenient gap between a couple of small fibre-glass sloops towing a long warp behind her. Jamie dropped the thirty-five-pound C.Q.R. anchor off the bow and Krister lowered the sails. As soon as Staff put the Danforth over the side of the pram close up to the rocks, we started to pull in on the warp, and the yacht slid neatly into position between the two sloops at the first attempt, with her bow pointing out to sea and a good length of chain and warp running to the anchors off either end of the boat.

We settled quickly into the way of life at Palma, it was everything we could have asked for. The town was handsome and no more than a fifteen-minute walk from the yacht club brought us to the market, which was laden with fruit and vegetables including exotic treats like mangoes, figs and peaches. There were no tourists at all it seemed, and a happy balance prevailed where the locals wouldn't build hotels until the tourists came and the tourists weren't coming until the hotels were built. The yacht club was a magnificent place, just a fifty-yard paddle from our moorings, the elegant swimming pool and surrounding gardens, together with the showers, bar and private restaurant were all put at our disposal without any extra charge. The island loomed sheer behind the town; it was rather drier than Madeira, but we were in no mood to quibble over more and warmer sun. Across on the other side of the harbour the commercial life of the port went on without impinging in any way on our pleasure, freighters came in and went out and fishing boats came home from distant waters.

We had stumbled upon the most westerly port of departure for small boats making for the West Indies, an air of expectation hung over the place, it represented the start line for the con-version of many a lifetime dream into reality: the next port of call was in Barbados a giant 2,700-mile step away. Every day the number of boats in the harbour increased, and the crews talked of the sea rather than the island which was clearly just a launching pad for their dreams.

Three weeks before there had been no boats in the harbour,

and soon they would all be gone once more; winter gales had sealed off the flow of newcomers from Europe and the hurricane season in the Caribbean was nearly at an end, and that in turn would signal the 'off' for most of the boats nodding impatiently now at their moorings.

On the right of the line lay a lean forty-five-foot white Giles ketch probably built of teak, with a square transom stern; and long headsail poles, for Trade-Wind sailing, which reached up along the silvery grey of the alloy main mast as far as the spreaders. She had three canvas dodgers laced along the after end of each side and her low racy spray hood was made of green canvas. Like the elderly Australian couple who owned it, this boat had a much-travelled meticulous neatness about her. She was the only one with a trip line to her anchor. They were homeward bound, via the Panama Canal, their concern was a good supply of sweet water and correct timing for their departure to ensure a faultless passage.

The next boat was a white German-built thirty-foot wooden double-ender ketch with yellow canvas on her decks, into which were squeezed a young Californian couple and their two daughters aged eleven and twelve. She was well rigged but had no self-steering, when they were at sea each person stood a watch alone. The parents were a couple of goers, they would make the best of everything and be an asset wherever they went. They were completely caught up in sailing, the husband had been a journalist and only thirty months ago he'd written an article on ferro-cement boat building in California. "We took dinghy sailing lessons on our park lake in L.A.," he said. "I'm still keeping in touch with my instructor."

The two children were made to work hard at their Calvert Correspondence course education, which the parents monitored for 'meaningfulness' (they told me an example of this was the substitution of long letters relating their experiences to friends, in place of the usual boring essays).

They had brought the boat over from Nova Scotia, where they had 'iced-in' during the previous winter, living aboard and sending the children off to school while they got jobs in a fibre-glass boat building factory (the wife typing and doing a time and motion study). They were heading for the Caribbean to look for another job in boat building. Like everyone else in the harbour they weren't really content with the boat they'd got and dreamed of changing it for another 'perfect' boat.

A few yards from the searching Californians lay another kettle of fish. A 1934 white-painted teak sloop whose owner had sailed her round the world. At sixty-five and ex-Royal Navy, he looked rather aloof, a tall thin balding figure with a bad-tempered short upper lip and hands rough like a gardener's. Most people would call him stuffy and rather proper, but he'd be fun to be with if you teased him, and hell to reef or winch for. A big tough pusher of a man whose standards could never be met, some would say a Briton from long ago—some wouldn't be so daft. He flew the Blue Ensign and his boat was properly managed, there was no self-steering gear, and when he went ashore he was always rowed about by one of his crew of two. Meticulous with his gear and precise with his prose, he had left Cornwall in fair weather and mustered the moral courage to put back into port when a gale was forecast. His boat was lean and hard as himself and together they had rushed downwind from Europe, driving the crew as they came. Usually he sailed with his wife but she was over seventy now, and too old for cruising—even what he called 'the milk run to the Caribbean'—so instead the old shellback had signed on a couple of fellows to sail with him as far as Barbados where his wife would fly out to join him for a cruise in the islands. In the spring—well that was a long way off yet—maybe he'd find another crew and sail home to his moorings in front of his house in a Cornish creek.

The shellback's companion was a lonely Home-Counties widower of sixty-five, a retired plumber surgeon with the look of Chichester, thin rather than lean he'd suffered the ravages of comfort. He talked volumes on boats but owned to having a hard time with the skipper—'a devil of a hard man to work for' as he called him. It was he who produced the 1920 squeezebox from its velvet-lined box at a party, and with a broad grin proceeded to wring every last bit of enjoyment from the occasion; and it was he who most impressed Jamie and Staff with his warmth of heart. Whenever he met Rebecca he entranced her with a sleight of hand trick involving the pushing of a knife into his right ear and withdrawing it from his mouth; he would be any child's favourite uncle. Paying his way on the voyage he too was suffering from the recession, his hard-earned savings were shrinking in tune with the stock market and his pension fell far behind inflation.

The third man on the boat was a paid hand in his early twenties. Fair hair cut short over a square friendly face, he was quiet and kept firmly in his place. But for all that he was always cheerful and seemed pleased to know where he stood, which surprised me, for I was born much later than the shell-back, into another different school.

Then there was an old black steel ketch with tall brown masts and yellow decks, her hull all streaked with rust. Forty-foot-long and once the proud status symbol of a Nazi bully, she now belonged to a very different German couple who had remarried each other for a second time after a divorce. They were both physical education teachers with beautiful bodies; the husband at thirty-one had been a skiing and swimming instructor at Hamburg University, he had a handsome moody look with deep-set pale eyes and sun-bleached fair hair. In sharp contrast his wife had jet black hair and soft brown eyes, she was twenty-five and had taught modern dance at Cologne. They had left the economic miracle of the new West Germany, because they disliked its materialism and the mechanical process of its educational system. They had rebuilt the boat, first stripping her down to the original frames and then completely replating her in a Hamburg shipyard. Now they were bound for they knew not where, in a boat painted brown and cream inside and hung with poems and pictures I couldn't understand; perhaps it would be the South Pacific, maybe they would find their dream somewhere nearer home—maybe they could never find it. They were very short of money and they were waiting to haul the boat up on the local slip to repaint her hull a bright red, but they had been at anchor longest of all the boats and they planned to wait at least until Christmas when their parents were flying down to join them. It seemed to me there was a danger the dream might end there in Santa Cruz, harsh reality and inertia combining to stop them from sailing any further. They were greatly taken by my idea that they should make for Buenos Aires, store the boat and head up into the Andes to teach skiing at Barilloche, and Krister gave them an address there from the time he had spent as an instructor at the ski-resort.

Next in the line lay a giant fifty-foot catamaran with white hulls and green decks. She belonged to a short stocky American oil man, whose face was almost entirely hidden inside a great bush of hair and curly black beard. He'd saved for two years while living in Norfolk and working the bitter North Sea oil rigs, then there had been a further year of preparation. Now at last he was homeward bound for Venice in Louisiana, with a plump dark-haired wife who burned with a vitriolic hatred of the North Sea version of the oil industry, two small children, a large collie dog replica of Lassie. Also aboard was a ginger shipwright in his early twenties who had recently finished an apprenticeship building sixty-eight-foot schooners back in Norfolk, to where his return ticket was paid from Santa Cruz. The boat was hung with nets of gear and dressed over all with laundry, on the stern floated an enormous American flag which had brought them trouble in revolutionary Lisbon. She was named *Crystal Tips* after a "far out T.V. cartoon about a little girl—why you just drive it like an automobile".

Yet another style of cruising was practised aboard a huge Taiwan-built schooner which lay out in front of the line of smaller boats. A pair of tall masts, the forward one only a little shorter than the main mast, and an extra broad beam made this fine white-hulled ship looked much bigger than her sixty-four-foot length. She was all wood fastened which gave a piratical look matched by her young owner, a tall slim twenty-four-year-old Canadian who wore his long black hair in a pigtail and affected a slim gold earring in one ear.

"Grandmother left me some money," he said, with a guilty look. "I tried business for a while but I couldn't stand it. So I bought a sixty-four-foot ketch, but I lent her to a friend for a weekend and he wrecked her on Haiti reef—a total write-off and uninsured."

Following this he thought he had learnt his lesson, and swore he'd keep clear of boats. But it only took a few months ashore before he began to hanker after that compelling mixture of responsibility, leadership and freedom that goes with owning a big boat and hired crew.

"Honey, you know I never could resist a bargain," he confessed one night in a long-distance call to his girl-friend. He'd bought his schooner with every cent of his remaining cash. Now he and the girl-friend, who was a canny New Yorker in her early twenties, lived out their hippy philosophy in the cavernous interior of the empty ship, along with three starving cats and whatever crew they could find as they went along.

The life and soul of the yacht basin was a long thin crow-like fellow with a matching long thin moustachioed face not unlike Sam Costa. He had been born in Scotland but had long since emigrated to New Zealand where he had worked as a carpenter and by gradually buying shares in a small building firm he had eventually become a partner in the business. Now fifty-three, he was on a voyage round the world with his wife, a sun-tanned open-faced sport who suffered from blood pressure. They had sailed to Britain and exchanged their boat for a sleek, teak-planked weekend racer which was proving a bit of a handful for them and they were not sure if they could make it down to Rio for the New Year where they planned to meet their daughter for a celebration. This rendezvous meant adding an extra 4,000 miles to their voyage home across the Pacific and through the Panama Canal. The ailing wife was also worried about her son who had left New Zealand and married a Eurasian air stewardess model. They had then both become Buddhists and were currently tramping through the Himalayas from one monastery to another and carrying their baby child on their backs. The skipper of the boat was philosophical about his son's behaviour but a little worried that he would sell up his land in New Zealand to settle permanently in India. But they were a big-hearted pair and I felt sure they would get down to Rio all right, after all, they had recently managed a plantation in the wilderness of New Guinea to save the money to make the trip, and I couldn't see them giving up too easily.

From my own point of view, easily the most interesting boat in the harbour was a massively constructed, white-painted wooden ketch. Fully fifty feet long, and broad with it, she had been built in Buenos Aires, and she was an updated version of the famous *Legh II* in which Vito Dumas had sailed round the world in the roaring forties during the early 1940s. Her Californian skipper was a short, square man, with a nut-brown tan and a bushy brown beard. He wore his hair long and the crown of his head was shiny bald. Now in his late forties, he kept himself fanatically fit with yoga and a diet consisting almost exclusively of brown rice and vegetables. A subsidiary reason for this sparse style of eating was that he lived abroad with his two young daughters aged nine and thirteen because his wife had been dead five years; they had with them an easy going Texan who was certainly no firebrand when it came to cooking, or anything else for that matter.

Since buying the boat in Argentina eight years previously, the skipper had lived aboard continuously, making a number of innovations and improvements to what was already a remarkable craft. He had cut and planed the sixty-four-foot, 1,400-pound solid Oregon pine main mast himself, selecting the tree personally in the forests of its native State. The sturdy winch complex fitted on either side of the mast he had built of tractor parts which he had hot-dip galvanised himself, but the mizzen mast was original, a 300-year-old church beam from the interior of Argentina. The whole boat was an expression of the owner's will and initiative, from the garden hose air line and compressor, which enabled him to dive a hundred feet to inspect his anchors or photograph fish, to the loose-footed sails he defended so strongly in American sailing magazines. The girls were pretty wild, they loved the life on the boat; although they were careless of the actual sailing, they longed to visit strange ports, and whenever their father spoke of selling their floating home to move ashore and put the girls to school they implored him not to. Between them they happily controlled the housekeeping from their cabin up in the bows, and the friendly Texan drawled his agreement with the decisions they reached on most subjects from diet to destination.

Their over-all plan was to sail on down to Beunos Aires via the Spanish Sahara and the Cape Verde Islands, there to refit the boat in readiness for a voyage around Cape Horn and up the west coast of South America and eventually back to California. But they were feeling the pinch for money and magazine stories and T.V. films were barely keeping them solvent.

"I reckon there's a real danger of loss of life. There are no landmarks to see, the shoals stretch twenty miles offshore with heavy surf, poor visibility and there's a lot of sharks." The skipper of the Argentine ketch and I were discussing the coast off the Spanish Sahara, and he was not optimistic.

"Well I'm thinking of going there next, but it'll be a bit

tricky without an engine," I said, pouring over the chart and absorbing the navigation warnings in the *Admiralty Pilot*. And I'm afraid the more the American exclaimed 'Outta sight' and 'something else', the more I resolved to give it a go.

The life at anchor in Santa Cruz was so pleasant that I could see a danger of staying too long, at the expense of some other part of our voyage. We had far to go and much to see, and although we didn't realise it at the time, these were the last yachts we would meet. From Santa Cruz we left the usual tracks of 'the milk run to the Caribbean' for much less-frequented waters. We had changed the glasses in the port lights and they were now reasonably waterproof. Also, we had recovered our Danforth anchor and chain which had come adrift from the warp one day, by using the Scuba apparatus we had brought for fishing later in the voyage, and at the same time had salvaged an ancient-looking pitcher which delighted Marie Christine, who decided we must bring it home with us. Becca had greatly enjoyed playing with the American children and could now plough up and down the swimming pool with her arm bands on which was some advance towards free swimming.

Although we never really explored the island of Palma we had found a wealth of interest among the other visitors to Santa Cruz, and became a part of a happy, small community of like-minded people who bent over backwards to help each other. Soon the mould would crack and things could never be quite the same, but it was grand being part of it while it existed.

7

On to the Sahara

THE MORNING of Tuesday, 29th October 1974, dawned soft and clear for us, as we lay at our moorings in Santa Cruz de la Palma. About 300 miles to the south-east lay our next port of call: Villa Cisneros, the principal and perhaps the only town of the southern part of Spanish Sahara, which is a small sparsely populated and almost unheard of country lying along some 500 miles of West African coastline; where the dunes of the great Sahara desert march into the Atlantic. The country's eastern border lies at the most 200 miles inland, and for much of its length only half that distance.

After the miseries of the trip from Funchal to Santa Cruz, aggravated by a night start in rough sea, we planned this next leg, down to Villa Cisneros, a little more carefully. While Marie Christine and Krister went ashore in the early hours, to catch the daily market and to buy a supply of fresh bread, everyone else got on with the last-minute details involved in preparing for sea.

We sailed at eleven o'clock in the morning, in hot sun from a clear blue sky, with just enough breeze from the east to fill our largest Genoa headsail. I felt unusually sad to be ending this little interlude in my life, and our departure was made all the more poignant by a spontaneous and quite unexpected show of farewell, by the crews from the other boats in the harbour. It was as if someone on each craft had been watching out for us to get under way. Perhaps they were anxious about a collision as we were the only boat without an engine; anyway, as soon as we drew clear of the line of anchored yachts and ghosted silently towards the end of the breakwater, the crews all dashed up on deck waving goodbye and sounding their foghorns. It was easy to identify each individual, and as it was most unlikely that I would ever meet any of them again, I would always be left guessing how each struggle, brave in its own way, would end.

Marie Christine, Becca, Staff and I were each doped up to the eyeballs with Dramomine seasickness pills, and the drowsiness resulting from this gradually hazed the spectacular scenery as we sailed slowly south along the coast, aiming to pass between the little islands of Hierro and Gomera some thirty miles away. There was a layer of fluffy white cloud lying all along and half way up the mountains, but this left the jagged peaks and the heavily cultivated lower slopes perfectly clear. We were visited by a large school of what we took to be small whales, about five miles out in the pale blue waters of the straits; they swam slowly past us with their cliff-like foreheads and curiously stiff-looking horizontal tails. Rebecca was hysterical with excitement, in spite of the seasickness pill, as one passed right under the bows where she was sitting, its back all scarred and brown in the clear water. I fell asleep in mid-afternoon, shortly after the whales had gone on their way. Perhaps it was the effect of the Dramomime but I was still feeling pathetically melodramatic about leaving Santa Cruz.

"John, we're on the wrong course!" swimming up from a drugged sleep I could hear Jamie's voice coming to me through a sort of fog from the chart table.

"You have applied the 11° of magnetic variation the wrong way," he went on. "You've subtracted it when you should have added it to the true course to get our compass course. We've been steering 22° too far to the east for four hours, and that's why Gomera is dead ahead instead of on our port bow," he ended at last—grinning with glee at finding me out.

I lay there, trying to look asleep, but all the while thinking up some excuse. "Just a little test!—Took you a long time to find out," I muttered lamely; Jamie and Staff snorted with laughter, not fooled for a second. Luckily the wind had continued only a light breeze and so we hadn't gone far out of our way. All the same I made a mental note to be more careful in future when mixing seasick pills with mathematical calculations.

The sun set like a ball of fire, and the swift-changing light showed Gomera as a squat black hulk, crouched above our southern horizon fifteen miles distant. Far away to the east we suddenly saw the majestic snow-capped tip of Tenerife's Pico de Teide, floating on the clouds 12,000 feet above the sea. We all tucked into a big supper of hot curry, 'to settle the stomach' smiled Marie Christine hopefully. But I was thinking of the last time I'd seen Pico de Teide, as a cadet homeward bound from South Africa on a battered old freighter, the *Clan Kennedy*, nearly twenty years before. Seated with a hated fellow cadet before the Ship's Master in his cabin below the bridge, I completely dried up when my turn came to recite Article 9 of the Rule of the Road, which concerned the intricate navigation lights carried by fishing boats. It was that failure combined with the magnificent view of Pico de Teide as I left the Captain's quarters in disgrace which clinched my decision to leave the Merchant Navy. Well, the hated fellow cadet would be a master himself now, if he was still at sea, and he would have chuckled to see me make the mistake with the magnetic variation so near the scene of his early triumph, he of course had recited the article quite flawlessly after my collapse.

After we'd washed the dishes, we all turned in except for Krister who was on watch. It was warmer now than Madeira, and I slept fitfully under only a sheet because of the afternoon sleep, and thought of the heat to come by the Sahara, when life might become unbearable in our cramped quarters.

Came the dawn, and we were becalmed close under the thousand-foot cliffs of Gomera. We awoke to the sighing of dolphins as they surfaced for air about our stationary boat, and the dead flapping of the sails as they slatted to and fro with each roll of a gentle swell.

A light zephyr of wind came out of the north-east in mid-morning but it was nothing much, and around noon we dropped all the sails and hoisted the spinnaker alone. And so we slid quietly across the calm sea beneath a cloud of red, white and blue, happily munching our thick sandwiches of fresh salami and tomato followed by as many bananas as we cared to pluck from the long stalks on deck, which were now ripening faster than we could eat them. For the first time on the voyage, I was able to show Becca a live turtle, as we passed a small one, dark yellowy-brown in the shelter of a drifting plank. During a calm spell in the late afternoon Jamie and I went in for a dip, bursting down through the palest blue and on past darker shades until there was nothing but inky black leading to the seabed 11,340 feet below, then turning to glide up towards the surface which from below looked like a sheet of mercury. Back on board I checked the chart to find out the nature of the bottom all that way beneath us: Globigerina Ooze the abbreviations Gloz told me, and the dictionary described it as a deep sea deposit of globigerina shells which are apparently 'a genus of foraminifers with calcerous shell of globose chambers in a spiral'.

We dropped the spinnaker before nightfall and put up the full mainsail and the No. 2 Genoa, which was cut high enough along the foot to be clear of any chafe in the conditions of the little or no breeze which persisted on through the night. Supper was a splendid mince, with potatoes, green peppers and onions followed by fresh fruit salad and all washed down with plenty of cheap red wine from Palma. Life seemed just about perfect; we had a couple of lights on in the saloon, and on the tape system Sinatra was singing 'I'm leavin', on a jet plane', which reminded us of colder nights in the Magellan Straits. Marie Christine had on a blue summer dress instead of her red duvet jacket while Krister and Jamie wore only swimming trunks as they sat on the main bunk. Up in the cockpit we could see the silhouette of Staff's racy pink sailing cap against a stunning full moon. The radio told us that far away in California ex-President Nixon was sinking after an operation for phlebitis, and I remembered the admiration I'd felt, on reading the book of his previous crises which I'd read on a cranky old riverboat four years before, on the Amazon . . . what could he be thinking now. . . ?

Next day was Halloween which Becca had been so keen to spend in Santa Cruz, since the American girls were going to visit all the boats in the harbour and have plenty of fun. Because we had had to leave them all behind, we decided to have our own Halloween party that evening, but first there was school work to be done in the morning and the oiling of the teak woodwork outside in the afternoon. Jamie and I grappled with various problems of position lines using a special plotting chart we had been given in Santa Cruz. We had two sextants on board, one good instrument which I used exclusively to take sights of the sun, and the other an inexpensive plastic model which served as a reserve and a workhorse for Jamie and the others to practise taking sights and comparing them with mine. Celestial navigation is like most things, pretty much magic until you do it yourself, and thereafter simple in everyday use but complicated if you really want to master it completely. I have never seen the need to progress beyond simply obtaining a position. Jamie was able to pick up the essentials without difficulty and often worked out his own sights to cross check my calculations.

In addition to navigation, the crew was learning, by practical experience, plenty of seamanship and general boat handling as well as the more subtle business of living with others in a small space. I was well aware that we would need to be a pretty handy crew to manage the stormy trip home from the Cape Verde Islands in December.

The wind was more or less non-existent, and it was only by the conscientious efforts of the watchkeepers that we managed to cover fifty-eight miles in twenty-four hours. The sun was hot for we were moving south only about a hundred miles west of the Sahara, but it cooled down in time for the party that evening. Marie Christine made toffee apples and Becca appeared dressed as a witch, in a white sun hat and with black lines of mascara on her face and wearing a yellow woollen pullover over a long black skirt. We all had to tell stories, and Staff led off with the tale of his arrival by air in Indiana for his year as an exchange student, when a woman rushed up to him and throwing her arms around his neck gave him a resounding kiss—only to discover that he had been mistaken for someone else, and his hosts were elsewhere in the airport. Once the case of mistaken identity had been solved he settled down for an interesting spell as one of the family of a small apple grower in the mid-west.

My story concerned the mechanics of a night parachute descent from a C119 over the wastes of arctic Canada in February 1963 when many of the stick of forty-two men had landed in snow-covered trees. Becca is keen on this sort of yarn for some reason. Marie Christine took up the threads after me with a long poem about witches, and then Krister gave a demonstration of half a dozen card tricks he had learned on a kibbutz in Israel, in South America and in Scotland which none of us could guess. Jamie couldn't think of any stories so we played a difficult game of grandmother's footsteps in between the bunk and the food bins on the rolling deck.

At last the party had to come to an end so everyone could get to bed, for at sea we were used to a stunning twelve hours of sleep from eight in the evening to eight in the morning. But I had trouble getting to sleep that night and so I went up on deck to sit in the bows as we moved imperceptibly forward at one knot with everything bathed in moonlight. I was becoming increasingly worried at the prospect of the voyage home to the north of Scotland from the Azores in December; in Santa Cruz the seasoned cruising skippers were frankly astonished at the idea and several of them had quietly said I ought to change my mind. At the back of my head I kept hearing the voice of a man I'd never met; this was the father of Krister's girl-friend in Durness back in Sutherland. When he was told what we were planning he kept silent for a minute or two and then pronounced, "It's all right for him—but he's no right subjecting the bairn to the North Atlantic in winter." I knew he was correct and the nearer we came to turning for home the more I doubted my own ability to carry the voyage through to its end. My mind went round and round in circles. What were my responsibilities? Should I fly Marie Christine and Becca home from the Azores? A letter from my wife's mother had arrived in Madeira, offering to fly out and collect Becca if we called in at Madeira on the way home.

Or was I just looking for something to worry about as usual? If it wasn't this it would be something else. . . . In the end I decided to go back below and sleep on it, there was plenty of time yet to work it out.

Next morning it was the 1st of November and we had the usual 'pinch and a punch, for the first of the month' followed by Staff's Australian response 'a hit and a kick, for being so quick'. Our day's run fell to thirty miles and I began to wonder if we would ever reach Villa Cisneros, never mind the Cape Verde Islands a further 600 miles on from there. We sat around watching the ships, mainly huge tankers, passing us on the Cape Town to the English Channel route. Fishing became the main preoccupation, and Becca took to this with all the enthusiasm of the successful mackerel fisher she is . . . only we weren't fishing for mackerel. We trailed a long red courlene line, more like rope than fishing line, and from this ran a six-foot leader of piano wire with a lead attached separately. The lure was a heavy red fish-shaped bar with a stout treble hook, which we'd bought in Punta Arenas but never used in the Magellan Straits.

"Look, Daddy—fish!" Becca was jumping with excitement, as we pulled in the line an hour or so after we'd put it out. A whole lot of big yellow-finned fellows with bodies like blue-grey torpedoes were coming in alongside the lead.

"I can't see why they won't take the spinner," I said, but suddenly it was all quite clear—the lure was gone, smashed at the split ring which had linked it to the piano wire.

"Look out!" I cried, "I've got to get the tackle tin," and I jumped down the steps into the cabin, every bit as excited as my daughter.

"They're still here, Dad!" called Becca. "They're just following the self-steering oar."

"Oh! Look out yourself," snarled my wife, as I knocked over a jug full of freshly made milk.

"Sorry!" I replied, scrabbling about in the engine compartment, which was now running with milk. At last I found the screw-top aluminium tin full of spare lures.

"Oh, they've gone," I heard Becca call out disappointedly.

"Well now you can just mop up the mess," said Marie Christine passing me the soggy dish cloth.

"Next time we must be more careful," I explained to Becca, later. "We will have a safety coil of line here on deck—when the fish takes it'll snap this piece of cotton and while the coil pays out we'll have time to pay out more line from the winder," I added, carefully attaching a big E.P.N.S. Woolworth's tablespoon, less handle of course, to the piano wire.

"That'll wobble deliciously," I said as we paid out the line over the stern, and Becca nodded wisely.

Staff was on watch when the fish took. The safety coil paid out fast, and before he could reach the winder to start easing off more line until we stopped the boat, there was a sickening jerk and it all went slack again. This time when we pulled in the line, everything had gone, the piano wire had cut through the line. What we really needed now was the big Norwegian trolling reel mounted on a plank, which I had left sitting on the shelf at Ardmore. We decided to give fishing a rest for a bit.

After supper Jamie was reading through the *Admiralty Pilot* to get an idea of the hazards surrounding Villa Cisneros. "Well it's your choice," he said looking up thoughtfully.

"There's a spot just here, that's missing a wreck," joked Krister, pointing the dividers at the point on the chart uncluttered with the half-ship signs which denoted wrecks up and down the coast.

"Well, we'll just have to read it through carefully—perhaps you could make a sketch of your interpretation of the buoyage system," I said to Jamie, and he nodded quietly before replying, "Pretty important we arrive there in the early morning—there's not much to go by in the dark and it seems to be all sand bars."

"We'll have a look anyway, if we don't like it we can always head on somewhere else, can't we?" Marie Christine suggested and everyone nodded agreement at this rather cautious approach to the idea of our visit to the Spanish Sahara.

The wind was more or less calm all that night, the moon was a blood-red colour, caused by the dust in the air from the desert, and next morning we noticed there appeared to be a more or less permanent yellowish haze which impaired visibility.

"Oh dear," I said. "This is what the *Pilot* calls 'the heavily breaking surf is often heard before the shore is sighted'." And nobody said much in reply—we were all hoping for some wind to at least give us some steerage way.

We had only covered twenty miles in the twelve hours from midnight to noon; the sea was a swaying carpet of blue, the sun burned mercilessly from a yellow-blue sky, we were out on the Atlantic Ocean and the smell was of . . . OIL. I had subconsciously recognised the smell for days, but it hadn't been strong enough to remark on. However, I could now see it! We had grown used to the black bubbles of semi-solidified oil which are nowadays nearly as common as sand on the English Channel beaches; the watchkeepers no longer remarked if they saw the brown marks of oil-staining our white hull along the waterline. All the same I was shocked to see that when a temporary breeze blew up after lunch, long channels of oil-slick smooth water lay between larger areas of the surface puckered by the wind. Since the closure of the Suez Canal, all the oil tankers have come round the Cape of Good Hope and the Atlantic is a much more difficult place to enforce the international laws concerning the discharge of persistent oils at sea than would be the much smaller and politically more sensitive area of the Mediterranean. My routing charts showed blue-shaded areas which extended only sixty miles offshore down most of the African coast, in which it was prohibited to discharge these oils, but there was also a footnote on the chart which stated: "Ships of 20,000 tons gross tonnage or more, for which the building contract was entered into on or after 18 May 1967 are prohibited from discharging oil anywhere at sea".

In spite of legislation there was no denying the presence of the oil on the sea and the persistent smell of it in the air. We were more or less becalmed in a remote part of a huge ocean, not far from an empty desert coast. Few people would ever be stationary in these parts, for although there were often three or four ships in sight at once, they were all making best speed for port with their valuable cargoes. For them, the passage of air over the ship at 15–20 knots would convert what was to us an oily smell, into a fresh breeze. There was one notable exception, a far from old tanker much in excess of 20,000 tons spent the entire afternoon lying stationary no more than three to five miles from us, she was not carrying anything like a full cargo at the time, in fact I thought she was empty.

All of the above may seem to be a fuss about nothing, after all of what use is a patch of empty sea? But as it turned out we were surprisingly close to a most valuable asset. That evening a fresh breeze sprang up from the north-east and by midnight we had pushed the day's run up to fifty-seven and a half miles and we were right among a giant fleet of fishing boats, big ocean-going ships much larger than the rusty trawlers which sometimes limp into the local fishing village at home in Scotland, seeking refuge to carry out repairs. There were fish on the surface too, a school of friendly dolphins raced around us in the dark, exploding from the water in a shower of phosphorescent fire as they played with the speeding hull. How would the dolphins be taking to the oil, as they inhaled air from the surface, I wondered, or for that matter would the oil be killing the phosphorescent creatures or the jelly fish floating on the surface, they are apparently all linked in the chain of ocean life.

The honest truth is that scientists do not know what the effects of oil pollution will be on the sea, but they do know that six million gallons of declared oil spillage are being absorbed annually by the oceans at the present time, and that figure is steadily increasing. We might be on the brink of causing irreparable damage—nobody knows—but a centrally heated house and a smart car full of petrol wouldn't be much use if there was no food on the kitchen table.

From the cockpit of the boat the watchkeeper has a circular horizon of about three miles radius, plus the height of the lights on any ship he sees. During the course of the night the number of fishing boats around us steadily increased from six at nightfall to thirty-two at five fifteen next morning.

"Land Ho!" cried Staff, and I was on deck in a flash. The wind was steady but light from the north-east, the sea was calm and if we did go onto a sand bar the wind was at least blowing offshore. It was just growing light, the desert lay like a long grey pall of smoke unbroken, for the entire length of the horizon ahead of us.

"I wonder if it's just a patch of calm?" I said.

"Give it another quarter of an hour and we'll know for sure," Staff replied, the light was increasing by the minute.

Twenty more minutes passed, then Staff called out again, "It's land all right!" and everyone got up for their first look at the Sahara desert. I reckoned from the chart that we were about ten miles off the coast in seventy feet of water. In front of us lay forty miles of low sandstone cliff—the edge of the Sahara. Apart from Villa Cisneros, forty-five miles south-west, the chart gave no indication of any human habitation. The coast bristled with wreck signs but ashore there was nothing but sand.

The sun came up out of the desert like a burnished copper shield. We altered course to run with the freshening wind parallel to the coast. Gone was the blue of the ocean, in its place a dirty chop of thick grey green. The water could be ten or a hundred feet deep for all the distance we could see through it. It was unusually cold in the cabin and rapidly warming up on deck. The trawlers lined the horizon out to sea, and we felt uncomfortable out of their company, in the knowledge that it was probably too shallow for them to operate where we were now sailing. The north-east Trade began to blow in earnest, and that wind is the key to the entire fishing puzzle. The same dust-laden air which permanently reduced the visibility also rolled back the surface of the ocean along the African seaboard, causing a mineral-rich upsurge of cold water from the great depths that lie offshore. Vast, but probably not inexhaustible quantities of fish, feed at the end of a delicate ecological chain along the edge of the continental shelf. The trawlers come from countries as far off as Japan to scoop up the fish, often staying on station for months at a time and discharging their catch into factory ships or simply icing the fish themselves until they can hold no more. In the background the problems of over-fishing and oil pollution lie unresolved.

"Look! Daddy, look!" screamed Becca, from her usual perch on the stern hatch cover. I looked to where she pointed, some fifty yards back in our wake, and at first I could see nothing. Suddenly, much closer, right by the spinner of the log line not ten yards behind us, I saw a familiar sight which sent a shiver up my back in spite of the hot sun.

"Killer Whale!" I shouted, and I could hear everyone running aft to get a look.

We were moving fast, five knots or faster. But it was the sinuous power of the black and white monster that made me catch my breath. Beneath the surface it looked like a black and white wall moving at great speed towards the back end of the boat, it was so close that there was no impression of any swimming motion, just a solid mass sliding towards us at a frightening speed. Then before hitting us, it swung up to the surface, made a sound like an air compressor at a garage, and shot away under water. We all looked about us but we didn't see it again. I think it was surprised and fled, keeping under the surface for some distance before surfacing again.

During the previous summer, Dougal Robertson had paid us a visit at Ardmore, and he described how his boat had been sunk off the Galapagos Islands following a collision with one of these whales. Also I had done an hour-long radio phone-in programme with Maurice and Marilyn Bailey which was mainly on the subject of their own sinking by a whale and subsequent 117 days' survival in a liferaft and rubber dinghy.

Both of these sinkings I had studied closely in the course of reviewing the two books *Survive the Savage Sea* and *117 Days Adrift*, for the *Sunday Telegraph*.

My conclusion is that these whales often cruise at a considerable speed without a great deal of thought as to where they are going. In the case of the Robertsons and the Baileys the whale that sank the boat was moving at speed at right angles to the hull. Perhaps at the last minute it saw the outline of the hull beneath the water and thought it was a mating rival or whatever, and attacked by reflex action. Quite possibly the whale simply collided with the small craft by accident, in which case the several tons of whale struck the hull on the relatively unstrengthened side knocking a large and unpluggable hole, which sank the boat and injured the whale.

In our case the whale was moving in the same direction as the boat, surfaced close astern and instead of attacking, it sheered off to port and fled in surprise. We had been lucky: how many small boat disappearances are because of whale sinkings, and the subsequent failure of the crew to launch a liferaft or dinghy in time, can only remain a matter of guesswork. I should add that we kept our Avon liferaft handy at all times, and if at all possible we would have had the Avon dinghy with us as well if the boat had sunk. It is not widely known that a liferaft is built to specifications which require it to inflate at very low temperatures, and this rules out the use of tough synthetic rubber used in the manufacture of the usual sport inflatables; in its place a material much closer to natural rubber has to be used and this is inclined to perish with long exposure to tropical sun. In these days of good emergency radio communications, the life raft is designed to remain at the scene of the sinking with the use of built-in drogues in the expectation of a rapid rescue following the transmission of distress signals; it is not intended to be sailed or rowed vast distances to the nearest coastline. In the event of a boat sinking, which is without the means to transmit distress signals, it is my opinion that the crew would be well advised to have some other craft as a back-up to the liferaft.

We kept a good look out for whales for the rest of the trip down to Villa Cisneros but we only saw one, a much larger beast far out on the port side between us and the coast.

It was difficult to fix our position accurately, because we had only the one radio beacon from Villa Cisneros, and that was ahead of us and coming across the Rio de Oro peninsula. On the land we passed occasional crude rocky beacons but we could not be sure if they were marked on the chart. One thing was certain; not far ahead the chart showed the sign for a "wreck over which the exact depth of water is unknown but thought to be eight fathoms or less, and which is considered dangerous to surface navigation", with an additional (P.A.) indicating Position Approximate which about summarised our own position.

All things being considered I was in a state of some edginess when Krister shouted, "Look at the wreck," pointing at the beach where a large fishing boat lay high and dry, almost obscenely lain on its side, forlorn and deserted. The sun was so high now, it was hard to look at the shore for long because of the glare from the intervening sea, and after looking away the water by the boat looked suddenly sandy coloured, as if we were about to run on a sand bar, this didn't help my nerves much either.

We ran along, speeding before a rising north-east wind over a grey-green sea flecked now with white. The daylight was running out as we raced close along the Rio de Oro peninsula, a low twenty-five-mile strip of crumbling wreck-strewn brown rock barely a couple of miles across, past the gaunt finger of the Arciprés light, daubed black and white in stark relief against the monotonous brown of the desert. At last we came to Punta Durnford at the southern end of the peninsula, it was four thirty in the afternoon and we had barely two hours of daylight left.

"Five fathoms below the keel," Jamie's voice sang from up in the bows where he was swinging the lead line. We were within a couple of hundred yards of the shore now, a smart blue and white fishing boat perched newly wrecked on the rocks, her bows slanting helplessly at the sky, two or three figures clambered over her like blow-flies on a carcass. They were probably members of the crew returned to salvage what they could before the boat broke up in the surf. The wind was strong indeed, whipping sheets of white from steep overfalling waves which told of eddies and currents and of sandbars not far below.

"We'll go for Cisneros," I said, answering the unspoken question. It was now or never. If we stood out to sea for the night it would mean being blown far down the deserted coast, and there would be no sense in a long beat back against the Trade Wind in time for what would probably be another night approach to the town, which lay some seven miles upwind of the Punta Durnford, on the sheltered side of the peninsula. No, we would reef our sails and make the most of the remaining daylight hours and trusting to our own vigilance after dark.

It was the wrong decision.

For a start the buoyage system didn't match up with the sketch Jamie had so painstakingly interpreted from the *Admiralty Pilot*. There was no sign of the buoys which were supposed to mark the entrance, over the bar, to the inland sea formed by the peninsula. The shallow bay was twenty miles long and five or six miles wide, but the navigation channel was narrow and tortuous and the *Pilot* warned that the sandbanks were always shifting. We took six rolls in the mainsail and put up the No. 2 jib, all the while watching the pale surf crash onto the broad sandy beach of the point.

"We're helluva close," Staff called. "Look at the size of those birds on the beach," and with a shock I realised we couldn't be more than seventy-five yards off.

"Four fathoms under the keel!" called Jamie, and I headed further out, frightened to go too far because of breaking seas over shoals about a hundred yards to seaward of us. It was a lonely place, and the isolation was somehow intensified by the crowd of black seabirds running up and down the wet sand in time with the white foam from each incoming wave. Eddies and whirls were all around, and the wind felt extra strong now we were beating into it. My legs were trembling and I wished we were somewhere else. The warm salt spray was stinging my face newly burned by the fierce sun of the day.

Across on the far side of the bay, steep cliffs glared white in the late afternoon sun, marching to the horizon left and right. Staff stayed up in the cockpit with me and continued the business of spotting for buoys. The tide was running out and the tide tables showed low water was not until eight thirty in the evening, so we were bashing along against both wind and tide, tacking at frequent intervals to keep within the narrow channel

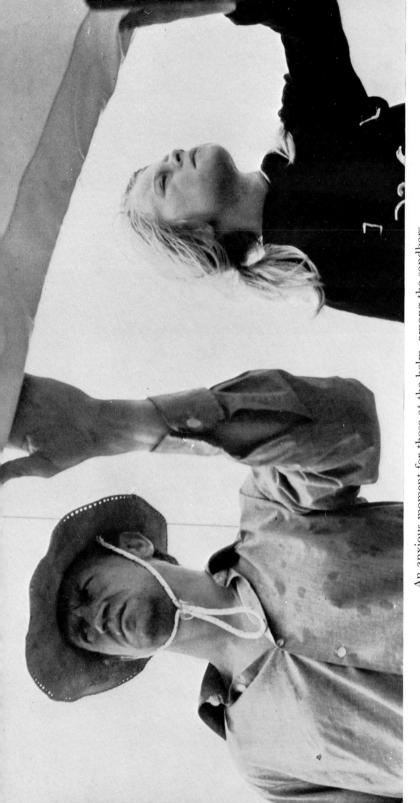

An anxious moment for those at the helm, among the sandbars off the Spanish Sahara.

Under full sail.

Approaching the Cape Verde Islands.

buoys which we weren't certain if we could trust, seeing as we had not seen any sign of the buoys at the entrance.

At sunset, Marie Christine dished up a welcome macaroni cheese and chicken suprême, just as an old-fashioned Spanish steamer with steep bow and long thin smoke stack, chuntered past us streaming a long plume of black smoke which left us with a strong smell of coal in our nostrils. She had taken a much wider sweep round Punta Durnford, which made me think we'd been lucky not to go around in a rough sea and falling tide, and as she butted up the channel towards the lights on Cisneros pier we noticed she was listing quite heavily to port.

"We don't seem to be getting on very fast," I said to Staff licking the crusted salt from my lips.

"Never mind, we've got the lights on the buoys now, we can wait till the tide turns if we have to," he replied reassuringly, which was particularly good of him since his favourite sailing cap had been blown away only minutes before.

We could see the steamer laid alongside the head of the T-shaped pier, and if anything the wind was easing a bit now the sun had gone. Although it was pitch dark, the lights of the town were bright and we agreed on a plan of action: to keep on tacking until we could slip into the shelter of the leeward side of the pier, then we'd heave-to and test the depth and if it was reasonable we would drop the anchor, and the sails, and wait for the morning before attempting to go any closer to the pier.

As we approached the pier, we were close hauled on the starboard tack and the spray came over the bows in sheets, from a short choppy sea. It was so dark that the lights on the three-quarter-mile-long pier blinded us from everything except the more distant lights of the town. Jamie and Krister donned their yellow oilskins and moved up into the bows with the lead line; they unlocked the lid of the main anchor-well on the foredeck, and then leaned forward peering into the inky black. Staff stayed with me in the cockpit.

We slipped into the lee of the pier, two hundred yards downwind of the steamer. I began to come up into the wind, to put the boat about so she would lie hove-to facing back into the channel. "Gently does it," I thought, "it's been a long day."

It was three minutes past eight, and with a slithering bump-

ing sound nine tons of boat ran sickeningly up onto some under-
water obstacle.

"Let go the sheets!" shouted Jamie, as I fumbled in the dark
with the jib sheet. Staff leapt into the stern and eased off the
mainsheet. The flapping sails thundered and the bumping
under the keel settled to a steady menacing thud! thud! as each
wave lifted and dropped the boat on the obstacle beneath.

"Ooh! What's that!" wailed Rebecca breaking into a flood
of tears in the cabin.

"We're just on a bit of sand," I replied to reassure her. Marie
Christine snapped on the light over the forward end of the
bunk, and almost immediately began reading aloud, with great
expression from *The Owl who was afraid of the Dark*. At the same
time the Rupert Bear tape sang from the stereo system. Becca
said no more, her attention was diverted.

Everyone else was thinking fiercely. Jamie threw the thirty-
five-pound main anchor as far as he could from the bow, in an
effort to prevent us from drifting further downwind into even
shallower water. "At least it's good for sand," I thought, trying
to imagine how even a C.Q.R. could get a grip on such a short
length of chain.

Krister and Staff dropped the sails and suddenly all was
quiet, except for Marie Christine's animated voice and the
ugly creak of the furniture in the cabin, the latter seeming to be
conducted by the tiller, which jumped in my left hand each time
we bumped with a wave.

"We'll have to kedge off when the tide comes in," I said
lamely, and Krister hurried to pull the lashings off the Avon
dinghy, where it lay on deck rolled up between the stalks of
bananas just aft of the mast and liferaft. Staff and Jamie
quickly produced the Danforth anchor, fifteen fathoms of chain
in a bucket and 240 feet of warp (one third of the 720-foot
length, mercifully cut up on Palma); then they joined Krister
in pumping up the Avon and launching it on the downwind
side of the boat.

I just stood in the cockpit, feeling the tiller jump in tune to
the waves, and trying to think of a quick way out of our problems instead of worrying negatively about what we would do if
the boat was badly damaged in this Godforsaken hole on the
edge of the desert.

Everyone was tired, and I had visions of Krister and Jamie losing a paddle from the dinghy and being blown away in the darkness, towards South America, some thousands of miles distant.

"We'll hang onto the rope—never fear," Jamie's voice called cheerily out of the night as Staff and I listened to the rhythmic plop of their paddles, and waited anxiously for their return.

At the first attempt they dropped the anchor too far away, upwind near the stern of the steamer, and they ran out of rope as they paddled back towards the stern of the yacht. Cursing their luck they hauled themselves back along the warp towards the anchor for another try. In the strong wind and noisy sea, Staff and I could neither see nor hear any activity except the occasional splash of a paddle, the harsh bluey-white lights of the pier blinded us and made our situation seem even bleaker.

"Do you reckon that noise is coming from out in the channel?' I asked Staff, hoping he would say no.

"They do seem to be taking rather a long time," he replied, his voice heavy with anxiety.

Down below in the cabin the story of *The Owl who was Afraid of the Dark* continued without a pause.

"I've been taking a line of the concrete water tower, the one that's all lit up over there, and this nearer building—we don't seem to be moving," I said to Staff. "The tide will be coming in now, so we'll soon be afloat if we can get the warp onto the stern to stop us from being blown down onto the bank against the tide."

As if in answer to my summons, the little dinghy, bearing two burly figures, appeared on a patch of glittering yellow water where the lights of the pier were reflected from the surface in front of our stranded yacht. They still hadn't enough rope, so Staff threw a coil of lighter warp which Jamie caught and bent on to make up the difference. Then they were alongside, and we led the rope through the fairlead on the stern of the yacht and forward round the winch; before the two fellows were back on board Staff and I had that rope cracking in protest at the strain.

"Should be on the make now," growled Jamie, "soon be afloat."

Krister slipped below to put the kettle on, a cup of tea would help calm our nerves while we waited.

For a long time nothing seemed to happen. Jamie saw some fish off the bow, but the depth of water on his lead line was the same as an hour before. In fact it was ten minutes to ten, nearly two hours since we'd gone aground, before the bumping began to alter its rhythm, with longer pauses between each thud. I pulled on the handle of the winch, steadily applying the pressure in the low gear, the anchor felt as if it was attached to the pier itself.

"She's going!" cried Staff, and with a few weak bumps she slid free. Jamie hauled up the anchor from the bow and the stern slewed round into the wind, which had risen sharply since the tide had turned.

I winched in eighteen feet of warp with the sea splashing over the stern; then we led the tail of the rope outside the rail and up onto the bow and made it fast. Letting go astern the bow swung up into the wind and suddenly we felt safe again. Marie Christine put her sleepy daughter to bed; Rebecca was half convinced it had been exciting.

Krister took the main anchor from the bow and paddled off into the darkness astern of us to drop it clear of the sandbank, while Staff and Jamie hauled us nearer the pier on the warp leading from the bow to the Danforth anchor.

It was quarter to midnight by the time we were all secure fore and aft, and everyone tumbled below, peeling off wet oilskins for a snack before bed. The boat was heaving up and down on the short sea caused by the tide flowing in against a north-east wind now blowing a steady force 4–5.

"At least we've been on the Sahara!" I said as I fell into the bunk.

8

A Sahara Town

As it turned out, it was lucky we did get off the sandbank; some of the times when I got up during the night we were shipping it green over the bows in a wind nearer force 6 or 7, and I thought gratefully of the broad flukes of the Danforth dug deep into the sandy bottom.

After a quick breakfast at dawn, we put up some sail and recovered the anchors. Within an hour we were tied up alongside an arm of the pier which pointed down to leeward of the main structure, our white fenders creaking and groaning between us and the dirty concrete wall. We had our Spanish courtesy flag, as well as the yellow hat, up on the signal halliards, and soon a smartly turned-out young corporal of the Sahara Military Police came aboard to check our documents. He told us he was from Malaga, doing a miserable two-year national service stint at Villa Cisneros. He called it the end of the world, and said the Saharans were Arabs and they didn't like Christians and wanted independence. The population of the town, which was only a military port, had been much greater but at least half the soldiers were now up on the Moroccan border 350 miles to the north, where everything but a state of open war existed between the two countries.

"Your documents are in order—you may go ashore if you like—but there is nothing much to see, we don't usually have yachts coming here," the mournful young fellow said, getting up from the chart table to leave. "It's like a prison," he added, and I smiled sympathetically remembering a similar spell in Bahrein more than ten years before.

No sooner was he on the pier than Marie Christine scuttled

up the ladder to try and buy some fresh fish from a rusty steel trawler, registered in Bilbao, which had come in early the same morning. Krister and I were delighted when she returned bearing five huge king crabs, as well as a plastic bag full of small lemon soles, squid, and some sort of bream which she had been given by one of the crew.

"Just like the old Austral restaurant back in Punta Arenas," laughed Krister, his hands running with juice as he cracked open another spidery red leg.

"They cook them up and keep them in a special cold room twice the size of this boat," Marie Christine added, putting down a glass of rough red wine and taking the hammer from Staff to break open the shell of her own crab. The sun was blazing down on us in the cockpit, and it combined with the endless wind to dry the sticky juice on our hands almost while we watched. Our luxurious meal was interrupted by the arrival of a fat Saharan 'Maigret' wearing dark glasses, who rolled up in a small sand-coloured Simca with some kind of official writing on its doors.

"Come and collect them the day before you leave," he called in Spanish, as he got back into the car, clutching our passports, and pointing at a square white fort at the mainland end of the pier.

It was very windy now and we decided to move the boat to the other side of the minor pier we were alongside, so we would be in smooth water. This operation took half an hour and we exchanged the use of the steps, which also served as a sailor's latrine, for a calm berth on which the coarse dust from the pier hailed down, immediately covering our decks deep in grey grit.

We soon realised we were an object of interest to the town people, for they drove down to the pier and gazed out of their cars at the strange sight of a yacht at Villa Cisneros. It was because of these visitors that we decided that someone must remain on board because it would be only too easy for a thief to clamber down and steal relatively inexpensive but irreplaceable items of gear. Krister, Staff, and Jamie strode off to see what was going on in the town while Marie Christine, Rebecca and I entertained the two fishermen who had given Marie Christine the fish that morning. They had had a fair bit to drink, square, dark men with scarred hands which looked inches thick. We sipped lemon tea, while they told us how they came from the Canaries on a two-month trip, or until they had 240 tons of fish iced up in the holds of the trawler. The only reason they had come into Cisneros was because the captain was sick—they were expecting a relief to be flown out within a few hours, and by morning they would be out on the fishing grounds again. The older, drunken man said his dream was to sail around the world with his wife and six sons, living only on the fish he caught to ensure his independence from the rest of the world. Then they warned us of half-inch blue mosquitoes on the other side of the bay which would send the 'bambino' to sleep for ever.

"Farewell—all the world are brothers," were their parting words as they hauled themselves up the shrouds and onto the pier. They had certainly been brotherly towards us, and we felt a little guilty at their emphatic claim that "the English eat no fish, it all goes to southern European countries". Marie Christine muttered something about "the way the price of meat is going, we'll be catching our own fish at Ardmore, never mind eating theirs".

After the fishermen left we felt a bit flat. It was a miserable place and miserable weather, I hated to see our lovely decks covered in the grit which also got into our eyes and matted our hair. The wind blew relentlessly, rocking the boat so much that I took the vane off the self-steering gear. I had a sore throat allergic reaction to the shellfish, and a skin irritation on my neck, chin and calves from the salt and sun. The howl of the wind made me feel as forlorn as the boat looked. We decided to do without supper and turn in early, before the fellows returned from the town. Then Rebecca collapsed into tears, saying how she was missing Pussy, and Noddy the horse. It was all too much for us.

Next morning we went ashore straight after breakfast, cadging a lift with a government official who had motored down to take a look at us. He dropped us in the middle of town; the street was dusty, the steady wind rolling paper bags and other refuse along the narrow alleys which lay between low white buildings. We scurried into a shop to examine the fruits of the Sahara: cameras, radios, tape-recorders, these mainly flooded into the free port by the Japanese; it could have been Aden,

Hongkong or Singapore except the soldiers were Spanish. Haggling to knock down the price, with sharp-eyed young Arabs in European dress was the accepted order of things, and we could think of nothing we wanted to buy. A sophisticated-looking negro was selling the colourful 'Bousbous' on a pavement. He looked away spitting contemptuously when Marie Christine tried to bargain for one of these voluminous blue national costumes. We stole away to have a look at the nearby fish and meat market.

It wasn't long before we felt we had seen all we wanted to of Villa Cisneros; towns are much the same the world over, if you are a stranger and have no one to show you around, they take some beating for loneliness.

We found ourselves in a small, well-planned park overlooking the pier, and Rebecca enjoyed her go on the swings and slides, but the grass was struggling to survive and the trees had a lop-sided sand blasted look about them; all the same if it hadn't been for the wind we would have been happy to sit there a while, watching the everyday life of the place go on around us. A stout negro woman walked past, her hair all done up in small pigtails, and there was a baby hidden from the dust in a pink sash hung round the waist and over a shoulder of her black dress. The corporation road-cleansing squad moved by in slow time, and I half expected them to suddenly galvanise into action and spray the streets with machine-gun bullets with weapons drawn from under their flowing boubous. Instead, the creaking steel wheelbarrow stopped and started, and one fellow became very involved in scratching his back with a broom handle, pausing now and then to throw back the tail of a long black scarf wrapped wisely round his nose and throat. The commander of the slow-moving wheelbarrow was the most interesting figure, a tall, thin man dressed in a stone-coloured sack falling abruptly from his shoulders to his black ankles, his head was cowled in a knitted grey hood which had a narrow horizontal slit for his eyes. Given a large red cross on his chest and he could have passed as a rather late Crusader.

We managed to persuade a couple of school children to take us to their teacher Señor Jaime, who we had been told liked to practise his English. After a few diversions we arrived at the teacher's small married quarters. He was not teaching until two o'clock in the afternoon and he ushered us into his living room. A small cubicle about eight feet square in size, this room was crammed with the material rewards of signing on for five years as an English teacher in the desert, and we were bombarded by eight-track stereo and dazzled by home movies; but his young wife agreed that it wasn't much like Seville. It was rather difficult to learn much about Cisneros from Jaime because it just so happened he didn't speak English and he was determined to keep on trying with it, with the consequence that neither of us really understood what we were talking about.

As we reeled out into the noonday sun, we realised it was lunchtime for everything was closed for the siesta. We were lucky to find a small bar-cum-restaurant, not far from the waterfront where we found ourselves the only patrons of the eating side, although a number of what looked to be teen-aged Army officers tottered about by the bar and the occasional Arab came in for a Coca-Cola; as drink is not allowed in the Moslem faith I wondered if the Coke might be laced with something a hint stronger, but this was probably an unworthy thought.

Once things got going, we realised that, of course, there is a whole rich pattern of life being weaved in Cisneros, just as there must be in any human community and we began to enjoy ourselves. The thin greying waiter with his tattooed arms and the only blue eyes in town, the villainous looking proprietor half-canned with his right arm in a sling under his shirt and his wife a semi-retired belly dancer type with a non-stop cackle and a voluptuous seventeen-year-old daughter who drew as many customers to the outfit as the booze and cuisine combined. The endlessly repeated Beatle tracks on the tape system, which were ignored by staff and clientele alike, as if the foreign language rendered them unboring.

We had finished a huge steak and chips, and were forcing down the tinned fruit salad which the waiter had drowned in Crême de Menthe, when Marie Christine suddenly grabbed my arm and said, "You know what that steak was, don't you? I've just realised, it was camel!"

We headed slowly back to the boat, after lunch, because there were several points I wanted to check on the chart and in the *Pilot* before making the tricky passage out to the ocean on our way to the Cape Verde Islands. I was well aware how easy it

would be to go aground on the way out, with far worse consequences than the gentle grounding we had suffered in the lee
of the pier. Also we had been asked out to the home of a
Saharaoise for tea at nine o'clock in the evening, and we wanted
to have everything ready for a departure early in the morning,
before our host arrived at the boat in his motor car to drive us
into town for the tea party.

We were just walking onto the pier when Rebecca asked,
"Daddy, why are the lights flashing on those buoys when they
are on the land?" Replying that I wasn't sure but I had an idea,
I walked quietly towards a short wiry looking man with grey
hair and a sun-wrinkled skin who was staring fixedly at the
lights with a stopwatch in his hand. After a minute or two, he
looked satisfied that the timing of the flashes was correct, and
putting the stopwatch carefully into the breast pocket of his
shirt, he strode rapidly towards the open door of his nearby
ground-floor office. His walk had the athletic spring of a man
who at his age must be putting a good bit of time into keeping
fit. As soon as he was inside the office, we followed, and after
knocking on the door we introduced ourselves. He spoke no
English, but chose French with Marie Christine, in preference
to our poor Spanish. Precise and bright eyed, Alfredo was most
interested to learn we were from the yacht at the pier. He was
not a pilot but the man who, for the last thirty years, had been
responsible for the lights and buoys all along the coast of the
southern half of the Spanish Sahara coastline. His French was
so fluent that he transformed Cisneros for us into a romantic
Foreign Legion outpost. The day was over, and he asked us to
come back for some tea at his home, so he could show us the
best way out of the channel.

We climbed into the dusty Land Rover, and set off through
the geometrical network of military married quarters, stopping
after five minutes or so outside a typical low white bungalow
made of concrete and set back some forty feet from the road.
The small front garden was well cared for, in sharp contrast
with the rolling desert of the narrow peninsula which began a
few houses away at the end of the street.

Alfredo's wife Anna came to the front door to meet us, and
once inside the door the desert was gone. We could have been
in an immaculate suburban home outside any city of the

Western world. A delicious tea of hot pancakes and honey, with tea drunk from delicate bone china cups was so quickly produced that we thought Anna must have known we were coming. A soft, comfortably built woman with a warm personality, Anna was clearly pleased to have strange visitors and she and Marie Christine were soon deep in family albums. Rebecca made friends with a well-fed ginger cat and looked at the photographs at the same time; unable to understand a word of the conversation she made her own story from the pictures.

Alfredo and I moved into his office next door; the walls of the big room were hung with large-scale plans of the various installations that were his responsibility, and I was amused to see that his first action on entering the office was to switch on the light at Arciprés Grande, the ninety-nine-foot black and white tower we had passed on our way south along the outside of the peninsula. It seemed so likely that he might have forgotten— maybe that was why there were so many wrecks out there! But then one look at Alfredo showed he wasn't the sort of man to forget anything, the lights and buoys were his life's work and he cared for them as if they were his children. With all the tools of the professional cartographer at his disposal he swiftly prepared a scale drawing of my route out of the channel, carefully noting down the relevant bearings and distances of the various buoys, light towers and marker posts along the way.

"Those two can buoys I was timing down at the pier—they are the east and west channel marker buoys. The bar has moved and they are in for servicing. Where did you come in?"

On the wall chart I traced our probable route, close to the end of Punta Durnford. Alfredo winced and peered at the depths.

"Seven feet at lowest water," he exclaimed, "what does your boat draw?"

"About six—maybe more," I replied quietly.

He looked at me. "Well you won't go back that way, you were lucky it was half tide," he shrugged and gave a mischievous little grin.

"Can you give me the tides for the next couple of days?" I asked, changing the subject; it would be useful to check the Admiralty Tables again, although I knew there could be no difference—but at least I could check the time zone for certain.

After some discussion we agreed that to be safe, I should sail at first light on the day after next, that would give me twelve hours of daylight if anything went wrong, and there were bound to be other boats in the area during that time. I decided not to mention we had no engine, and as we left the office to rejoin the others in the house, I wanted to ask him if, in thirty years, he ever had forgotten to switch on the Arciprés' light but I hadn't the nerve. After a quick look at his astonishing collection of photographs, those of a lifetime's skin diving in the bay and long journeys by Land Rover through the desert, it was time for us to go back to the boat. Marie Christine would have dearly liked a hot bath, but she hadn't the nerve to ask either.

On the yacht, the dust was thicker than ever, and I hated the scrunching sound of our feet as we walked along the decks; we called goodbye to Alfredo who kindly stood in the dark up on the pier until we were safely in the cockpit, before returning to the Land Rover and driving back to his home.

Jamie was looking after the boat and Krister and Staff were ashore, but they returned just in time for a big supper of all the remaining lemon soles, which Marie Christine fried up in no time. Jamie had been looking through the *Pilot* again, and he was now very pleased to have the plan Alfredo had drawn to check with his own interpretation of the book.

When our friend Gamoudi sounded his horn on the pier above, at nine o'clock sharp, we were still checking the chart, so he came down for a cup of instant coffee as an aperitif to his own tea party.

"Try and fix up a trip into the desert," Krister whispered later, as we followed Gamoudi back up to his waiting car. Staff, Jamie and he were staying on board for the rest of the evening to write letters and so they looked after Rebecca for us; they felt they had exhausted the town's possibilities and now they wanted to explore the desert. It wasn't going to be easy.

Gamoudi's car was a small new saloon, a Ford Escort or the like and it contained every gadget I'd ever seen in a car. As we sped along, Bob Dylan protested to us from somewhere under the steering wheel, while the needles of rev counters and compasses whirled on the dashboard. A tall fellow in his early twenties, with a soft persuasive voice allied to a generally charming manner, we had met Gamoudi only that morning in

one of his father's several shops, where he was dispensing everything from lipsticks to tape-recorders, and although we had
bought nothing he had asked us to his home that evening to
practise his English.

The fact that he was a Saharaoise and we were driving in the
dark gave me a feeling that we were on an underground
mission, and this was only enhanced by our almost furtive
arrival at the back of a non-descript block of square, flat-
roofed two-storey buildings. We parked the car, and I noticed
a light burning dimly through a curtain in an upstairs window
as we darted across the street towards the house. The stairs
immediately inside were narrow and nearly vertical; at the top,
from a small unlit landing we went through the right-hand one
of three doors, and found ourselves in a long room with a blue
carpet on the floor and sofas lining the walls. There was a
definite smell of incense burning, though I couldn't see where;
our host bade us be seated then he excused himself for a minute
to arrange for the tea to be brought in. Marie Christine and I
sat together, gazing at the covers of left-wing international
magazines neatly laid on low tables in the centre of the room. I
half expected military police to arrive at any minute.

The place had a strangely ambivalent atmosphere, it was
charged with emotion like an active guerilla headquarters; on
the one hand there was a massive quadrophonic Blaupunkt
tape system with its flickering amplitude needles and rolling
tapes and beside it stared the empty grey face of a giant colour
television screen, set in the wall as if poised for Big Brother to
appear and give us the orders, while on the other hand the
incense, carpet and soft hand embroidered cushions spoke of
the studied good manners and timelessness of another age.

"This room is a meeting place for our relations who come in
from the desert," smiled Gamoudi, as he came in leading a shy
Arab boy of about eighteen, who wore the traditional flowing
blue bousbous and carried a primitive charcoal burner in his
hands, "and this is my cousin, he has recently come here from a
small desert village in Mauretania where he has lived for most
of his life, he is going to work in my father's shops."

Two other young Saharaoise friends of Gamoudi came in to
join us. They were both dressed in the casual European style of
slacks and open shirt and because they didn't speak English,

Gamoudi translated the conversation for them. One was a medical student working in the military hospital; he was well on the way to becoming a doctor and he was the most extreme leftist of the three friends, professing an admiration for Che Guevara, whom he closely resembled in appearance. The other friend wanted to be a journalist, he was quieter, but perhaps that was because he understood no English, whereas the medical student appeared to always have the general drift of the conversation before it was translated by Gamoudi.

Meanwhile, the shy desert boy was busy making the tea in a battered kettle over the charcoal burner which was now set on the floor in a corner of the room. Quite clearly it was a long drawn out ceremony and one which Gamoudi told us was carried out four times daily by the nomadic tent dwellers in the desert.

"The tea-drinking is really the basis for periods of discussion during the daily life of our brothers in the desert, it is meant to take a long time and we always drink three small cups one after the other, without milk of course. The first cup is taken without sugar, it is bitter like Life. The second cup has a little sugar in it and is bitter-sweet, like Love. And the third and last cup has much sugar and is sweet like Death."

Gamoudi told us this with reverence. While we sipped the tea, we also nibbled biscuits from a large square tin of assorted Huntley and Palmers, and delicious toasted almonds which were heaped on a plate.

Our conversation was simply political. The three young men were certainly in an interesting situation, because of phosphate. Imagine the Spanish Sahara, a strip of land 500 miles long and 150 miles wide with a population of 100,000 Saharaoise, many of whom live a primitive nomadic existence, and 50,000 Spanish soldiers, and compare this with Britain, perhaps twice the size but with a population of 55,000,000. For centuries nothing much happened in Spanish Sahara, and then about the time when every small nation is being granted independence from colonial oppression, phosphate is discovered, a considerable percentage of the earth's remaining reserves is proved to exist in this little country.

Gamoudi and his two friends fervently wished for the 50,000 Spanish soldiers to be gone, but at the same time they wanted

Spanish military protection from the fifteen million Moroccans who were suddenly keen to absorb their small neighbour. All three friends were studying a university correspondence course, Gamoudi himself was reading law: they all stood to play a significant part in the emergence of an independent Sahara nation and they openly supported the leader of their Liberation Front, who was an active enemy of the Spanish operating from Mauretania immediately to the south of Spanish Sahara. Quite clearly there was going to be no desert expedition for us!

Gamoudi said they disliked the U.S.A. as much as Russia, that Israel was simply an American presence in the Middle East and that Allende the dead ex-president of Chile was their greatest hero, murdered by the Americans. They preferred Wilson to Heath, but they didn't really think about Britain at all. They looked forward to a referendum in 1975 when they expected to gain their independence from Spain, then they felt they needed a benevolent dictator to pull the 100,000 people together. The nomads should give up their hard simple life in the desert and join in the future of their country, every family should have Land Rovers instead of camels. There was to be a headlong rush into the blank wall of materialism, all because of the phosphate.

And so the conversation went on, and would have continued all night had the medical student not had to return to the hospital for duty, and had Marie Christine and I not pleaded exhaustion in the strange climate. The boy from the desert had long since left us in spirit, he sat in the corner with a far-away look in his eyes, and Gamoudi said his relations were all like that when they came to visit his father from the desert. He said, "Many of them will only sleep outside, where they can see the stars."

9

Salt Island

0530 HOURS Thursday, 7th November 1974, forty-one days out of Ardmore.

I wake up for the sixth time in the cramped curved bunk, the luminous dial of my Rolex says it is five thirty in the morning. I nudge my sleeping wife, "It's time to get up," I say grumpily, she sits up quickly—always good at reveille. The kettle goes on the cooker, and I crawl up onto the gritty deck and start washing my way forward, throwing buckets of water quietly up ahead to swill away the dirt so I can avoid that awful scrunching sound. The boat is just about ready to go, I spent all yesterday checking it. In the bleak light glaring from tall street lamps on the pier I take off the mainsail cover and undo the sail ties securing our No. 2 jib to the guardrail up in the bow, it is all wet with a heavy dew. The north-east breeze is light, making everything seem a deal more friendly than the harsh wind we have known up to now.

"After five thirty, fellows, tea's nearly ready—let's get going," I call down softly through the open forehatch.

"O.K.," Jamie calls back, as cheerfully as his gruff voice allows.

Ten minutes later, and we are away, drifting under the jib alone across a pool of light between the minor piers. At the end of the 'T' on the head of the main pier, a tiny spot of light waves a circular goodbye; it's a sentry, cigarette in hand, we can just make out his silhouette leaning against the rail.

No one says much—the tea hasn't really soaked down to the toes yet. The full mainsail goes up quietly, plastic luff slides clicking faintly in the mast track. I stay at the helm, heading for

Getting ahead in the Cape Verdes.

The Cape Verdes: Rebecca
makes some beach friends,
above; below, with Marie
Christine visiting a salt mine.

the pale white flashes marking the main channel buoy. Jamie
and Krister change the headsail for the No. 2 Genoa.

It's high tide. We reach the channel buoy and turn away to
starboard, the breeze is still light on my cheek. Up ahead, just
as Alfredo's plan reads, the lights on the buoys stretch ahead in
line, right on our compass course of 220°m.

The new day is born, the air seems to buzz with the increasing
light. Out of the Sahara, on the far side of the bay, the sun
comes up fast—a flat-topped orange ball. A flock of terns fly
past, low and silent over silver water.

By seven thirty it's broad daylight and Galera light tower at
the end of Punta Durnford is nearly abeam; when it is we must
alter course 90° to head directly towards it, keeping the light
and the Sarga marker-stick in line. But the wind is light and
feathery now, and the tide runs strongly out of the bay, glee-
fully jumping over the sandbars which try in vain to check its
rush. We turn for the light and the tide continues to push us
sideways; oh, for a bit of that wind we despised yesterday. Out
on the port side we see the eddies and whirls, and the spiky
waves breaking ominously over the sandbanks. Krister and
Staff heave the Avon dinghy up over the lee rail to increase our
speed, but it's left inflated and ready just in case. . . .

The tide-rip lies close on the port bow, a flock of gulls wheel
over a patch of fish; we are unable to keep the stick in line with
the more distant light tower. The stick moves steadily away to
the right of the light—we're slipping badly.

And then it's over, we're through, smooth as a bullet from a
barrel. Out on the ocean we pick up a lazy swell, the sun is hot
without the breeze and the Cape Verdes lie dead downwind
550 miles to the south-west. Krister streams the log and sets up
the self-steering gear. I feel the Dramamine taking effect, it's
time for a sleep. . . .

When I awoke a couple of hours later we had only covered
five miles or so, but Punta Durnford looked a good way off in
the haze. Up on deck, I noticed immediately that everything
was spotless and the Avon was neatly stowed away on the deck
aft of the life raft. I was delighted, Cisneros was an oppressive
place and tempers had been getting a little short in the cramped
dirty conditions. Now the air was clear again and we were on
our way.

During the next night the Trade Wind returned and we picked up speed, rolling along with the full mainsail out to port and the No. 1 Genoa boomed out to starboard. Life settled down for three days of high-speed running before the wind: 130, 148 and 143 miles per day, under a brassy sky full of dust from the Sahara. Rebecca spotted for the white cuttlefish floats, so beloved by caged budgerigars back in Britain; then we moved into the flying fish belt and she spent hours watching them take off in silver clouds out of our way, as we barrelled along with big blue-green seas overtaking us from behind, picking us up and bearing us along in the surf for a few seconds then letting us down and passing on. Down below, Marie Christine found the rolling motion made cooking much more difficult, even dangerous; hot soup or scalding porridge kept crashing off the stove and splattering thick and sticky across the cabin floor. Standing at the cooker, jammed inside the supporting waist belt, she had to wear a long plastic Newcastle Brown apron and seaboots to shield her against getting burned.

We soon sailed clear of the fishing fleet and away from the shipping lanes too. The ocean was a great rolling empty place and no amount of flying fish for breakfast or dolphins at the bow could remove the feeling of desolation brought about by the Harmattan, that dry dusty wind from the African interior.

No one slept well on the night of 10th November, it was hot and humid, we had a clear R.D.F. bearing off the radio beacon dead ahead on Ilha do Sal, a narrow rocky island some sixteen miles north to south and five miles east to west, but we couldn't be sure of the distance. In spite of the arid mountains, which rise sharply to 1,300 feet the *Admiralty Pilot* insisted "the haze over the whole group is often so thick that the surf is sighted before the land".

"Land Ho!" Krister called out at 0930 on the following morning. The sky was cloudy and it looked like rain. The jagged mountains were high in the sky and we could see the surf, a thin necklace of white.

Straight away we went onto hand steering and altered course to the north-west, aiming to pass round the northern end of the island and sail down to the small port of Palmeira on the west coast which should be sheltered from the wind and swell.

"Will there be a supermarket, Daddy, like at Santa Cruz?" asked my daughter. Was this the greatest wonder she had seen after a quiet childhood in the Highlands? I looked across the three miles of rough water to the desert island. A ruined tower and a pair of roofless houses were the only signs that men had ever visited the place; inland, cone-shaped hills of dust stood sentinel over an empty plain strewn with rocks which we tried in vain to turn into bushes with the binoculars.

"No, I don't think so Rebecca—there might not be very much here at all," I replied, anxious not to frighten her, remembering how Krister's stories about the slave trade in the Sahara had made her too frightened to enter the mosque in Villa Cisneros for fear of being kidnapped and sold to giant negroes. I wondered if there would even be a village, let alone a supermarket at Palmeira.

"What would it be like to be the Portuguese discoverer of these islands, sailing downwind to the edge of the world," mused Jamie.

"It doesn't look much good for farming," replied Staff, realistically.

We realised just how fast we were moving as we closed with the coast along that five miles of northern shore, massive combers smashed ceaselessly against a low dark brown reef of tortured volcanic rock, and we fairly whizzed round into the shelter of the west coast.

"Palmeira is only about four and a half miles—less than an hour," I said to Jamie. "Let's get the dinghy inflated and over the stern, in case there's any bother anchoring."

"We haven't got a very good record for coming into port," he laughed back as he scurried up onto the deck to undo the lashings on the Avon with Krister.

"Don't you steer so close to the rocks! How do you know there isn't a reef out here?" scolded Marie Christine from on top of the stern locker, where she sat as usual with Rebecca.

"Because the chart shows it drops straight down to fifty fathoms—that's why," I snapped back, heading a little further off shore all the same. The wind seemed to sweep right over the island unhindered, and we were moving along at what must be nearly the boat's top speed.

"Oil tanks, that'll be it," called Jamie from the bows.

"It doesn't look much of a port to me," said Staff, "four oil storage tanks—that's all there is!"

"Where'the tunny fish factory, Daddy?"

"Over there, Beck, the new place with the red roof," I replied, heading towards four huge mooring buoys obviously intended for visiting tankers, and lying nearly a mile off shore.

Even taking into account the tank farm, the empty tunny factory, and a few scattered huts in the angle of the bay, there was a strange atmosphere of being nowhere at all.

We sailed in through the buoys towards a sweeping sandy beach, and the water turned a milky green colour over sand thirty feet below. The surface became suddenly smooth, but it was as windy as ever and we headed in as close as we dared with the lead readings steadily falling to 'twenty feet below the keel', before dropping anchor.

The Cape Verde archipelago lies 280 miles off the coast of Africa, to the West of Dakar, in between the latitudes 14°–17°N. There are ten islands and five islets divided into two groups windward and leeward. The island of Sal (Salt) is the most north-easterly of the windward group. When we were there it hadn't rained for seven years, and had it not been for the fact that the only international airport on the archipelago was sited on Sal, it was difficult to see how the population could survive. There was fishing, but political uncertainty had caused foreign investors to withdraw support from the new tunny factory when it was only half built, so it stood empty. Of course there was the salt, but that didn't appear to be a particularly valuable resource; but there was nothing else on Sal.

It was already after mid-day, and pretty hot out of the wind. We had a bite to eat and waited for someone to come out from the shanty town to give us clearance to go ashore. At half-past three a battered red aluminium launch came past, and on board as well as the two ragged fishermen, there was a fat black policeman who looked at our passports briefly, and then said we could come ashore with him if we wished.

"Let's buy some fish," Marie Christine said brightly, pointing at a box of red mullet in the boat, and the fishermen were pleased to sell. Staff and Krister decided to stay on board to write letters, so we tied the dinghy behind the fishing boat for our return, and accepted their offer of a lift for the quarter-mile trip to a small pier, standing beside a reef which guarded the entrance to a sandy bay.

Once ashore, the first thing we noticed was the single tarmac strip of road which ran straight out of the village and into the dusty hills towards the airport which lay somewhere in the interior. There were no roads in the village, which was built in neat blocks of rough one-storey huts and houses, divided by a network of dusty spaces which were not paved in any way. Two or three clumps of palm trees were the only sign of any vegetation at all, for as far along the coast as we could see, and scrawny goats, donkeys and chickens all scratched about in the dust eating the refuse. The donkeys were so thin that when looked at from head on, they seemed to have no body at all, just a grey head and long ears supported from the ground by two thin sticks. In among the cluster of tin or straw roofed huts, with cracked white or rouge plastered walls, we became objects of embarrassing interest. A group of ten or fifteen children formed up behind us, fascinated by the sight of a little white girl with shoulder-length blonde hair. We came to a shop and almost barricaded ourselves inside a small walled terrace which sported a few long unused tables for coffee drinkers, while we waited for the shopkeeper to return and sell us some bread. It was already well on in the afternoon and school was finished for the day, more and more black children came to stare goggle-eyed at Rebecca, who had herself scarcely ever seen another black child; several mothers arrived to lean on the terrace wall, while holding babies in their arms and straight away there was a bond, a common interest, between them and Marie Christine, they became friendly with a speed that Jamie and I would have found impossible to achieve had we been on our own in the village. Barriers of race, colour and language fell immediately before the common experience of motherhood; how much trouble would be avoided if only men could communicate with each other so easily.

Sal is a very poor island, but the families are large and modern medicine has cut infant mortality almost to nil. Among the squalor of Palmeira the people laugh a lot and they hold themselves proudly as they walk, every inch the noble African negro. They wear their hearts not on their sleeves but on their chests with T-shirts boasting support for P.A.I.G.C. the political party which won Guinea Bissau its independence from Portugal in 1973. These people are descendants of Guineans who have settled in the islands over the centuries; they feel themselves to be Guineans and they want, and will almost certainly achieve, unity with Guinea Bissau. Beyond that the future is more cloudy, economic support will have to come from somewhere: Africa, Arabia, America, China or Russia, wherever it comes from there will be a price in human terms which the laughing, optimistic people of Palmeira may not have considered. Whatever happens they feel sure it will only be better than the centuries of neglect they had under Portuguese colonial rule.

We hitched a lift with a local merchant who was returning to his home in Santa Maria, twelve miles away on the southern tip of the island. Jamie and I bumped along in the back of the old Peugeot pick-up with a couple of locals, while Marie Christine and Rebecca rode in the cab with the smiling merchant. As we bowled out of the village, I saw a flock of plover-like birds rise from a scruffy football pitch which had forty-gallon drums for goal posts; and we passed several small boys who were walking in along the road from the desert rolling wooden casks of water bound with motor tyres from some distant well, rather as an English child might roll a hoop.

The modern airfield complex lay about three miles inland on a totally barren plain, raised a hundred feet or so above the sea and dominated by a substantial military cantonment. Here we did stop by a supermarket, and Rebecca ran towards it as if it was some magical palace. Sitting in the back of the truck I heard the screech of brakes and caught a glimpse of my daughter's face as she froze with terror in the middle of the road. Then I just saw the shape of the Land Rover as it shuddered past. I shut my eyes, sick with shock, and when I opened them again she was standing on the pavement screaming for her mother. Rebecca doesn't have much to do with traffic.

We drove on along the road following the higher ground which formed a central ridge along the island, rather like a backbone. Everything was scorched, a few black crows flapped aimlessly about the sky, tossed by the ceaseless wind. Before entering Santa Maria, which was about three times the size of Palmeira, the road came down to the coast and followed the curve of a huge empty beach of golden sand and then passed through a grove of palm trees and out by an area of salt pans with many small windmills whirling bravely in the wind. The sun was already dipping towards the sea as we came to a halt outside a Belgian-owned hotel; it was a big place, laid out like a motel and it was clearly intended for rich custom from the airport, but it stood more or less empty except for the crews of the South African Airways planes, which were unable to arrange for alternative landing facilities on the mainland of Africa.

After a round of drinks the merchant said he must go home, clearly expecting us to put up for the night at the hotel, which was just about the last thing we had in mind; and after some discussion, we arranged with him to pick us up from a small boarding house further up the street at nine o'clock that evening and drive us back to the boat. In the meantime we went on a tour of the village, in the care of a young bank cashier who had hitched a ride with us down from the airport in the pick-up. First we saw the diesel-powered water distillation plant, which pumped water out of the sea, evaporated it in huge boilers and then condensed the steam to make fresh water, which was then sold at the rate of about £2 for 1,000 litres. Then we went on to see the tuna factory, which Rebecca was most excited about; although it was a small place we were pleasantly surprised at its cleanliness. The fish were brought in each day and they were cleaned, chopped, boiled and canned in quick time. While Marie Christine was busy buying twelve large cans of tuna for our stores, we saw the mounds of fish, meal and bone heaped in the yard at the back of the factory. The entire operation seemed to be run most efficiently by the Portuguese manager.

It was now too dark to go and see the salt pans but our guide explained that sea water was run down into bores in the ground where it dissolved the rock salt and the solution was then pumped up by the windmills to evaporate under the wind and sun in the salt pans. By the end of all this we were looking forward to our supper, and after thanking the friendly cashier for his hospitality we went along to the boarding house. Our invasion had clearly been a bit too much for the lady of the house, who looked rather flustered throughout the couple of hours we were in her home. Nevertheless she provided a welcome meal of fish soup followed by fried fish and potato with a fried egg on top, and wine to wash it all down. We were just eating our fresh oranges when Augustine, the rich and now not so smiling merchant arrived in his new Mercedes, to drive us back to the boat in his new rôle of taxi driver.

In the dark, with the shiny Mercedes, a symbol of his prestige on the island at risk, he drove with great care. Gone was the laughing élan of the Peugeot, and in its place the bongo drums from Africa—Radio Guinea, turned up to full volume as if to emphasise the power of Black Africa. Every car which came along the road towards us sent him scuttling off the tarmac until it was safely past, there was no conversation and he was clearly upset that we weren't rich enough to stay at the hotel.

Next morning we awoke to find another boat in the bay, a brand new luxury motor yacht well over a hundred feet long, lay about a quarter of a mile further out to sea; but there was no sign of life aboard her so we went ashore to meet a taxi the policeman had kindly arranged to take us to visit the salt mine on the other side of the island. We had to go via the airport to change some money, and so the driver returned home to Palmeira while we waited for the bank to open. The airport had that prestigious anonymity of international airports the world over, outside all was barren desert but inside there was the usual bustle, with the passengers, who were all smartly dressed blacks waiting for what was possibly the only plane of the day. The whole place echoed to the clamour of rock music and the more way-out fliers danced frenetically with their transistor radios, and the mindless gaiety of it all was dramatised by the absence of a clock in the terminal.

Life was much slower at the salt mine. We arrived at a tiny artificial harbour in time to see a crate of lobsters, langouste to be precise, being packed alive in boxes for the daily flight to Lisbon. The men handling them wore long sleeves and thick gloves to protect their arms from the rasps on the waving antennae with which the unhappy clawless creatures tried to stop this fatal business.

By the harbour stood great mountains of white salt, which blew into our eyes and lay like snow over all the machinery which powered a bucket conveyor system, bringing the salt down from a hole in the side of a mountain a mile or so inland.

We drove along a rough track beside the overhead conveyor and on through the tunnel into the crater of an extinct volcano; then leaving the car, we walked a few yards further to a bend in the track which zig-zagged steeply down to the square fields of drying salt. Apparently, a saline solution is pumped up from a hundred feet below the bed of the crater and spilled into salt pans which look rather like paddy fields. It takes three months for the evaporation process to be completed and then the salt, up to 30,000 tons of it each year, is taken down to the harbour in the conveyor buckets for shipment, mainly to Africa.

As we drove back across the desert to Palmeira the driver told us that before the drought in 1967, there used to be fields in place of the barren wastelands, and 1967 seemed such a short time ago. Overhead the sky had plenty of clouds but no rain ever fell. Away to our left a little donkey trotted along, kicking up a small cloud of dust as its master, who rode side-saddle, tapped its rump with a switch.

After a swim that afternoon, Staff, Marie Christine, Rebecca and I decided to pay a visit to the motor yacht on our way back to *English Rose*. As we passed under the flaring white bows, I realised for the first time just how large the ship was. The wind was blowing strongly, and we had trouble holding onto the long ladder hanging down from the ship's side.

"C'mon up!" a voice boomed from somewhere up above, and we struggled up onto the deck.

"Hallo, I'm Alan Gray." I shook hands with a slim grey-haired man of about forty-eight who looked as if he might be the owner.

"They call me 'Dirty Charlie'." A huge barrel of a man thrust out his hand and I shook it as he added, "I'm the chief engineer around here."

"And he sure lives up to his name!" laughed Mr. Gray.

Everyone was introduced, and we moved through a door opposite the head of the gangway, to find ourselves looking at an onyx-faced bar with no drinks. It was like entering a new luxury hotel just before it is opened to the public.

"Would you like to see over the ship?" Dirty Charlie boomed.

"Yes please," said Marie Christine, "we'd love that." And so began an extraordinary tour. Charlie explained that we were aboard a 126-foot Feadship specially built in Holland for the

Canadian owner. They were delivering the ship from the builders in Rotterdam to California, but engine failure had forced them to put in to Palmeira to wait for parts to be flown over from Miami.

"My contract stipulates that I don't reveal his name—but I guess you could say he's one of the rich men of the world," he added casually as we entered one of the kitchens, which was fitted with micro-wave cookers, an icemaker, a fridge, and a deep freeze. Across the passage was a laundry containing two enormous washing machines, and there were ear muffs for the user to deaden the sound of the ship's engines which lay through the next door we entered.

"See that chrome plate?" Charlie roared in my ear, pointing at the gleaming silver sides of two giant engines. "Well that plating alone cost 20,000 dollars!"

There was the usual rumble of machinery, but it was only some small part of the gleaming complex, a generator or a pump perhaps; the twin eight-cylinder Caterpillar DE379 diesels stood quiet under the expressionless eyes of several close-circuit T.V. cameras which monitored the entire engine room from the bridge. I didn't understand a bit of what it was all about, it looked like all the other ships' engine rooms I had ever been in, maybe it was a bit cleaner, but it's not only rich ships that have clean engines; but all the same I left the room regretting that so much of the technicality had escaped me.

A few stairways above, we found ourselves in the dining room and here the sheer weight of money was easy to understand: there was a thick glass table, teak chairs carved to look like cane, crystal glasses, dark wooden walls, deep brown carpeting and hydraulically damped sliding doors. From there it was a short shuffle through cream carpets to the spacious gracious main saloon, complete with giant colour T.V. video and the ultimate in eight-track stereo, a massive onyx fireplace and, if you should feel like a drink, which I felt a few of the future passengers might, there was the computer cocktail bar ready to serve you. Pick up a card, for a Manhattan say, from the index, slip it into the slot on the cabinet and in a few seconds out comes your mixture. We took a brief look over the lavish barbecue on the poop deck before moving to where the real luxury began—the owner's stateroom.

"I knew the guy was rich when I saw the gold hinges on the lavatory seat in his private BAC 111 which flew us over from the States," cracked Charlie, as we followed him down the stairs which led to paradise.

"See these doors—he flew a man over from California to Holland just to hand paint them," Charlie's voice was hushed now, as if we were in a church, he showed us the mighty satin-sheeted bed, hand-printed silk wallpaper, mothproof cedar wood cupboards, the bathroom with its centrally positioned Jacuzzi whirlpool bath flanked by top-class loos on either side. The guest stateroom aft was just the same, every room had the colour T.V. and every last hinge was plated fourteen-carat gold. On we went into the owner's study, coloured dark brown to suit the sombre power of the great man who needed three telephones of different colours to communicate with his domain. Should he perspire at any time, or feel the need for cleansing, then he could slip discreetly through a side door and stew in his sauna.

Up on the bridge we had a regal view of the world; over on Palmeira beach the poverty-stricken black children played happily.

"We have three echo sounders," Charlie interrupted the hopeless direction of my thoughts. "They're for Canadian waters really, one for floating logs, one for those half afloat, and one for logs which are submerged but only a few feet under-water—we gotta be careful—the Prime Minister of Canada will probably be on this ship."

I nodded and smiled, thinking of Bernard Moitessier, who dropped out of the 1968 single-handed race which I'd been in; he'd sailed onto the South Pacific rather than return to the 'snake-pit' of Europe to claim his prize. He said he dreamed of the day when a country of the modern world had barefoot ministers—he'd ask for citizenship right away.

Well, it was all a bit much really, we paddled back to our boat, pushing hard against the wind, each of us thinking on what we had seen.

After supper Staff returned to the floating palace, to ask if a couple of the crew would like to come back aboard *English Rose* for some Gold Brand . . . Nescafé! and we spent the evening listening to Dirty Charlie's desperate scrapes while he polished off our meagre supply of liquor including Lucy's bottle of home-made anisette.

I sat on top of the food lockers champing at the bit to be gone from the international airport atmosphere of Sal Island. What I had come all this way for was now only half a day's sail further south across the sea—Boa Vista, the seldom-visited desert island of the past.

We sailed at seven next morning.

10

Boa Vista

WE ROLLED SOUTH, down the thirty-six miles to the island of Boa Vista at an average speed of six knots, running before the Trade Wind again. Staff took a whole Dramanine pill thinking we were going for the 130-mile trip to Praia, the capital of the Cape Verde's on São Tiago, and so he spent much of the time asleep. Marie Christine, Rebecca and I thought we would do without the pills and put up with the sickness. The seas were slate-grey beneath heavy cloud, and an ominous black fin shadowed us for a while: it was a miserable trip and the three non-pill eaters were all sick, while Jamie and Krister looked on quite unaffected by the violent rolling motion.

The dotted line on the chart, which indicates the limiting danger line around the island which is roughly a dozen miles in diameter, extended quite a distance offshore; and the *Admiralty Pilot* spoke of many vessels being swept onto the rocks in poor visibility by the south-westerly current, and also of very heavy rollers which rendered it unsafe to anchor.

The sun came out and the island appeared black and yellow just before noon, in its unique style it slowly grew into one of the most beautiful sights I have ever seen. It was as if we were sailing back into history. The craggy mountains dropped sharply onto a desert plain extending deceptively into the sea, a rusty ship lay wrecked on a deserted beach lashed by majestic surf. Rounding a low headland at the north-western corner of the island, we began, for the first time, to see signs of human life: thin poles stuck on the peaks of a range of hills. Then, quite suddenly we saw a church and manse, standing all alone at the head of a bay, perched on a small desert hillock and backed by gaunt mountains. It was pale and tall with an everlasting look about it, as if a band of faithful monks lived there still, oblivious to the jangle of the modern world.

Turning the black-brown cliff which sealed off the monastery bay, we saw in the distance the town of Sal Rei (Salt King), low and incredibly old looking with a bright blue church standing in the middle and slightly above it. At the end of the town on a rocky promontory, rather where one might expect to find a refuse tip, there was a neat white-walled cemetery; and across a shallow half-mile-wide channel lay a narrow brown island with little hillocks rising to ninety feet or so along its mile of length, on one of these stood a crude stone tower holding the only light on the coast.

"There's a trading schooner down there, look—at the anchor in the bay," Jamie shouted excitedly, pointing through the channel and beyond the island. And we all looked, we might have been back in the Middle Ages; lateen-rigged cutters were sailing to and from the schooner laden with cargo, the broad-based triangles of their canvas sails framed beautifully by the shallow pale green water.

For a while we passed along outside the red-brown reefs off the island, and then we saw a low round fort guarding the approaches to Sal Rei; although it was now filled with drifted sand its long black cannons still pointed menacingly out across English Reef half a mile to seaward. We tightened the sheets, and sailed under the guns towards the schooner, which looked to be making ready for sea, its business done. A string of wrecks spread along the six-mile curve of broad white sand beach, and the pounding rollers reminded me again of the *Pilot*'s warning about remaining at anchor. The north-east Trade was blowing as strong as ever, and we were still a mile off the town when we dropped anchor in twenty feet of water, and even then I was worried at being so far inshore of the schooner.

We ate a late lunch in the cockpit and looked around us. A range of arid mountains ringed the horizon ten miles inland, and in front of them a great tract of lovely white dunes marched into the sea. It was all bathed in a pale washy light, for the sun had disappeared for good behind dull grey clouds, but this only heightened the effect that had begun when I had first sighted the lonely church further back up the coast. There was an untouched look about it, as if the rocky coast deterred passing ships from calling and the island was consequently left to its own devices.

There was more to this feeling of isolation than I imagined, as we found out when we eventually scrambled up onto the town's rickety wooden pier after a rough trip against the wind using the Seagull outboard motor on the back of the Avon dinghy for the first time since far-away Madeira. The policeman was hard put to hold back the crowd of inquisitive islanders which thronged the pier.

"Welcome to Boa Vista," said a grizzled half-caste old man holding out his hand in greeting. "I am the harbourmaster; perhaps we should go to my office," he added in surprisingly good English, and we picked our way through staring negroes towards a row of tall elegant stone buildings fronting onto a short but wide seafront boulevard, tastefully shaded by spreading green acacia trees.

"We are a very poor island," apologised the harbourmaster, who we learned was called Alfonso, once we were all gathered inside the high-ceilinged gloomy room which served as both his office and his living quarters.

"We have the lowest standard of living of any of the Cape Verde Islands, one, maybe two, sailing traders comes here each month, sometimes they don't come at all for months at a time and we run out of food. The doctor is supposed to come for one day a month, but it is not enough." As he spoke I noticed he was shivering, and yet at the same time there was a film of sweat on the tight parchment-thin skin of his forehead.

"Are you not well, Alfonso?" Marie Christine asked sympathetically.

"It's the malaria—it'll pass, I have no tablets." The old man waved his hands in an expression of profound hopelessness.

"Next time we come ashore we will bring you what we have," my wife said firmly and poor Alfonso cheered up a bit. He took us next door to the tunny factory where the day's catch was being gutted by a team of women, and he smiled when we brought his attention to the incongruous inflatable speedboat which lay to one side of the building.

"Fruits of the sea," he laughed, "a recent wreck, she lies on the north coast of the island. We get all sorts of things," he added, pointing to some sections of deck steam pipe piled up in a corner below the black sail of a sailfish nailed to the wall above.

It was getting dark and so we decided to return to the boat after a hurried cup of coffee in a back street shop, the owner of which managed to get us some bread rolls from the bakery which had already closed. When we got back to the boat the schooner had departed, and Krister lit the hurricane lamp in the bows for the night.

We were woken by a gruff cry just after dawn next morning, and as I peered out of one of the portholes above our bunk I saw a small lateen-sailed fishing boat speeding along our port side.

"He's trying to sell us some fish I think," I said to Marie Christine, as I hauled myself over the rail and onto the cabin floor, pulling on some clothes at the same time.

By the time I reached the cockpit the fishing boat was scudding across our stern. As soon as he saw me the old man handed the tiller to a boy he had with him, and after fumbling about in the bows for a moment he held aloft a fearsome-looking barracuda, fully four feet long and still rigid in rigor mortis. We couldn't possibly eat all that and after some quibbling, while he tacked to and fro, the old man sailed away in disgust, and I was left standing half-naked on the back of the yacht wondering what a parlous situation it was when a Briton couldn't afford to buy a bit of fish on a desert island.

We waited all morning for Alfonso to come out on one of the sailing boats to guide us through the sandbars to an anchorage nearer the pier, but when he didn't appear we got on with the work in hand. Marie Christine and Rebecca settled down to their schoolwork; Staff and Krister got in a good long sleep; Jamie set off in the Avon to take some Codeine and Aspirin to Alfonso in case he was still unwell, and I got on with worrying about the journey from the Azores to Ardmore—a hobby which was consuming more and more of my free time.

Jamie returned shortly before lunch with some shells and coral from the island which he'd visited on his way back to the boat. He told us that as Alfonso was feeling pretty low, he wouldn't be coming out that day, so I agreed to stay and look after the boat while the others went ashore for the afternoon on the island.

Berthing in the Azores with a Portuguese giant astern.

Left, at the hot mud springs in the Azores; right, exit with pineapples. L. to r. John, Rebecca, Staff and Krister.

Leaving the Azores for Ardmore, December 10.

It was my first spell alone in the forty-eight days since we had left Ardmore, and I enjoyed five delicious hours of total relaxation in complete silence except for the sound of the wind in the rigging and the waves gurgling past the hull.

I thought of Becca and how the voyage had affected her so far; she had certainly done well on the previous day with an early start and after a prolonged period of either feeling or actually being sick, she had still come ashore with us, enduring the frightening fifteen minutes of soaking in the dinghy and the trip back in the dark, with plenty of spark. She had come a long way in cramped conditions for a child of seven who was used to unlimited space to play in. I realised it was so easy for the five adults to forget what a plague it could be for a solitary child to be told to do this and not do that by everyone who spoke to her. She seemed to have overcome her initial fear of the sea, and was now willing to have a go at almost anything on the boat, particularly enjoying the cooking and cleaning with her mother. Above all, she was an excellent companion, always full of fun and never bearing a grudge against anyone. On the other side it was difficult for her parents to tell if she was being spoiled or not, and the fellows were always very patient in dealing with her. Perhaps in the rough and tumble of life with other children, she wouldn't get her way so easily, but then things certainly didn't go all her way on the boat with five grownups pushing her around all the time. Was it fair to take her along on the trip home from the Azores . . . ?

I woke up to the noise of the approaching dinghy. They had plastic bags full of shells—the kind you see in coffee-table books of tropical sea shells—and they were all delighted with their afternoon. We lit the paraffin lamp to save electricity and had a grand supper of onions and mince with fried rice, and plenty of rough red wine from the plastic jerry can we had bought in Palma.

Next morning the wind was blowing even more strongly than usual off the desert, and the trip ashore in the dinghy was so wet that we wore only swimming gear and oilskins, changing into dry clothes in Alfonso's office. Poor Alfonso was definitely not in high spirits, so we decided to invite him to a lunch party in his own office. After a dose of Codeine the bout of malaria subsided, and we coaxed him into eating a bit of tinned octopus we had brought from somewhere along the way and fresh bread from the bakery, but he wouldn't touch the wine.

"I'm very happy you are here," he said quietly during the meal, and we were absolutely delighted. He told us he came from Sao Antão, the second largest and furthest west of the Cape Verdes, he'd been a customs officer for thirty-five years and at sixty-three he had only another couple of years to serve in Boa Vista before retiring to resume his bachelor existence on his native island. He had picked up malaria while serving on Sal, and he desperately wanted to get home, because he felt ill and deserted on Boa Vista. We could only promise to report his plight when we reached Praia, which was our next port of call, but his lot seemed a pretty miserable one and our hearts went out to him.

When he had cheered up a bit he told us something about Boa Vista in the precise English he had taught himself on the lonely island outposts on which he had served since 1940. He believed that Boa Vista was the first of the Cape Verde Islands to be discovered by ships serving Prince Henry the Navigator of Portugal in the middle of the fifteenth century, and he pointed to the well-planned streets of Sal Rei as evidence that it had been the capital of the Cape Verdes until 1700, when Praia on São Tiago, the largest of the islands, had replaced it. The present population of about 4,000 were mainly descendants of Guinean slaves brought over by the Portuguese five centuries before, and they lived in six villages around the island with Sal Rei as their capital. Before the drought came in 1967 it used to rain during three months each year; and ships would come to collect the salt, cattle and castor oil seeds which had been the main exports. Nowadays it was just the salt, and some lime for cement which left the island, and things were slowly sliding from bad to worse as the sand silted up the bay and even the fishing was not as good since the drought began.

After lunch we left Alfonso to rest in his sombre room, and set off for the fort island across the channel in the dinghy, returning to the deserted sandy beaches which lay at the head of several rocky inlets. Rebecca played hopscotch on the hot sand and we tried to catch octopus and small fish in the rock pools, taking care not to tread on the spiny black sea urchins which were almost everywhere. Staff and I swam 150 yards with flippers

and masks to a reef, lying off the sheltered south-eastern corner
of the island, on a line between the yacht and Sal Rei. The water
was clear and shallow around the reef, which was exposed at
low tide, a series of rocks in a circle no more than fifty yards
across. We had seen shoals of small fish, like swaying curtains
of silver when diving at Palma and snorkelling at Sal, but now,
for the first time we saw big fish close-to. There had been nothing but empty sand on the swim out, and the first sign that we
were approaching the reef was a fair-sized shoal of yellow and
brown fish. They were some sixty or seventy feet clear of the
rocks they appeared to be circling.

Staff and I were both comparative novices at this sport, and
the size of the barracuda the fisherman had tried to sell us that
morning didn't improve my confidence. Tales of sharks and
sting rays were discounted by Alfonso, but then I hadn't seen
him doing much swimming. Closer in to the rocks there shimmered a silver shoal of lean fast-looking fish about the size of
mullet, but they took little notice of us, appearing to move clear
of us more out of good manners than through any sense of fear.
We were on the surface, close together, but the fish were also so
near to the top of the shallow clear water that we felt we were
more among them than over them, and with a weighted belt
from the scuba gear hung around my waist, it took only a kick
of my flippers to send me down to the sandy bottom.

Aiming for the reef itself, Staff and I split up, circling the
group of rocks which were now well awash, in opposite directions to minimise our disturbance of the fish. I lost all track of
time, completely absorbed by what I saw; it was all and more
than I had hoped it might be while coasting along the edge of
the kelp beds at Ardmore during the summer with Jim Vale our
scuba instructor. The sea was warm and the sun gently toasted
my back; the water was so clear it seemed as if I was flying
rather than swimming, and the fish were so numerous and so
brightly coloured I really thought I must be dreaming. It was
quite unforgettable, but the overall impression I have is one of
free movement in a fresh environment which perfectly suited
me, there was absolutely no aggravation or discomfort and for
once I had that elusive feeling of perfection.

Swimming carefully along the steep wall at the eastern end of
the reef I was most interested by the solitary grey fish which

swam quite close without any real sense of alarm, when I moved too close to them they moved off lazily and not in the state of panic which I remembered was the reaction of smaller fish in other parts of the world. These grey fish, at one and a half to two feet long, were the biggest fish I had yet been aware of when swimming, and I suppose Jacques Cousteau would have thought me rather pathetic as I moved warily along that wall, diver's knife in hand, almost ready to jam it in the gaping mouth of an attacking shark. The sense of exhilaration was grand.

Rounding the end of the reef I came to the southern side, which was a mass of tumbled rocks, overhangs and yawning crevices. I took a deep breath and swam easily down, aided by the lead belt, and began to explore among the rocks hardly ten feet below the surface. Childhood years of spotting the chub beneath Thames-side bushes on summer fly-fishing expeditions, has left me with a keen eye for just the situation I was now in. Sticking out from an arch formed beneath two dark rocks which had rolled together, I noticed the thin antennae of a large langouste, a type of lobster without claws; they were waving gently like a pair of black whips over the white sand. To catch this creature would be a prize indeed, for only that morning one of the locals had tried in vain to sell us at vast expense, a couple of smaller langouste from a floating crate he kept by the pier. I swam cautiously round to the other side of the rocks and dived. The creature's broad tail was spread fan-like on the sand before me, within just an arm's length. It showed no sign of alarm and I was sorely tempted to grab it from behind there and then—but once back on the surface where could I put it until Jamie returned from the yacht with the dinghy? And also I remembered the men handling those langouste near the salt mine on Sal—they had worn gloves and long sleeves for protection. I marked the position from the surface, so I could show Staff later; at the same time I saw Marie Christine and Rebecca playing on the beach—they seemed to be part of another world.

Bursting with confidence now, I began to explore the other rocks, fully expecting to find more langouste which I would mark out as a sort of living larder for the remainder of our stay at Boa Vista; oh, it was just grand—what larks! Of course, it was necessary to look closely, it was no good just cruising about aimlessly, I had to get right down there and poke my nose into every little corner. "Scourge of the langouste, huh, we'll live like kings," I thought, gliding beautifully among the rocks. If Krister could stay under for a whole minute, surely I could too —with a little practice.

I came smoothly up across a pile of rocks and along the bottom of a small valley. A large boulder barred my way ahead, I swung up close to the rough brown surface of the rock, supple-limbed, master of my environment. Suddenly my back broke through the surface of the water. I breathed out, blasting the water out of the snorkel tube, and took in fresh air in its place.

In the few seconds it took to complete the change of air in my lungs, I had lost concentration, I was past the boulder now and looking down into a long crevice about an arm's length beneath the surface.

Then the bottom of the crevice moved!

Rolling onto its side in alarm, and exposing its twin lines of grey flank and white belly I found myself staring straight into the rat-trap jaws of a huge conger eel. I couldn't go up, for I was already on the surface; and I couldn't go back, because the gentle swell was lifting me firmly forward, towards that snake-like head—its small black and white eye gazed cold and motionless, poised to strike. I kicked out wildly, threshing for deep water, desperately hoping the vicious conger wouldn't attack.

Once clear of the reef, heart still knocking in my chest, I turned and looked back, dreading I might see the hideous thing ribboning after me. There was no sign of it.

I swam much more carefully now, keeping the broad knife in front of me, and never going too close until I was sure there was no chance of cornering something which might turn and attack me. I was suddenly keen to rejoin Staff again, and so I started to move more rapidly along the southern side of the reef. But when we did meet up he preferred to stay on his own, so I got a grip and continued exploring by myself. The sight of three langouste side by side on the sand at the foot of an overhanging wall restored my enthusiasm a bit, and I dived down to size up the chances of capturing them by hand at some later time; they didn't seem too anxious as I swam slowly past them, and I thought it might be possible to grab one, but the others would surely escape. Further along the wall was the black entrance to a cave, and I swam past it at a safe distance; when I was level with it I looked inside and saw a really big fish, about the size of an alsatian dog, its leathery mouth opening and shutting like a white deck quoit. It didn't look fierce, more like a vegetarian sort of fish, but it was certainly the largest fish I'd had swimming around me.

I felt it was time to go home for supper and think about the next stage in catching the langouste, or maybe holding a stout line and dropping bait in front of the cave. Staff and I made one last trip along the other side of the reef, seeing a small yellow and black moray eel which sent shivers of memory down my spine, and then we finned back to the shore to rejoin Marie Christine and Rebecca who were patiently waiting for us. Jamie was already half way to the beach from the yacht by the time we waded ashore, and in no time we were all back in our floating home waiting for supper to cook.

Once again the days were slipping past, if we wanted to visit other places we must move on. We gave ourselves two more days at Boa Vista, when I would have liked much longer to concentrate on the underwater fishing. Señor Aquilles introduced himself next morning, while we were down at the public washing-troughs where Marie Christine and Rebecca washed a lot of their clothes along with several local women, who were very helpful in explaining their method of scrubbing on a stone rack. Aquilles, he spelt his name this way on a piece of paper for me, was the Administrator on the island, and he asked us if we'd like to join him that afternoon on a visit he was making by Land Rover to villages in the interior; of course we accepted. A slender intelligent-looking fellow of around thirty, he was already accompanied by three policemen who were all jammed into the front seat of the battered Land Rover when we arrived outside his home at the appointed hour, and it was something of a squeeze to fit all of us, except Jamie who was on the boat, into the back, but then we had to take a local girl as well and the groaning springs kept bumping on the chassis as we lurched across the desert on a rough much pot-holed track.

The village was twelve miles from Sal Rei, on the other side

of the mountains, and the reason for the visit was law enforce-
ment. It seemed the storekeeper was hoarding sugar supplies to
force up the price. The Administrator knew he had been
supplied with the sugar but the villagers contended the storekeeper would not sell it. As we rattled down the dusty single
street of the village, which was more like a hamlet built with
small poor houses lining the track, there was already a sizeable
crowd outside the store, and this transferred its interest to us in
the back of the Land Rover once we had come to a halt. As in
Sal they were particularly amazed to see Rebecca, and a wall of
black faces and round staring white eyes soon hemmed in the
back of the vehicle. They were good-natured people, but very
poor, their stone-walled fields turned to dust by the drought
and only a few groves of date palms and the occasional clump
of acacia trees seemed to be surviving. The endless wind blew
whirls of dust about the stony ground and there was the familiar
sound of cockerels and braying donkeys. The hearing of the
case was rather protracted, and Aquilles kindly took us to visit
another village for a glass of beer and some biscuits while it was
going on. Despite the drought some of the houses managed to
maintain trellises of bright red bougainvillia around their front
doors, and it seemed incongruous when the woman selling the
beer made a great play of putting a bowl of plastic flowers on
our table.

We had the same bumpy trip home across the arid wastes,
and to speed us on, Staff and Krister started a sing-song which
went down very well with the police and Aquilles.

Staff, Jamie and Krister were all keen to move on to Praia on
São Tiago, because their mail would be waiting for them there,
forwarded from Madeira and redirected from Ardmore since
mid-October. It was the enthusiasm for mail as much as a feeling of passing time which made me regretfully decide to sail on
after only one more day of relaxation at Boa Vista.

11

Homeward Bound

"WHAT WILL IT BE LIKE on the trip from the Azores to Ardmore?" Staff mused, looking into his mug of coffee and thinking of the suffering he had already endured from seasickness.

"Well, we could do what he did," Krister laughed, tapping the cover of Chay Blyth's *Impossible Voyage*—the book of his single-handed voyage around the world into the wind.

"Oh, Gawd!" I muttered, expecting some ghastly impossible suggestion for the seasick sufferers to put up with.

"No," Krister continued quite seriously, "when Chay and his wife arrived at the Azores in December 1968, remember she joined him in South Africa to sail *Dystiscus* back to England with him when he gave up the race at Port Elizabeth—shortly after you put into Brazil, John—they left the boat at the Azores and flew home!"

"Yes, that's right," I said, remembering. "Chay flew back and sailed the boat home when the weather improved the following June." In fact it was not quite like that, Chay and Maureen had set out from São Miguel in the Azores and headed for Portsmouth but the weather was so severe they abandoned the idea and returned to São Miguel after two days of appalling storm.

I didn't know of anyone who had ever sailed from the Azores to north-west Scotland in December—but we were about to find out if it was possible. We'd had our touch of sun, and now the time had come to pay the price.

The hundred-mile trip from Boa Vista to Praia had gone

without a hitch and Praia itself had been interesting for a couple of days while we picked up our mail and wrote letters and cards to friends. We told the authorities of Alfonso's illness on Boa Vista and much of our time was spent sitting in a park-side café in the middle of the small town, which is the administrative capital of the Cape Verde Islands, drinking coffee and listening to homesick Portuguese soldiers and farmers tell their tales of woe. At night shots were fired in internecine strife between the two political parties who sought to control the islands after the independence, which was expected almost daily. There was an air of decay and uncertainty—we longed to be on our way, to get to grips with our own problem.

We sailed at 1017 hours on the morning of Thursday, 21st November 1974. Ahead of us lay 3,000 miles of steadily deteriorating weather, the first 1,500, to the Azores, would be sailed into the wind, against the north-east Trades on whose back we had been rolling south for the past couple of months. The other 1,500 miles, after the Azores . . . well, we'd first get to the Azores and see about that when we got there.

Slipping out from Praia we ran straight into a strong north-east wind, just as we expected, and we covered four miles in the first three-quarters of an hour. Then, quite suddenly, we found ourselves in the lee of the thirty-mile-long island, a barrier of barren mountains running up to four and a half thousand feet, which shielded us from the wind. In the next thirty hours we only logged seventeen miles. The sun blazed down on us, the cabin was airless and unbearable, even in the swimming gear we all wore. The stark mountains shimmered above us—there was nothing for it but to get on with something to pass the time until the wind returned; Marie Christine sewed up the seams in Jamie's bunk, Staff and Jamie changed the corroded aluminium filter in the drinking water pump, Krister and Rebecca were out in the cockpit trying to whistle up a wind, and I fiddled about with *Admiralty Pilots* and routeing charts also seeking to solve the problem of the absent wind.

There was much talk about one particular letter I had found awaiting me at Praia. It had come from American Samoa in the South Pacific, from Nick and Julie Grainger, a young couple in their early twenties who had been with us for two years at Ardmore. Nick had become keen on sailing, which he had never done before coming to Ardmore and he had bought a second-hand twenty-one-foot clinker-built mahogany boat for £250 in Thurso. She was a registered fishing boat built in Orkney and Nick had had her decked over by Bob Macinnes our local boat builder in Scourie; then in July 1973, he and Julie had set sail directly for Madeira which they reached in thirty-four days. Marie Christine and I met them out in Madeira that autumn. They were in good spirits and pleased with their boat *Aegre*. From our apartment, a thousand feet above the sea, I had watched them sail across the far southern horizon, their tan sails a tiny speck on the broad ocean. After a spell in the Canaries they'd crossed the Atlantic to Barbados and on inevitably, to the Panama canal and through into the Pacific. Some 4,000 miles later they arrived at the Marquesas and then sailed on to Tahiti; by this time they were calling the boat "God's little *Aegre*"—all this in a boat in which it is hardly possible to sit upright below the deck. The letter waiting for me in Praia concerned the next leg of their voyage: they had set sail again, heading ultimately for New Zealand, and one night while Julie was at the helm, and Nick asleep below, they were capsized in a big storm. The internal buoyancy kept the boat afloat, and they managed to right her again but she was dismasted and much of their gear had been lost in the night, including the Avon dinghy and sextant. They now had a waterlogged boat or nothing, their navigation gear had all but disappeared and it took them a dozen exhausting hours to bale out the boat and get her sailing again under a jury rig. With only a watch, a compass and navigation tables to help them navigate they at last saw the peaks of Samoa rise over the horizon after four weeks and sixteen hundred miles from where they had been capsized. There was nothing for it but to run for the shore and hope to make it ashore through the surf, but a few miles out they had met a Japanese freighter which they had gone aboard. *Aegre* was badly damaged in the subsequent tow into harbour at nine knots. In their letter they said they both felt a lot older and wiser than when they had left Ardmore!

At Ardmore we had all been hoping the Graingers would eventually make it right round the world and back to Scotland; old Bob Macinnes had newspaper cuttings from Glasgow to

Tahiti pasted up on the wall of his ancient workshop. The news of their misfortune came as a bitter blow just when we needed encouragement. "It would be a hell of a lot worse in the *Aegre*," we used to say, when the weather was bad, and now the *Aegre* was finished; "we've completely lost confidence in her", the letter said, and this seemed to throw extra doubt on the ability of *English Rose* to complete the voyage we were on.

We dropped the sails for the night, to stop their dreadful slatting noise, and next morning it was as calm as ever. The pressure of frustration at getting nowhere was increased by sunburn from long hours on deck in swimming gear and a restless night in sweat-soaked sheets; as a result tempers were a little short. Krister and I had widely divergent ideas about the voyage. For him it represented a holiday, a means of visiting strange places, a return to the nomadic timeless life he had enjoyed on his own for a year in South America, after the icecap expedition with us in Chile. He felt no weight of responsibility and he wasn't one to worry unduly about his long-term future; neat and self-contained he was always careful to avoid personal entanglements, which might restrict his easy-going bachelor life-style, preferring to keep his many friends by copious correspondence rather than joint participation in any special project. On the other hand, I seemed to feel the burden of responsibility increasing daily, in the hot cramped conditions prevailing on the boat.

Unhappily, I had a growing belief that things were going to go wrong. The problem was really one of communication and without appearing a fussy old man I couldn't seem to bridge the gap of years and experience. I was thirty-six and they were twenty-four, twenty-two and twenty-one. This difficulty existed particularly in my relationship with Krister (24) and Staff (21), neither of whom had been to sea before. For example, in the frustrating heat of the calm at the start of a 3,000-mile voyage, experience told me the way to get sailing was to use every two-minute puff of wind to edge through the wind-shadow of the island and out into the Trades once more. Krister's style in contrast, was to relax and enjoy the day, to make the most of the present and deal with the future as it came along—the wind would come in time and no amount of fussing would speed its return. In the confined incendiary conditions of sweat, sunburn

and impatience, there was bound to be something of a clash—
and while it took place all right, it was conducted in the muted
tones of two individuals struggling to retain calm self-control.
The results of this suppression showed themselves in different
ways. I became increasingly impatient and Krister began
teasing and even bullying Rebecca which led to an inevitable
subdued clash with her mother.

Staff (21), was the youngest and least experienced of the
crew. Long periods in hospital following a broken neck and
other illness had left him with an iron self-discipline, which
coped with the almost insurmountable problem of his chronic
seasickness. The efforts he made in this direction were reflected
in his quiet earnestness, which precluded many flashes of wit;
and with the natural self-confidence of youth his judgments
were sometimes too hasty and final—and occasionally entirely
incorrect. In the fifteen years that I was older than him, much
had happened to me; the cares of life rested gently on his
shoulders and he was occasionally a little short with me for
worrying. I felt perhaps he had come half way round the world
from Australia to work at Ardmore after his suffering in hospital,
in the hope that I would measure up to his idealism. The
familiarity of our life together aboard the boat bred something
like contempt when he found my feet were of clay like so many
others!

Jamie (22), and I had known each other for seven years,
since he had left school. Weak academic results and conflict
with his parents had made him shy and introverted, lapsing
into black moods which sometimes lasted for days, he relied
greatly on his strong physique to prop an unnecessary and
negative sense of failure. I could see much of myself in all this,
and so I was pleased to see how much confidence he had gained
from the Gosport to Ardmore trip over the New Year, and how
he seemed to feel as if he was coming out of a long dark tunnel.
Of the six of us on board, Jamie was best suited to the confined
conditions, and it was he who perhaps gained most from the
experience. He always spoke in a very quiet voice, and he
avoided arguments and clashes of personality most skilfully by
retiring to his bunk in the forward cabin to read or sleep whenever he felt in a rare black mood, which never lasted beyond
the length of a four-hour watch.

Marie Christine was keenly aware of being the only woman on the boat; the absence of proper washing facilities, the carpet of beard trimmings and hairs which covered everything as a result of having three beardies on board, and above all, the lack of privacy made things very trying for her. Added to this was a continuous feeling of seasickness accentuated by her self-imposed cooking duties; there was no need for her to keep a watch on deck so she spent over-long periods in the cabin. Ambivalent as most people are, she feels at her best when alone with Rebecca and me in her home at Ardmore, but at the same time she is the first to admit how much she enjoys the interest and excitement of a more risky way of life. Her strongest asset, psychologically, was an ability to avoid clashes by remaining interested but non-committal in argument; she would say, "Well, I think . . ." in a reasonable way, because she is a strong believer that things once said in the heat of the moment can never be unsaid. Perhaps her weakest point was her loyalty to me, only with the greatest difficulty could she resist a raging counter-attack on anyone who criticised me, no matter how fair the reason; my shortcomings could always be justified by the overall pressures to which I was subjected as the captain of the boat. "It makes my blood boil!" she would say to me at night in our bunk when we were as near as we ever were to being on our own, and sadly I would usually have to agree with the opposition.

Sometimes she felt Staff was a bit arrogant, but the only open clashes she ever had were with Krister over Rebecca. Krister was one of a family of eight children, his father was a foreman in a Swedish aluminium smelter; there was never too much money to go round and the young Krister was brought up in a good straightforward strongly disciplined way in which what the parents said, went, and that was an end to it. The method had worked well for him and he could see no reason for it not applying to other children too, Rebecca included. He had learned some of his English at school in Sweden, but mostly through common use at a Kibbutz, on which he had worked in Israel before coming to Ardmore in 1971. One of the more unfortunate sayings he had picked up and commonly used in conversation with Rebecca was the mild 'shut up!' His way of saying this sometimes gave the impression of bullying, to which I usually responded with a weak plea for peace—not so Marie Christine, who more than once urged him with barely concealed rage, to leave the upbringing of the child to its parents.

Rebecca was seven years old; she had little experience beyond the remote life at Ardmore, with the result that nearly everything which happened was either exciting or frightening, but usually new. This was tiring for her and whenever we were in port she had to keep the same late hours as the adult crew, occasionally on returning to the boat she would get beyond herself. Staff, Krister, and Jamie were all in their way most considerate towards the little girl and each of them spent long hours either reading to her, playing games or teaching her practical things about the boat. Her greatest asset was her self-sufficiency, learned in long television-free days alone at Ardmore, which had made her both sensible and observant of the small things of nature which surrounded her. She could spend long periods sitting quietly on deck absorbed with her surroundings, and seldom did she ever complain of boredom—in fact I don't think she has ever heard of the word.

It would be easy but unfair to end this critical evaluation of the crew without some mention of my own failings. On each of the expeditions I have led I have always had the overall successful completion of the project uppermost in my mind; and this has inevitably meant pushing on when others would have preferred to linger and enjoy the pleasures of strange places. This was the case again on this voyage, from Krister's and Staff's point of view, but not Jamie's. Success and safety in the past had come, in my view, from careful planning beforehand, a pessimistic outlook regarding what might go wrong in the future, and an irksome attention to detail throughout the course of the expedition and particularly in the latter stages when people are tired and confident of success before it is actually achieved. A common example of this on most of the expeditions has been the way an old military lesson has come to mind from Sandhurst days, "more soldiers are killed on patrol when returning to their lines after successfully completing the mission, than are ever killed on their way out towards the enemy lines". I have found it particularly true that the race is never won or lost until the finishing line has been crossed.

In my efforts to succeed, and as a result of the general attrition of effort over the years, I have noticed the fraying of my nerves and a decreasing stock of patience can be particularly trying to others in a confined space. Arrogance, intolerance and selfishness also feed the flames of determination.

The return of the wind was signalled by a dramatic sunset as we lay becalmed a mile or so off the coast of São Tiago in the late afternoon of 22nd November. Dolphins gamboled around us in the milky blue water and they left us just as the sun turned blood red beside the dark triangle of Fogo volcano, whose 9,000-foot cone loomed high over our western horizon more than thirty miles distant. As it sank into the ocean the sea became a crimson sheet of silk paling to gold as the last rays turned the sky to copper; on the shaded eastern side of the boat the colour of the water was purest indigo, against the ginger of the mountains, each of which had a white volcanic plug at its summit. The wind came with the night, from 0–5 knots in as many minutes, and before long the smooth water turned rough once more and poor Staff was being sick. "What goes down must come up," was Krister's laconic note in the log, referring to both the wind—and Staff's supper.

We crashed north all night into the steady north-east Trade and I took Staff's watch from four to eight in the morning as he was still deeply involved with the black plastic bucket in the forward cabin. The day was lumpy with tall, green seas and Rebecca was sick twice, but we covered the hundred miles north to the five-mile channel between Razo islet and São Nicolau island by mid-afternoon; then once again the wind fell away. We were becalmed under the 4,000-foot Mount Gordo, which we could just make out through the thick yellow haze which partially obscured the channel as well. Again the dolphins came to play and again the wind came up at sunset; as it grew dark we crept past Razo, close enough to see the surf exploding against the sheer cliffs of that uninhabited islet. Once through, nothing lay between us and the Azores, 1,400 miles away to the north-west. We reefed down and settled ourselves for a long bash to windward.

"Isn't it sidey!" said Rebecca, early next morning, referring to the steep angle of heel. All the seasick sufferers met in the cockpit that morning for a couple of hours of empty grinning at each other, and watching white breakers mounted on blue chargers hurling themselves against *English Rose* in endless succession under a clear, brassy sky. We felt awful; whoever would want to go against the Trades like this? We wouldn't do it again that was quite certain.

A measure of change in motion, is that Staff had to do 240 strokes with the double action bilge pump to clear the water that we had taken in during his watch. Clad in faded jeans, and old yellow shirt and with a red neckerchief neatly knotted at his throat he looked plumper than during the summer days at Ardmore, but he was having trouble keeping his macaroni down after the pumping session with his head between his knees. After a lot of searching by Jamie, we discovered the leak —it was pouring in through an outlet valve high on the port side, which I had forgotten to close after removing a spare bilge pump before leaving Ardmore. In other words we'd had this large hole in our port side for two months and over three thousand miles, but only now were we going sufficiently hard to windward for the water to come in in any significant quantities. Looking down through the engine compartment during the search for this leak, I could see sunlight through the fibre glass alongside the line of the keel at the stern of the boat—we were certainly heeled well over.

For the next nine days we covered more than a hundred miles in each twenty-four hours; to begin with it was stifling hot because for the first time in ages we had to keep the forehatch shut because of the spray. Without a current of air passing through the boat it was muggy and miserable, but gradually the yellow mantle of haze left the sky and as we clawed north the air grew clear and cooler; out came the woollen hats and polar sweaters for night watches, and our talk turned more and more of home as we pulled sleeping bags over the sheets on our bunks at night.

"I'm taking after my Granny," laughed Rebecca as she won yet another game of pelmanism. Cards became part of daily life and she never tired of playing anyone at anytime.

It rained on us for the first time in many weeks on 1st December, when we were still 400 miles south-east of the Azores, but the water failed to wash out the long sandy streaks staining the

Cold work on the foredeck.
The North Atlantic in
December.

A lull between the storms on the homeward leg. Jamie, Rebecca and Marie Christine.

Entering Castlebay, Isle of Barra.

big sails which we had had to put up when the wind failed. Our speed dropped to thirty-eight miles in twenty-four hours, but this gave us an opportunity to carry out some of the work we thought necessary before we encountered bad weather. Down came the spinnaker net we had rigged between the forestay and the mast, and the liferaft was moved back into the cockpit along with jerrycans of survival supplies, in case the worst came to the worst. We rigged the safety lines inside the cockpit for the first time, Staff greased all the winches, and a spare jib halliard was rove through a block at the head of the mast, just in case the existing galvanised wire should part. Down below books were stowed away, and safety tapes were fitted to all cupboard doors which were left tied in a reef knot, as an extra security, in case the normal fastenings should fail. We rehearsed various drills for abandoning ship and each person was given duties to perform to make sure we could leave the boat at maximum speed if necessary.

We were not a day too soon in our preparations. By noon next day it was blowing force 9 or more from the north-east, the strongest wind we had had since leaving Ardmore and the worst weather any of us except Jamie and I had ever seen at sea. After a livid red sunrise, Staff had started to be sick again at nine o'clock just as soon as the wind began to rise from the south-west; we sailed on through the morning, on slate-grey seas now in place of blue, as the wind steadily climbed to around force seven, reaching north-west under the No. 2 jib and a heavily reefed mainsail. Krister was on watch when the boat was suddenly knocked over, with the main boom firmly held aback by a kicking strap which we had made up by rolling in a green canvas strap with the mainsail, as we reefed it.

What had happened was that the wind, which had built up a big swell from the south-west, suddenly came from exactly the opposite direction, the north-east, and in mighty gusts, too. By the time I reached the cockpit, the new wind was moving like a sheet of hot steel in a rolling mill, with the torrential rain steaming off the surface of the sea. The big south-westerly sea was stopped in its tracks, the waves were literally being blown backwards over themselves in sheets of spray.

We lay over on our port side like a stranded whale, but

luckily Krister was just handing over the watch to Jamie as it happened and they were quick to let the jib sheet fly, dash up to the mast and drop the main and then the jib. We came upright again, made fast the sails with sail ties and just lay a hull riding it out with no sail up. Down below I quickly made the decision to abandon the idea of going to the Azores. If this was the sort of weather we might expect, it was just not worth it without an engine to help us manoeuvre in a strange port if the weather was rough. I had taken the precaution of ensuring we had adequate supplies and water for the complete 3,000 miles from the Cape Verdes to Ardmore and now was the time to carry the plan out—before we had an opportunity to give up in the Azores.

"As soon as we get home, I'll cut all the rockers off the rocking chairs," Marie Christine was promising. The violence of the onset of bad weather had badly shaken us, after all, we still had 1,700 miles of worsening weather to come.

The wind veered and decreased in mid-afternoon, and we set sail once more. The Azores were up ahead and everyone was looking forward to fresh meat and vegetables, the things we hadn't seen since leaving Palma. I read through the *Admiralty Pilot* and set up the four excellent charts we had of the archipelago, the wind was now a warm soft breeze from the south-east and it had soothed away all trace of the mid-day madness.

"Horta's out—*Pilot* says it's no good in a south-west wind— we could try for Delgada on São Miguel, the best port in the Azores—it's about 270 miles due north," I said, from the chart table, waiting for some reaction.

"Well, I'm for it," replied Jamie, "we can fill up with fresh water and finish getting her ready for the rough weather."

"Oh yes, me too—it would be a pity not to see it," Krister added, and Marie Christine and Staff nodded their approval. Of course, poor Rebecca would have to go along with whatever the adults agreed . . . and suffer the consequences.

"O.K. then, Delgada it is," I said, snapping the *Pilot* shut, "we could always go into Santa Maria, its forty miles nearer— and it has the international airport for the Azores." I didn't need to say what that meant.

"No, Rebecca and I will stay with you—won't we Beck?"
Marie Christine said quietly, and Rebecca nodded.

"What about you, Staff?" I asked, "you've been so sick, and
the weather's only going to get worse, we could always go on
without you."

Staff shrugged, saying nothing. Selfishly I hoped he would
stick it out; the last 1,500 miles from the Azores to Ardmore was
my main reason for carrying such a large crew. The original
idea had been for only Krister and Jamie to be in the forward
cabin; this would have given them much more privacy as one
of them would have been on watch for two-thirds of the time,
with me doing the third watch. A lot of the pressure we'd felt in
the hot weather had been owing to cramped conditions; but
I'd thought it all worth while for a powerful crew on the last leg
home. Against this I was secretly worried that Staff's health
might crack up, he sometimes looked really dreadful after three
or four days without food or drink during the endless bouts of
seasickness. The strange thing was that he hadn't suffered
unduly at Ardmore where he had crewed for me for much of
the summer, while Jamie and Krister sailed *English Rose IV*, but
now at the first sign of rough weather he was violently and
continuously sick. At the back of my mind was the serious record
of hospitalisation he had suffered in Australia. A small yacht on
the North Atlantic in winter was no place to become dangerously ill.

"John, you mustn't leave your wet oilskins on top of the food
bins," Marie Christine scolded, from her place by the cooker.
I replied with my version of a delicate moue and looked
away.

A few minutes later I suddenly thought of something.

"Hey! Wait a minute! My oilskins aren't wet—we must have
a leak!" I jumped out of the bunk and began scrabbling about
among Rebecca's bedding on top of the food bins. Sure enough
the sleeping bag was wet. A few seconds later I discovered the
cause—water was dripping steadily from the bar and trunnion
in the deck-head which secured the starboard mainstay (supporting the mast) to the deck. I felt a surge of sickness in my
stomach—this was exactly the trouble which had put me out
of the first single-handed round the world race six years before,
when I was leading.

"Oh you needn't worry about them," the salesman at Camper and Nicholson had laughed at my fears, "those fittings will see the boat break up before they part!"

But there it was, rain water dripping into the cabin.

"It must have happened when we were knocked over yesterday." I stared miserably at it.

"But it's only coming down one side—there's no sign of any real strain—it'll just be the caulking up on the deck that's split, we can reseat the plate again in Delgada. It'll be as right as rain," Jamie said, seeing nothing to panic about.

"Mate, a shroud plate changed the course of my life—I'm just a bit sensitive to them," I grinned. Yes we'd fix it in Delgada.

I could hear Staff up in the cockpit, singing to cheer me up:

"We were down by Bondi pier,
Drinking tubes of Foster's beer,
And we'll chunder in the old Atlantic Sea!"

He was a plucky fellow all right.

We were closing on Delgada, and already past Santa Maria which lay hidden by mist out on our starboard beam, the wind had backed to the east and it was blowing a gusty force 5–6. It was already well into the afternoon, and the butterflies were stirring in my stomach; we had about fifteen miles to go and no more than three hours of daylight left. The clouds scurried low overhead and there was the ever-present danger of bad weather, I cursed my luck for another race against time. This was no place to heave-to for the night, with an island dead ahead whose coast spread invisibly eighteen miles on either bow. The *Pilot* warned of giant storms which might sweep up from behind us at any time. No, we must crowd on the canvas and try to make it before dark.

"What d'you think it costs from the Azores to London by air?" Staff asked me quietly, as we sat in the cockpit trying to keep back the rising seasickness. It was Jamie's watch but he was up at the mast preparing coils of mooring warps for our entry into Delgada harbour.

"About a hundred pounds single, I suppose. You'd have to go via Lisbon," I said thoughtfully, "but you could hitch from Lisbon, and save the air fare."

"Well, I'm seriously thinking about it," Staff said earnestly.

"Well, I can't make up your mind for you," I smiled, trying to sound as friendly as I could. "You'll regret it if you don't finish the trip on the one hand, but on the other it's going to be a hell of a trip for seasickness. You must do what you think is best for yourself—we could get by on our own—be quite sure of that." I had provided the loophole, there was nothing more to be said.

12

Azores

"LAND HO!" Jamie's gruff voice called from the bow.

And there it was, well up in the sky, suddenly coming out of the mist.

Rebecca scrambled out from the cabin to get a look, keeping hidden behind the sprayhood and peeking her head round the lee side.

"Well what do you think of that, Beck, fifteen days of nothing and there's the town dead ahead, d'you think you could do it?" I asked smugly. She looked at me and shook her head slowly. I hoped very much that she was thinking I was just great—but she wasn't letting on.

"About ten miles?" said Jamie, clambering back into the cockpit, his oilskins dripping with spray as he unhooked his safety rope from the deck wire and clipped it onto his belt.

"About that—it'll be a close thing," I replied, trying to identify the radio beacon tower out to the east of the town, through the binoculars.

We were all in need of fresh rations; everyone looked tanned and fit but we had lived on a more or less continuous diet of dehydrated rations since leaving Palma forty-two days before; the desert had had little to offer in the way of fresh food. Our eyes had become accustomed to the glare off the sea and land had come to mean barren yellow-brown rocks in the ocean, inhabited by poverty-stricken people who could grow next to nothing themselves, and who had to rely on imported foods to supplement a basic diet of fish.

The sight of São Miguel, affected me in a way I could not

remember since Chay Blyth and I first saw the green of the Aran islands off Galway after ninety-two days rowing across from America. It was just the tonic my spirits needed, a long well-rounded countryside of neat green fields rising steeply up green-clothed mountains whose tops lay hidden in the clouds. I was reminded of Southern Ireland and the Yorkshire dales, it was 'home' country so different to the parched yellowness of what we had known in the Cape Verdes. The port of Delgada looked neat and small, surrounded by those blessed green fields —like one of those rural scenes used by Ovaltine to advertise their country factory.

With only a few minutes of daylight left, we rounded the end of the port's massively built mole, with heavy seas pounding all along its three-quarter-mile length. The harbour was wide and more or less empty and we were surprised to see a small pilot launch patiently waiting to guide us to a mooring. The pilot had a hand megaphone and spoke good English; he sheltered behind a doghouse and his smart naval officer's hat was held firmly on his head by a chinstrap.

"We have seen no yachts for three months—they won't come here again until next April," he said, once we were safely tied up alongside the quay in front of a huge trawler, which was busy unloading sardines for the island's cannery. He wouldn't come aboard, and we held our conversation while I filled in the necessary forms, leaning on the bonnet of one of the cars which had already driven out from town to see us.

"Where are you bound for?" the pilot asked, craning his dark handsome head.

"Scotland—we've got to be back for the New Year," I smiled, my legs feeling a bit wobbly on solid ground.

"It ees not possible!" stared the pilot. He said nothing more for a few seconds, just looking at me. Then he made a suggestion. "You can leave your boat here—we have an American yacht," he gestured towards a tall-masted blue sloop up on the shore. "The owner left her here until next June when he will return—he is a wise man."

"Yes, I've heard of that before," I thought of Chay and Maureen Blyth, who had left their boat on that very shore and flown home. "But no, we must get home, it is important," I added.

"You are lucky, the pressure is high now, soon the bad weather will return and then . . ." he made an extravagant gesture at the mighty harbour wall, "the waves break right over there."

"We must not be here then," I replied, speaking slowly so he would be sure to understand we were going on.

He gave up. "Well, if you or any of your crew would like a shower, please don't hesitate to come to the pilots' quarters at the end of the mole, it will be a pleasure to help you," he said kindly, then flashing a charming smile he bade me goodbye, and was gone into the dark.

The Azores must be one of the most bountiful places on earth. Every inch on São Miguel was turned over to agriculture, not in the desperate terraced manner of Madeira, but in small fields rich in deep green grass which grows continuously all the year round. There was no sign of the poverty we had seen everywhere else we had been on the voyage; the Azores produced an over-abundance of food. Although based on a strong dairy industry, the island of São Miguel grew all manner of good things besides, and being so far from European or American markets, the islanders got on with the happy business of consuming much of the produce themselves.

We scurried ashore for a quick look at the town that first night, leaving Staff to tend the moorings. The narrow cobbled streets were thronged with townspeople out to look at the shops all lit up for Christmas.

"Excuse me! Do you know of anywhere where we might get something to eat?" I asked a man who was looking at a tray of engagement rings in a jewellery shop, as if checking the prices before deciding whether to try for a Christmas engagement with the absent girl of his fancy.

After a moment's thought—or was it a return to reality—he nodded politely and led us down a dark back street.

"This is the place," said Marie Christine tugging excitedly at Rebecca's hand, long before we reached the restaurant, "I can just tell by the smell."

We thanked the man as he waved us into Alcide's, an unprepossessing looking place, both outside and in, it looked like a railway café outside Reading station. Half a dozen locals were sat at plain brown tables, the walls were dirty cream and uncluttered by any pictures or time-wasting stuff of that sort; the business was eating and the decks were clear.

"Ooh! It looks like a heap of chips," Rebecca cried in disappointment, when she saw the waiter bearing three steaming plates towards our corner table.

We dug in and found the chips were only a thin covering for enormous steaks lavishly garnished with a rich garlic sauce.

"I think this is the best steak I've ever had in my life," said Marie Christine, taking a swig of red wine between mouthfuls. "I would have been satisfied with just the soup, but this is delicious."

"I bet they don't use frozen meat here," I said.

"Oh no, this is absolutely perfect," she went on, it was difficult to stop her, and when thick rings of fresh pineapple came later, it just finished off one of the most memorable meals we had ever had. We agreed that on the next night we'd make sure the boat was well secured and then have a party with everyone from the boat together, to prepare ourselves for the long haul home.

We were all three feeling pretty tired as we plodded along the mole in the dark, and we were in no mood for a chat when a sentry came out of his box, which stood in the shadows under a warehouse. He was guarding a huge consignment of wine which was contained in large wooden casks, stacked one on top of another. He must have seen us coming in the light of the tall street lamps which stood all along the wide road running in the shelter of the mole wall. I suppose we didn't look like locals and he thought he'd better check. It was cold and the collar of his heavy grey greatcoat was up about his ears, a pistol bulged ominously in its leather holster at his waist. When we explained we were from the English yacht lying against the wharf, his eyes widened with interest.

"*Aventura!*" he exclaimed.

"You can say that again," remarked Marie Christine, watching Rebecca skip along the road towards our floating home, now only about fifty yards away.

I awoke next morning at five thirty, long before it got light. I was full of a strange exhilaration, brought about by landing safely at this green and friendly place. My mind raced with all sorts of plans for the future; there was no staying in bed, I got up quietly and dressed.

"John! What are you doing?" Marie Christine stood in the cockpit in her nightdress, and stared in amazement as I sat on the wet deck writing furiously by the light of a street lamp.

"I couldn't sleep—so I came up here to write down my ideas —before I forgot them," I grinned sheepishly.

"I woke up and wondered where on earth you'd gone," she replied. "I'll make you a cup of tea!" and with that she disappeared back into the cabin.

As soon as the sky streaked with the first light of dawn, I was off, heading for the shore to look for Miguel Vidal, Michael Zino's friend whom I'd met in the red boat *Marlin* on the day we left Madeira. He had said he might be in Delgada at about this time in December. I almost ran along the mole, exulting in the clean fresh air of the silent dawn, it was going to be a still sunny day, the sky was clear and I'd seldom ever felt so alive. On my way towards the town I passed several fishmongers, short dark chunky men wearing black berets which made them look French; they carried their fish in panniers at either end of a stout wooden pole balanced across their shoulders. Once or twice I was passed by ponies and carts containing fish or vegetables for market. I hurried on across a tree-shaded square with a bandstand in the middle and on down through the cobbled streets until I came to a square surrounding the great bulk of a stone church or cathedral, and facing this imposing house of God were the Banks of Mammon. On the far side, where silent single-decker buses lined the pavement, awaiting the day's passengers for outlying districts, I saw a small café, and hurried in for a breakfast of hot coffee and cheese rolls. The proprietor, who stooped heavy shouldered by the coffee machine, was Bob Hope, or someone very like him. He wore a pale shirt with a subdued tie, barred green and brown, a few strands of hair laid thinly across a nearly bald round head. As he gazed at his customers through heavy lidded eyes half a smile played on his lips and a cigarette hung from one corner of his mouth. The place was busy with locals waiting for buses or shops to open. A woman came in with a basket of fresh baked cakes and I wished I'd not already eaten the cheese rolls. Life was just grand.

I went to the bank as soon as it opened, the sun warming my

back in the street and this time it was Cliff Richard who changed my money. I just knew it was going to be a good day as I walked to the hardware shop which held the agency for the brand of gas Miguel distributed throughout the Azores, Cape Verdes and Madeira. I walked in through the open doors and there he was not a yard from the door, casually reading a leaflet as if he were waiting for me to arrive. His business was finished and he had a couple of days to spare, there was nothing he would like more than to show us over the island, which he liked so much himself, that he was thinking of moving his family over from Madeira.

We picked up Marie Christine and Rebecca in his car, arranged to meet the fellows at Alcide's for supper and drove off to a sumptuous lunch at his hotel, the São Pedro, which he said was more like a home than a hotel. It was the old and stately home of an American landscape gardener who had lived on São Miguel in the previous century. The stone over the fire-place was engraved 1812, and the whole place was lined with fine woods, the timber floors were so highly polished that we hardly dared tread on them.

That afternoon, Miguel drove us, together with the wife of a visiting pineapple buyer, to the eastern end of the island to see some boiling sulphur springs which lay at the bottom of a huge tree-lined volcanic crater. Along the way we passed the fields which are the source of the island's wealth, and Miguel pointed out the various crops; sugarbeet in great mounds like turnips, chicory root which is ground to mix with coffee, tobacco, and great long glasshouses which grow pineapples the year round. We saw tea plantations up on hillsides where horsemen rode to milk their cows carrying twin milk churns slung across the saddle. There were more horses at work on São Miguel than I had seen anywhere in the world. Maize, wheat, sweet potatoes and several vegetables are also grown in their season.

The Furnas Valley, twenty-eight miles east of Delgada, which in spring is covered by azaleas and rhododendrons, has twenty-three different hot springs which are used for cooking and medicinal purposes. In the middle of the valley there is a large park of artificial gardens created in the last century, the centre-piece of which is a steaming thermal swimming pool of about thirty yards in diameter. This is roofed by the boughs of the enormous trees surrounding it. Fat carp cruise indolently along narrow, curved pools built to show off the exotic plants, bushes and trees to their best advantage, and quiet, shaded avenues lead to obelisks and monuments. We were the only people in the gardens, except for a handful of old men busy with brooms rhythmically sweeping the hard black grit paths free of leaves. It was far from the sea and there was the scent of autumn in the still afternoon air, the autumn we had missed at home. Later, high up on the rim of the crater, on the way home, we saw thin spirals of wood-smoke, rising vertically from foresters' fires; and puffs of steam from some of the scattered houses led Miguel to remark that the hot springs were actually piped into them for heating purposes.

"Here they have oranges all the year round," he said wistfully, and Marie Christine and Rebecca listed all the fruits on the island: pineapples and passion fruit, oranges and bananas, custard apples and guavas, apples and pears, grapes and plums, the game went on for a long time; until Rebecca saw another horse up ahead, then she lost all interest in fruit. At a tiny laneside dairy we persuaded a man to sell us each a mugful of creamy milk, straight from the churn.

We met Krister, Jamie and Staff at Alcide's, and we were just finishing an enormous meal of soup, steak and chips and pineapple (all there ever was on the menu) when Miguel arrived together with the pineapple buyer Augustino and his wife Pieto.

"Do you think you could run through the menu again?" I asked, and huge smiles lit three bearded faces.

During the meal, we decided to sail on 10th December. Surely three weeks would be long enough to reach home for the New Year? Krister had managed to find the British Shipping Forecasts during the day, while searching the wave-bands for Radio Sweden. "Gales in all sea areas," he laughed, mopping the gravy from his beard, and I wondered if Staff had been to the airline office.

The next three days were taken up with eating, and visits to places of interest, between meals. We saw the Seven Cities Lakes, two great sheets of water of different colours, one green and one blue, from the narrow track which runs along the rim of an extinct volcano containing them. Far below, on one side, we saw six white fishing boats, small dots on the broad ocean, and way down on the other side the two lakes set in rich farming land, glittered in the sunlight, fresh after a recent shower. We had to imagine how it would all look in the spring, drenched in blue hydrangeas, but nothing could change the melodious sound of the bells which hung from the necks of the Fresian cows.

Daniello Machado, kindly showed us over some of his hundred-year-old greenhouses, each containing 900 pineapple plants. A big friendly bear of a man with short fair hair and blue eyes which always seemed to be smiling, Daniello explained that a plant bears only one fruit, and each pineapple takes two years to grow in the rich volcanic soil. He cut four unripe pineapples for the boat, saying they should be ready to eat over the New Year at Ardmore; and just before we left he picked some orchids for Marie Christine from a collection of seventy-six varieties he grows for a hobby. We later learned that Richard Burton, the film star, was growing orchids commercially on Santa Maria, close to the international airport, so he could fly them to the American market.

In the village of Rio Seco we stopped in the main street, and peered down into a large hole at a street junction, fifteen feet below we saw the top of a fountain, all that remained visible of the original Rio Seco which was buried by a volcanic eruption in the seventeenth century.

In spite of the wondrous sights, it was the food and the friendly people of São Miguel which I remember most, as in most remote communities the people were never too busy to stop and talk, or help us to find places. Eating was a serious business in small inexpensive eating houses which were always full, even though we never saw any other visitors on the island. The food was fresh: meat, fish, vegetables, dairy produce, fruit; there was no sign of canned, frozen, dehydrated or even preserved food. The ubiquitous pineapple, proudly claimed to be the best in the world, soothed away the digestive problems which otherwise might have troubled us after rich Portuguese and French cooking.

Perhaps it is necessary to endure six barren weeks on a small yacht to really appreciate the bountiful Azores.

The day before we left, a Monrovian oil tanker tied up alongside the wharf just astern of us. She had come in unexpectedly for fresh water after taking on bad water in the Mediterranean, which had caused some sickness among the Pakistani crew. Strangely she was carrying 19,000 tons of Russian oil from the Black Sea to New York, which must say something about the state of the world oil crisis. The young Irish captain of the ship had his wife on board with him, and we exchanged some of our books for her old newspapers; Marie Christine felt very flattered when the captain's wife said she'd heard the food was good at Ardmore, it seemed a most unlikely situation to receive such a compliment.

Too soon came the morning of our departure. Marie Christine, Rebecca and I went into the town for a last stock of fresh bread and vegetables, while Krister checked the post office for the latest weather situation and confirmed that the high pressure area still covered the Azores—at least we should be able to clear the archipelago before heavy weather returned from the south-west. Staff had been to the airline office, had thought about the business of flying home, and for the simple reason that he didn't want to let us down, he decided to stick it out and come on home with us.

It was a bright sunny day, as all our days had been at the Azores, and Daniello was on the pier in his old Volkswagen beetle, when we returned to the boat laden with armfuls of provisions. With him were his wife Maria, Antonio his son and his friend Frans; they had come to see us off—luckily for us as it turned out.

Jamie and Staff had made the boat ready for sea, and the Avon dinghy was rolled up and stowed away in the engine compartment. We shook hands with our friends, smiling sheepishly as Daniello shook his head and warned of high winds due in just a few hours' time by his reckoning.

It was blowing force 4–5 from the north-east in the harbour, as we let go the warps fore and aft. Krister and Jamie pulled us out along the rope and chain leading towards the Danforth anchor, which we'd laid off our port beam to prevent the boat from chafing on the wharf, as she rode the ever-present swell. We had the No. 2 jib up and flying loose, and Staff was at the sheets in the cockpit, ready to haul in the sail just as soon as the anchor was free.

Jamie picked up the blue coil of floating rope with the boat-hook, this was the anchor tripping line—but it didn't trip the

anchor. We swung round head to wind, the anchor chain tight
as a bow string, and our stern suddenly lay close under the
flaring bows of a freighter, the cross trees on the mast swaying
dangerously close to the ship's side as we rolled.

"Take in the jib, Staff, I'll sail her up a bit," I muttered. The
boat heeled to the wind, and the cross trees narrowly shaved
past the towering steel wall as we crept forward.

But it was no use, the anchor was firmly jammed among the
rocks on which the mole was built. "Oh, for the Avon," I
thought desperately. We were in a tricky situation, one touch
of the rigging against the ship and we would be in serious
trouble. I looked across at the pier. Daniello had already turned
the car, he knew what to do, and he was on his way.

Ten minutes later a powerful white launch appeared on the
scene, butting through the choppy water and sending sheets of
spray over the doghouse, behind which sheltered Daniello and
half a dozen boatmen. Jamie threw them the tripping line, and
they paid it out until it was at an oblique angle to the anchor;
the anchor came away the moment the line tightened on their
stern. We were free.

Daniello realised we would have to tack several times across
the harbour before we could clear the end of the mole, so he
had the launch tow us right out until we could sail out on one
broad reach, then he spoke to the man at the tow rope and it
went slack. I pulled the tiller up towards me and the bow swung
away off the wind. Staff tightened the jib sheet while I did the
main, and we were away. Up in the bows, Jamie hauled in the
tow rope, rolling it into big coils in his left hand, while Krister
tightened the main halliard at the mast winches. Marie Christine
and Rebecca waved frantically to Daniello in the launch and
Maria and Frans on the end of the mole as we dipped towards
the open sea.

Antonio was the only person on top of the massive concrete
wall as we turned west to run along the island's southern shore,
a lonely figure in a dark raincoat with hungry combers surging
up through jumbled rocks as if to engulf him.

13

Looking for Trouble

"WHAT DO YOU WANT in your roll, Staff?" Jamie called up from the cabin.

"What is there?" the stocky Australian replied, enjoying every minute at the helm, trying to decide in the bright sunlight if what he saw on the horizon was the bridge of a ship or a submarine.

"You can have cheese and tomato, or marmite, or peanut butter and jam!"

"I'll take the lot, one after the other," and we all laughed at his nerve, for we knew as well as he did that he had only an hour or so before the suffering began again.

We covered the fifteen miles downwind to the Ferraria light, perched high on the cliffs at the western end of the island in quick time; as we turned north so we met the full weight of a north-easterly gale. There was nothing for it but to put up the storm jib, reef the main right down to the top row of holes, and try to slide across the wind in a north-westerly direction, taking care not to make too far to the west though, because the rocky bulk of Terceira Island lay some seventy miles north-west of São Miguel. Staff lapsed into convulsive sickness. Marie Christine, Rebecca and I felt awful. Jamie alone tackled the steak and eggs which he fried up that evening.

"It's not much like last night is it?" said Marie Christine miserably, as we huddled together in the bunk. I shook my head. Our friend Miguel had had us to dinner at his hotel, and I'd worn my suit for the first time since leaving Ardmore seventy-three days before (mind you I hadn't worn it for some months before that either!). Marie Christine and Rebecca had

176

enjoyed dressing up in their long dresses rather more than I. There had been only two other tables occupied in the elegant dining rooms of the São Pedro that night, and our table for eight received the maximum attention. The food was excellent; the waiters wore white gloves, and between courses they had removed the crumbs from the tablecloth with a sort of hand-powered 'it beats as it sweeps as it cleans' device—made of silver of course. I smiled, how carefully we had tried dusting the pineapple with cinnamon to see if it removed the acid taste—those days were over.

It was a lumpy night, the heavy seas sometimes knocked on the hull with the sound of a sledgehammer. I'd asked them to build me the strongest boat in the world—this was the sort of treatment she was made for—but it was frightening to be there in the dark and listen to it. We had already come 1,500 miles to windward, it didn't seem fair to start off with gales to windward on this last leg, the wind was meant to be from the south-west pushing us along—not the north-east beating us back.

Rebecca was in the bunk with us, and she became so frightened at one stage that she began a dreadful keening noise, which, she wailed, was because she was homesick for Pussy. She and I had a long talk about the cat in question, and at last she went off to sleep after some discussion about whether or not Pussy was vexed if he wagged his tail in his sleep.

Krister slept on the floor of the cabin, the steadiest place in the boat, and when I went on watch in place of Staff at four o'clock in the morning, Jamie moved in to sleep on top of the food bins. This meant five people were sleeping in a cabin originally laid out for one.

Out on the port bow I could just make out the loom of the main light on Terceira, as it pulsed faintly on the horizon every ten seconds; this was good, I could keep a watch on it, and once past it we were free all the way to the Hebrides. Not so good was the way the boat sometimes fell off the waves, the slamming effect of the seas kept us shuddering for much of the time, but if we wanted to keep pushing forward there was nothing for it but to hold on and hope for the best. When the really bad weather came, as it surely would, I wanted to be well clear of the land.

Surprisingly, towards the end of our third day at sea, the

wind began to ease and veer to the east, and Staff began to come round again; he'd eaten nothing since the fresh rolls on the morning of our departure and he was in a pretty weak condition. We hung up six pineapples which Augustino, the buyer who had flown back to Lisbon, had had delivered to the boat just before we sailed. Although they made the cabin smell rather better than it otherwise might have done under the prevailing conditions, they looked pretty lethal as they swung to and fro from the handrails in the cabin directly over the bunk and the food bins. I foresaw one of those incongruous personal disasters, where someone would be blinded by a direct hit in the eye from the spear-like projection of the two-inch cut stalk at the bottom of the weighty pineapple; so we tied a string between each stalk to lessen the chances of disaster. The orchids were less of a problem; we bound their stalks and wrapped them in newspaper, then they were stuck through the hole in the top of the white glass shade on the small paraffin lamp, which hung in gimbals at the head of our bunk. I didn't say as much, but when I came down off watch in the early hours of a morning and saw my wife's sleeping form beneath those green- and yellow-speckled orchids, I was always impressed by the tomb-like effect.

"GO CAREFULLY!" was written in large letters across the head of the log, and arrows pointed down to FRIDAY and 13 and December. And go carefully we did, the wind fell away to nothing at all and Staff tottered out on watch, eating again at last. St. Kilda, the islands on which we had nearly been wrecked on our journey up from Gosport almost a year ago, lay 1,080 miles north-north-east. It was a bad Friday 13th at home the news told us, with gales everywhere and fishermen drowned off East Anglia and a tug sunk in the Firth of Forth, but we tried to be cheerful at our candle-lit supper party. The candles were not so much romance, more an economy: owing to an oversight (or was it over-eating?), we had not bought any more petrol for the generator in Delgada, and our estimate was that we could only put another three full charges into the pair of 102 amp hour batteries. Luckily we used the electric navigation lights only when too close for comfort to shipping, normally we used just the paraffin lights which Lance had fitted to the bows before we'd left Ardmore. Although it was reassuring to be able to switch on the deck floodlight when we thought there was any danger, it was far more economical to use the paraffin lights normally.

The calm lasted for an unbelievable five days. On the 14th December, we only logged five point two miles, but it gradually improved through forty, ninety-eight and ninety-nine miles and towards the end of this poor Staff began to feel groggy again, so we installed him on the floor of the main cabin and I took over his watches. It was much colder now and we all wore our full winter rig every day. Krister was hit in the back by a stormy petrel one night which gave him a bit of a fright; we thought it must have been blinded by the hurricane lamp which we kept hung in between the backstays as a stern light. Rebecca and Marie Christine emerged on deck to try their hand at catching Portuguese man o'war jellyfish in a plastic bucket, or just to watch the dolphins as they rolled about under our bows.

The calm got on our nerves a bit, but we were all getting on together far too well to have any clashes. It was just that during this time the forecast for all up the western seaboard of Britain was continuously hovering around storm force 10, and I couldn't stop thinking of the cliffs, and of those moving hills of white water we had encountered during the hurricane on the rowing trip from America to Eire—and that had been summer time. Over and over again I juggled with the various approaches to Ardmore, was it better to keep right out in the ocean until we were level with the Butt of Lewis and then turn sharp east? The disadvantage of this was the chance of being blown on further and further north by ill-timed southerly gales, and I well remembered Jamie growling at Brian Cunningham as we lay to the warps in a southerly gale off the Butt the previous January, "It looks as if you'll see Iceland again, Brian!"

Another approach would be to more or less follow the course we'd been blown onto at that time, and pass between St. Kilda and the Hebrides, aiming to keep about twenty miles from either, and then sail on up north past the Flannans, and then east round the Butt. This meant being close to the coast for quite a long time.

A third possibility was to aim for Barra Head, which had a convenient and powerful radio beacon for homing purposes. From Barra we could either rush pell-mell up the Minch, inside the Hebrides, or if the weather was too bad we might try for a run up the outside of the islands to St. Kilda—just as we had on the trip up from Gosport. Given fair warning we might even put into one of the handful of small ports along the inside of the Hebrides, but it wasn't right to chance 'fair warning' so I discounted this idea.

Round and round these ideas went; it was important I came to the right solution, and there was little else to occupy my mind as we wallowed about in the light airs, waiting for our comeuppance. The lines I drew on the huge North Atlantic chart usually seemed to end at the lonely unlighted rocks of St. Kilda —mainly, I think, because this course allowed a greater clearance of the west coast of Ireland.

0600 hours, Tuesday, 17th December, it was still dark and I was on watch. We had the No. 1 Genoa boomed out to port and the mainsail far out the starboard side and she was snoring along nicely before a fresh south-westerly. Our position was on the same latitude as the middle of the Bay of Biscay; about a thousand miles west of La Rochelle on the French coast, a little closer to St. Kilda. The Azores were more than four hundred miles astern now and on the present north-easterly course we should clear Ireland by something a little over a hundred miles.

It was cold and I was struggling to keep awake in the dark, every half hour I forced myself to go down below and make up a peanut butter and marmalade sandwich with a couple of biscuits; then a quick swig of cold water from the tap, a shake of the head and back up for another half-hour battle with sleep and the cold. The sea gurgled noisily along the waterline, and I wondered just how much the carpet of inch-long goose neck barnacles around the stern would be slowing us down. I wished the light would come, but we had gone back to G.M.T. for convenience on the radio, and my watch would be finished at eight o'clock, well before the first glimmer of dawn. Staff was sleeping better now he had moved to the cabin floor, and I hoped to get him back on watch for the four to eight p.m. spell in the evening.

The minutes ticked by. . . . How could it ever take so long from six o'clock to six thirty, when I must go down below and listen to the weather forecast, using the earphones so as not to wake the others.

Six twenty-five, I peer at the watch again to be sure. Yes I'll have to rush or I'll miss it.

"There are warnings of gales in all sea areas," the distant voice spoke without any trace of emotion, "except Biscay and Finisterre." We were way out to the west of Finisterre but I noted they were to have variable winds force 3–5; I listened on out of habit, Hebrides were having north-west gale force 8 to storm force 10—it was no day to be close off the west coast of the Hebrides, nor in the Minch either for that matter.

I returned to the cockpit munching my sandwich, no need for the water now—I was grappling with the best approach problem again, and I had noticed the barometer was beginning to fall at last, after a whole week at between 1025 and 1030.

We managed ninety-nine point nine miles that day, and Staff did come back on watch. Although he felt pretty rough, I thought he would be far better if he could get back into the swing of things. It was time to use the full power of the crew, so I introduced the idea of the four of us doing two-hour spells in place of the old system of three men working four-hour watches. by supper-time that day, the radio was reporting hundred mile an hour gusts at home and the glass over the chart table was slowly falling. There was no doubt that we were in for it, and there was an air of excitement as we shovelled down our hot stew and tatties by candle light; morale was high as we ran through the foul weather procedure yet again, debating whether to stream warps, lie a-hull, or run under bare poles in extreme conditions, for the hundredth time.

Next day, the glass dropped ten points and we were bowling along before a southerly gale under the storm jib and a scrap of main. Staff stuck to the two hourly routine and seemed the better for it. It was rough and spilly down below in the cabin; coffee, porridge, curry, scrambled eggs, milk and wine all crashed to the deck at different times during the day. Marie Christine and Rebecca were in great spirits; we had all caught something of the drama and excitement of the present—this was it, the essence of living to the full, we knew well that none of us would ever forget the fight which lay ahead of us.

Another seven points were lost on the following day, but the wind eased a bit in the evening and the stars peeped out for a while through racing clouds. But it was only a temporary lull; when the wind returned in the early hours of 20th December, we rolled away the rest of the mainsail and lashed the boom amidships, as a support for the man on watch when he looked forward over the sprayhood. The glass fell another eleven points to 994 at midnight.

My two hours on watch that afternoon were a tremendous thrill. I stood astride the cockpit, facing forward, one foot on either seat and my left arm hooked over the main boom. The Hasler steering gear worked easily, even though the alteration line wheel had somehow got crushed. We were running along before a severe southerly gale force 9. I judged our speed to be five or six knots, but the seas were now so high, that we just couldn't stop the log line from tangling, as the waves kept throwing the spinner forward out of the water and on top of the line. We tried a longer and a shorter line, with a new spinner, and we oiled and cleaned the clock with the right oil, but the line kept on tangling and the clock under-reading.

It was cold even though we were running with the wind, and I had all my warm gear on under my superbly tough Equinoxe yellow oilskins and boots. A blue duvet hood kept my ears warm under the oilskin hood which was drawn tight beneath my chin, and a towel kept the drizzle and spray from working down my neck, but my feet had to keep moving or I lost all feeling in them. I wrapped the tail of a jib sheet round either hand, then leaning back I took the strain on my arms, swaying from leg to leg as we rolled, my life harness clipped to the cockpit safety wire.

The sliding cover of the main hatch was pulled shut, and a heavy perspex dropboard filled part of the vertical entrance to the cabin, the rest was covered by an orange oilskin jacket to keep out the flying spray. Over my head, slung between the backstays, the diamond-shaped aluminium radar reflector drummed in the wind, spinning this way and that each time we climbed to the top of a wave. It was hills and valleys now, great grey-green slopes stippled with streams of white foam.

Looking forward over the sprayhood, as we slid headlong down one of these long grey walls, I watched a fulmar gliding stiff winged and camouflaged pale grey and white, like a miniature spitfire in the valley below. General George S. Patton

must have felt something like this riding on his tank at the head
of the allied advance through Europe.

By noon next day, the 21st December, we were 240 miles
west of the south-west corner of Ireland. Krister was now able
to produce quite a good position with the Consol system, and
we were getting the odd radio beacon at extreme range; this was
just as well, because the ragged sights I had managed on the
few occasions when I'd been able to use the sextant, were not
up to much. I taught Rebecca how to use the callbuoy emergency radio, and she soon got the hang of making it work.

"If you find yourself alone in the liferaft, work the radio and
wait for the kind gentleman on the other end to come and pick
you up; then you'd better tell them tea and pineapple juice
have gone for a swim," I said to her after we had gone through
the drill several times. I was tea and Marie Christine was
pineapple juice in a rhyme she had made up:

> I like coffee (Rebecca)
> I like tea (Daddy)
> I love Mummy (Pineapple juice, somehow!)
> And Mummy loves me!—when I'm good.

At supper that night we heard on the news that the leader of
the Saharan rebels had been captured on the Mauritanian
border; Gamoudi's tea party in Villa Cisneros seemed far away
and I wondered what he'd be thinking now.

Things were getting just a bit confused now. We had had
winds of gale force or more for much of the past four days, it was
wearing us down—we thought we were thinking straight but
we weren't, the cold and the uncertain future were getting to us.
Navigation calls for clear thinking, the one thing we wanted to
avoid was dipping to the right of our course and coming too
close to Ireland. I had a nice clean chart of 'Newfoundland to
the Faeroes' on the table; I'd marked in the arc of maximum
range of the various Radio Beacons: Mizzen Head, Eagle Rock,
Toky Island, Barra Head and the Butt of Lewis; they were all
there, ready for our approach to the land. Then I switched to a
grubby Consol chart of the British Isles which was overlaid with
the red, blue and green lattice of signals from Bushmills,
Ploneis and Stavanger.

I failed to notice in the poor light that the line of Krister's

Consol positions was curving remorselessly towards the rocks of Achille Head on the western edge of County Mayo.

The glass dropped to 991, but the wind paused to gather its strength again for an hour or so at nine o'clock in the evening. The radar reflector had broken its lashings and crashed to the deck, but the wind was still too strong to put it up again satisfactorily. When I came on watch at ten it was already rising again from the south-west and I wondered if we'd done right in changing the storm jib for the No. 2 jib. There was a giant swell running but it wasn't at all confused, the veer of the wind from south to south-west had taken place nice and gradually, but both wind and sea were now edging us ominously closer to Achille Head. I'd decided to go for Barra Head by this time, because the weather had allowed no good sights of the sun, and the log was under-reading too badly to be of much use for Dead Reckoning. We were relying far too much on Consol for my liking; so if I could pick up the Barra Head Radio Beacon with its 200-mile range, I could home right down its beam, which was preferable to trying for the unlighted and beaconless St. Kilda, after 1,500 miles in this thick weather.

By dawn the No. 2 jib had to be replaced by the storm jib, as it had lost a number of the piston hanks which clip it to the forestay, and those remaining were all undone.

"What I really miss is not having any chocolate," Jamie said thoughtfully, as he scraped the last traces of porridge from his plate next morning.

"You'll just have to wait and see what Father Christmas brings you then, won't you?" teased Marie Christine, and he smiled ruefully.

Christmas was now pretty big business in the cabin. Rebecca was much concerned with making and hanging gay paper decorations along the handrails and in and out of the remaining hanging pineapples which now included the four Daniello had given us. This show had to be paid for and Rebecca insisted that everyone present their specially made tickets when they crossed an imaginary line drawn between the chart table and the cooker. All this was all an infinitely more serious matter to her mind, than the way the grown-ups went on worrying about the weather.

Krister was delighted to find Christmas was pretty big

business in Sweden as well; he heard on Radio Sweden that fifteen 'Father Christmases' had gone into a store in Stockholm, filled up fifteen sacks with toys, and then left the store again to distribute their presents to the children on the streets. Police had arrested fifteen Father Christmases.

On watch that afternoon, the gale seemed to be dying, we put up the No. 1 jib, but kept the main down—just in case. The swell remained the same size, sliding past as if some giant was rolling hills at us from somewhere over the horizon; but gone were the urgent riffles that always scuffed the grey surface into white streaks when the sea was building. Around us flew a large number of sea birds—perhaps they were used to following the trawlers, some of whom might have returned to port for the Christmas holiday—sadly we had no fish to throw to them. The pert little kittiwakes were all young, with the distinguishing black line behind the eye and zig-zag black line along the wing top; perhaps with age they grow wiser and fly south nearer to the sun. As well as the bull-necked fulmars, gliding and banking low over the surface, hardly seeming to fly at all, there were a few wheeling goose-sized gannets with their long pointy beaks and handsome golden heads. Here and there for the first time, I saw the odd bullying great black-backed gull, like an old man lurching heavily with whitish feet cocked, like hands groping for a fob watch.

By the time I handed over to Staff at four o'clock it was already getting dark, and the wind came with the night. The forecast at five minutes to six offered our area, which was now aptly named Rockall, south-west force 6 to gale 8 and later backing south and increasing to severe gale 9, becoming cyclonic. The only bit I liked of this was 'backing south'—that should keep us clear of Achille Head. The glass which had rallied nine points during the day, began to dive at the rate of a point each hour, but this increased later to two points an hour. There was one final thing for us in the shipping forecast; a low of 984, positioned 450 miles west of Finisterre, was moving rapidly north to be in Rockall for noon the next day.

That night of Sunday, 22nd December, we had the worst weather so far. It was cold and frightening. The sea seemed to have discovered an extra explosive ferocity. At ten o'clock, Jamie and I dropped the storm jib, as it had also lost a few piston hanks, and in its place we put up the tiny spitfire, which we shackled onto the forestay at the head and foot as an extra precaution. After he'd gone below, I headed a bit further to the north, taking the wind and sea a little on the port quarter. This should keep us clear of Eagle Island whose radio beacon lay twenty miles north up the coast from Achille Head, and was seventy miles from us bearing 043° True. Once clear of Eagle Island, the coast fell away to the east in the great bight of Donegal Bay; and with a wind from anywhere except the north or north-west we should be reasonably safe.

The self-steering gear struggled now, the angle of the boat and the small headsail making control extra difficult in the huge quartering seas. Every so often the gear would react too slowly, unable to anticipate like a live helmsman; then there would be a screech of grinding cogs as the latch lifted unable to hold the weight of the boat against the power of the sea. The watch keeper became more of a helmsman as the night progressed; this was just as well as far as I was concerned, because I got an awful fright every time the sea gained control over the boat. The wind increased its shriek in the rigging two-fold whenever the hull twisted round to lie broadside onto the hungry seas, and leaping white arms of spray reached out of the dark as if seeking to drag me over the side.

I found that when I stood up to look forward over the spray-hood, I had to crook my arm around the main boom which had roll upon roll of terylene mainsail wrapped round it, the discharge of static electricity from the wet terylene was so fierce that I could not keep my hand on the sail.

"There are two different worlds: one out there, and one in here!" Staff said, as he came down into the cabin at the end of his watch at ten o'clock next morning, Monday, 23rd December. He stood at the cabin entrance, the spray glistening wetly on his yellow oilskins, while he re-adjusted the orange oilskin jacket to cover the gap between the hatch cover on top and the perspex dropboard below. Krister was now on watch until mid-day, when Jamie would relieve him; it was hand steering now and the tall, bearded Swede was revelling in the wild conditions.

This was the sixth day of gales, and I felt my colours were fast running dry. The glass was down to 984, and still falling. The forecast for Rockall at 0630 in the morning was south to south-west force 7 to 9 to storm 10. There were three areas of low pressure on the go: south-east Iceland (filling), Hebrides (filling) and the one which was now due in West Rockall at 6.00 that evening.

Jamie's efforts with the radio direction finder at ten thirty in the morning put us somewhere about seventy miles due west of Eagle Island. It was blowing around severe gale 9 or more from the south, maybe even a bit east of south—but after six days we were becoming used to this new style of life, dangerously so!

"We're level with the southern shores of Donegal Bay," I said to Jamie who was still at the chart table. "Let's head more for Barra—what'll that need?" I asked from the bunk where I was playing with a very cheerful Rebecca.

There was silence for a few moments, while he worked out the course, sliding the protractor across the chart and whirling the dial.

"Fifty-five degrees compass will do it," he growled, and I called up to Krister to see if he could make this new course. In view of the forecast and the prevailing conditions this was a mistake.

"What's that?" a yellow head poked through the gap it made between the orange oilskin and the starboard side of the cabin entrance. The tumult of whirring wind and roaring sea made it hard to hear and he had the oilskin hood pulled tight by the drawstring at his chin, so only a small oval at the front of his face was visible.

"Can you try for fifty-five compass?" I shouted again.

"Okay, I try," he grinned and the head disappeared.

We weren't running directly before the wind on the present course of 030° compass, and another twenty-five degrees to the east at 055° compass would have us riding a gaint switchback, with the wind well out on the starboard quarter of the stern. At first nothing changed, while Krister tightened the strings holding down the bottom corners of the orange jacket shielding the entrance to the cabin. This was a tricky business as it meant taking off soaking wet gloves, securing them, holding the tiller and fiddling with chilled hands at slip knots in the string.

Then we were away, up and down and across in a new racing twisting motion.

"Yes, I can make," the Swede bellowed from the cockpit.

It didn't seem right to me. I should have done something—but I didn't. We plunged along under the tiny spitfire jib, and nothing seemed to be going wrong, so I left it. "After all," I thought, "Krister's in charge up there, he's as safe as anyone I know and its broad daylight."

Marie Christine left the saloon with a bowl containing a little warm water and went into the loo compartment for a wash, pulling the curtain behind her. Jamie heaved himself up onto the food bins and pulled on his blue down sleeping bag. Staff was already asleep in his bag wedged in the angle between the cabin floor and our bunk where I lay stretched out under a pile of red sleeping bags and a tartan rug, and with my head up at the forward end. Rebecca and I were on our centenary game of I-Spy, which I could nearly play with my eyes shut because by now, I knew the exact location of practically everything it was possible to spy from our bunk. We had an argument about whether the single remaining orchid should be 'O' for orchid or 'F' for flower and I felt tired.

"Look Rebecca, old top, I've got to have a gonk—I'm on again in a couple of hours," I said rolling over on my back; and I pulled the soft down sleeping bag over me in preparation for a delicious warm sleep.

"All right, you cuddle down," crooned my daughter, now adopting the role of nurse as she knelt in the bunk beside me. She was leaning back against the bookshelf, holding the disgusting red and yellow orchid in one hand, and soothing my brow with the other.

Quite suddenly the little hand stopped dead, it fell away from my forehead. I opened one eye—we were heeled over to port and instead of the cabin roof I found myself looking directly at Rebecca's face, her mouth hung open. For a few seconds—which stretched on and on—I couldn't bring my mind into focus. Rebecca's pale blonde head seemed frozen, her blue eyes stared at where the orange oilskin had been over the cabin entrance. Horizontal lines of white foam streaked the air between her head and the bookshelf.

Then like a slow-motion film I turned my head and came up

into a sitting position. A wall of water blocked the way out to the cockpit. For an instant I glimpsed Krister's worried face, then it was gone. The cabin suddenly filled with the sound of roaring water.

"Block it—Jamie—Block it!" I heard myself call in a low urgent voice, as if it were a move in a game of ice hockey. Out of the corner of my eye I saw that Staff was already on his feet, the water streaming from the blue sleeping bag in which he was still cocooned as he stumbled towards the cabin steps in a vain effort to block the gushing gap.

Jamie had swung his sleeping bag over the edge of the food bins and I was on my way over the bunk rail when the boat came upright, and the incoming water subsided to a trickle.

"Go to your mother, Rebecca—just keep calm!" I called back to my daughter, and she scrambled over the rail like a little wet monkey, still clutching the obscene-looking orchid.

I could see the cockpit was just a swimming pool, still brimming over into the cabin. The boat lay low and water-logged—the danger was obvious—if we got hit by another whopper, and more came into the cabin—we'd go down like a stone.

Jamie was already scrabbling in the oilskin locker for the wooden dropboards which should have been in place all along, suffocation or not, with the kind of conditions we'd been having. The orange jacket had disappeared—at least this gave Jamie more light for his desperate hunt.

I looked round to see how Rebecca was. The curtain to the loo was swept back now and the child stood in the entrance with her fair hair slicked flat and wet against her head and the icy North Atlantic swilling round her legs. She thought a huge wave had broken a hole in the side of the boat and we were sinking—she was staring at me with a fixed intense look of horror as if hypnotised.

"Keep calm—it's only a little splash," I heard her mother say soothingly.

"It's not, Mummy!—You can't SEE—it's a waterfall," wailed Rebecca.

I saw a pair of arms pick her up and mother and child disappeared from view, to sit on the loo and console each other.

Krister was already baling furiously in the swimming pool with the black bucket, in a desperate attempt to have us floating

better for the next whopper. Jamie was dropping the dropboards into their slots in the cabin entrance, as I turned my
attention on the drowned radio gear which was so essential for
navigation. Meanwhile Staff was pulling the small portable
pump and hose out of a locker, and while I mopped down the
electronics, he and Jamie frantically started pumping.

I snapped on the radio—it sounded hopelessly 'mushy'. In a
panic, I began stripping it down, drying it with some loo paper
which Marie Christine passed back from another locker.

We didn't feel at all cold, the shock saw to that, but Jamie,
Staff and I were only dressed in soaking wet underwear, and I
was kneeling in our bunk which was just a trough of icy water.

Gradually, I was filled with an enormous sense of personal
outrage that the sea should have dared to invade 'the other
world' as Staff had called the cabin.

Rebecca sat wrapped in a damp grey blanket on the food
bins, shivering furiously and still hanging onto the orchid.
Through chattering teeth she kept asking quaintly, "Whatever
is the world coming to?" in between wails of self-pity.

As soon as the cockpit was emptied below danger level,
Krister dropped the spitfire jib which he had let fly as soon as
he'd thought of it after the knockdown. Then he made a check
of the boat and called down the damage, while we carried on
below.

"The sprayhood is flat all the seams burst and torn, I can't
get it up again. The lee dodger is flapping free—all the lacing
is broken—LOOK OUT!" he shouted, and another whopper
hit us, surging across the cabin roof and sending a torrent of
water in along under the hatch cover.

He started pumping again. "It's not too bad," he called. "At
least it's done the washing up!" and we heard him laughing.
"It's all gone, not a trace of anything at all." He finished
pumping the cockpit dry and then he lashed the tiller and came
below. We let the boat lie a-hull.

It took the six of us three hours to sort out the chaos. Practically everything on the boat was soaking wet except for
Krister's gear, which he had kept on his top bunk in the forecabin. Of course he had got soaked from the waist down, but he
kindly dished out bits and pieces of his dry clothing for others
to wear, and Marie Christine found a grip full of dry stuff

which included duvet jackets. We decided to keep on our wet clothing and let it dry on our bodies, and we heaped all the wet gear up into the forecabin out of the way.

After hot tea and a bit to eat, Krister, Rebecca, Marie Christine and I huddled together for warmth in the bunk and Jamie and Staff shared the space over the food bins. Outside the storm raged on from the south, and every so often a whopper came in and hit the boat sending a jet of water down onto the chart table. Between sleeps, we discussed what had happened, while Jamie read through Adlard Cole's *Heavy Weather Sailing* like a schoolboy doing some last minute swatting before the exam.

"If the wind veers sharply as the depression goes through, that's when we'll have to watch out—if there's a cross sea set up," I said, we had talked about this many times before, but now we might have a real live situation. The glass was right down to 981.

Each of us had seen the situation rather differently. Krister told how he had been watching the sea carefully, and that the heavy displacement boat had given him no cause for worry, as she was riding across the waves very steadily.

"Then I saw this much larger wave quite a long way behind us. At first I didn't worry, but as it came nearer it looked like two or even three waves one on top of the other—so I called out and headed the boat straight down wind."

"Yeah! I heard you shout," Staff interrupted.

"I didn't," I said.

"Nor me," Jamie peered over the top of *Heavy Weather Sailing*.

"I did, Krister," piped up Rebecca.

"Well, just as we neared the top of the wave, it seemed to break and everything started to happen rather fast. My first thought was to get to the Helly Jacket and stop the water from going down into the cabin—but the wave picked me up—and only my harness stopped me from going over the side."

An indication of how wet it was in the boat is that Marie Christine's hair was soaked as she stood in the washing compartment. Krister's gloves were washed off him by the wave and he found one later, up on the bow, while he was dropping the spitfire jib.

Sadly, the forecast at five minutes to six gave Rockall south-south-east 8–10 veering west 9. We had been hearing of all sorts of trouble at sea, and now the weather was so severe that the Swansea to Cork ferry was cancelled for the night. We certainly needed our supper of mince and tatties and I decided we should lie a-hull for the night.

It was a pretty rotten night for us, but we managed to sleep. Jamie stayed down at the chart table end of the bunk and took the weather forecasts. Marie Christine and I kept Rebecca between us for warmth up at the other end. Rebecca was warm and cheery but she looked a pretty odd sight with Marie Christine's polar pullover as a sort of dress which reached well below her knees, a navy Damart hood and my polar mitts on her feet. We were warm enough but wet, cramped and sticky with the salt—we kept thinking of the hot peat stove at Ardmore still 350 miles to the north.

The luck was not all bad and the wind veered gradually to the south-west and fell away to something like force 5. The fears of dreadful cross seas proved groundless.

"Land ho!" Jamie called next morning, "Achille Head again —it looks a bit nearer than it did on the first of October!" This brought me up into the cockpit all of a dither.

"It's a hell of a long way off, all the same," I muttered and retreated below to get the D.F. bearing off Eagle Island, so we could cross it with a visual bearing of Achille Head for a fix.

"Fix 1030 hours 24 Dec 74 LOG 5345", I wrote on the chart ten minutes later. We were twenty-eight miles to the west of Eagle Island.

Christmas Eve was spent rolling north-east before a south-west wind force 5–6 and under the No. 1 jib alone, on a slate-grey sea towards Barra Head, which was 200 miles away at noon. Malin was the sea area we now listened for on the shipping forecasts. It was bitterly cold but thick oilskins kept our body heat sealed up inside them, even though our clothing was rather damp. The barometer climbed up and up until at midnight it reached 1,000, when we had the tri-sail and No. 2 jib pulling for us, but it started to fade away again as Christmas Day came in.

Marie Christine made a great effort to give us all, and especially Rebecca, a happy Christmas. We stuffed her stocking with all sorts of goodies and even Staff, Krister and Jamie found socks full of chocolate, tangerines and miniature bottles of liqueur. The log read 'MERRY CHRISTMAS TO ALL OUR READERS' across the top and breakfast was French toast made with *real eggs*, specially kept for THE DAY. Lunch was frankfurter sausages and Jamie's version of bread (cooked in the pressure cooker) and slightly salty Christmas cake.

"It's the rottenest Christmas ever!" was Rebecca's estimate of it all at one stage, shortly after losing at cards, but this was later revised to, "I quite like it really, I'd rather be with you."

The barometer fell all through Christmas Day, and this combined with a forecast south-west severe gale force 9, and the certainty that we should reach Barra Head around midnight, took a bit of the fun out of the day for most of us. All the same, we were delighted when Staff produced two tins of nuts for the crew; even Jamie came out with the remaining cans of his Tennant's lager. Marie Christine dished up a splendid supper of tuna fish pie, spinach and mashed real potatoes, which had all been cooked in our one remaining saucepan. We had a bottle of wine we'd bought from a soldier in Praia, Cape Verde, and the last of the 'ripe' pineapples. Staff's delicious box of walnuts finished off the extravaganza.

"I can see it!" shouted Staff at 2230, "it's half a finger above the horizon already!"

So much for seventeen miles visibility. At 683 feet above the sea it was probably in the cloud—shades of that awful shock Brian Cunningham had given us when he'd suddenly sighted it on the afternoon of 4th January!

By midnight, the barometer had fallen fifteen points during Christmas Day and I was feeling pretty jumpy. We went onto double watches, with a man on deck and the other constantly on the radio direction finder; and with an hour on each of these duties followed by a couple of hours' sleep, it was a poor night. Marie Christine and Rebecca moved up into the bows to sleep on the spare bunk, but they were thrown about so much they had to return to the bunk in the saloon at five o'clock in the morning.

14

Into the Beer

I HAD SOME COLD THINKS on watch before dawn. The wind was blowing nearly a gale from the north—the forecast gave it as veering to the east and increasing to force 9 later. Castlebay on the island of Barra was no more than eight miles away—the radio talked of cars being blown off the motorways and ships in distress. . . .

"We'll go into Castlebay," I called down through the hatch to Staff, and he grinned back, cheeks hollow in the dim chart table light.

Dawn found us tacking in towards Muldoanich Island off Vatersay Sound, the channel leading to Castlebay. It was a spectacular morning, one of those grand crystal-clear winter days, with never a cloud in a peerless blue sky. The mountains on Barra wore their yellow-brown colours of winter and the sea was a livid ice green; in the distance, Atlantic surf boomed on the long-deserted sandy beaches of Vatersay Island. I caught myself looking nervously down towards Barra Head ten miles to the south: there it lay, the very last vertebra in the hundred-mile skeleton of islands which make up the Outer Hebrides.

The wind died away to almost nothing, and it was one o'clock in the afternoon before we finally ghosted in under all sail up alongside a black Seine netter by the lofty pier at Castlebay.

"Merry Christmas!" called Krister to a group of young lads, dressed in faded blue overalls, who were doing odd jobs aboard the silent fishing boat.

"Aye, Aye!" one of them called back, and although they showed no outward sign of surprise at the strange arrival of a small white yacht in the dead of winter, there was a general move across to take a look.

"Do you have any customs or police here? We've just come direct from the Azores," I asked the nearest fellow, a shaggy-haired twenty-year-old.

"Ach no! We've no customs—the policeman lives in the wee house up there." He briefly withdrew one hand from a pocket and pointed to a grey council house among the cluster of old buildings surrounding the bay, which made up the sleepy village. "He'll be down if he's interested—but I doubt it."

After the weather we had been enduring for the past week or so, we found Castlebay unreal with a kind of fairyland quality about it; bathed in sunshine and flat calm, even the locals were speaking in whispers lest the spell should break.

"There seem to be a lot of boats crossing over the sound to Vatersay," I said to the grey-haired owner of a small store, where we bought fresh groceries.

"Oh aye!—it'll be the first time in about a month they've been able to get across," came the soft smiling reply.

With fresh provisions safely aboard in bursting cardboard boxes, our attention turned to thoughts of hot baths. "You'll be all right if you've got a 'Lady Godiver' (fiver)," said the same young fellow who'd told us about the policeman, pointing this time at a decidedly closed-looking hotel on the hillside.

Half an hour later Marie Christine, Rebecca and I stood forlornly outside its huge double wooden doors, listening to the doleful echoes of the bell we had pulled again and again. Suddenly a window shot up high on the wall above the door, and a tousled head peered down over the sill, "It's Jamie, it's Jamie!" Rebecca cried, jumping up and down with excitement.

"Lovely hot bath I had," chortled Jamie at the three of us shivering below, "I'll come down and let you in," he added, and the window slammed shut again.

The hotel was a big rambling old place, shut down for major improvements to meet the new fire regulations. The whole crew had hot baths which worked the Christmas spirit back into our limbs—we were on the land, for the moment we were safe and it was Boxing Day. In spite of the short notice, Mrs. Mcleod made us all very welcome and we had a big supper in the family's own living room, tucking into fresh meat and plenty of sprouts picked from the garden just outside the front door. The room was hung with Christmas decorations and there were cards and presents everywhere; it all seemed so warm and friendly after the sea. Mrs. Mcleod, a grey-haired homely mother of nine children, told us of the excitements of the previous summer when the yachts in the Round Britain Race had made Castlebay one of their few scheduled forty-eight-hour stops; the weather had been so bad that several boats gave up the race and some even stayed in the little port for three weeks. There had been plenty of drama with newspapers and tele- vision men, as well as doting parents, wives and girl-friends cooped up in the hotel, waiting anxiously for the storm to end and boats to arrive.

The weather changed abruptly in the afternoon, and while we phoned relatives and friends from the dark hall that evening the front door rattled on its hinges as yet another gale swept across the island. We had nowhere to sleep except the boat and Marie Christine was keen to have one good night's sleep in a proper bed before we made the last dash for home; foolishly we had left our oilskins on the boat and by the time we left the hotel to search for accommodation it was raining fiercely out- side. Running pell-mell down the road towards the home of the lifeboat engineer John Allan, we got drenched by sheets of rain which slashed across the pools of light thrown from the street lamps. I'm sure it was only when Marie Christine let the bath- towel slip down over her stomach, beneath her soaking duvet jacket, to make herself look pregnant, that poor John Allan was finally convinced that something really must be arranged. He made a couple of hurried phone calls and it was agreed that the lifeboat coxswain would take Marie Christine, Rebecca and me to Mrs. Macneil's wee croft in his car, while John rowed Krister, Staff and Jamie out to the yacht which had been moved to a safer mooring beside the lifeboat in the lee of the castle, which stood on a rock in the middle of the bay.

When we awoke next morning the storm was gone, and over a large breakfast at Mrs. Macneil's we agreed to sail on home if the forecast was anything like good—we couldn't bear the suspense. At four thirty in the afternoon, in failing light we fairly shot out of Castlebay, under the No. 2 jib and a scrap of main-

sail; once into the sound we bore away and rushed along the
three and a half miles towards the Bo Vich Chuan buoy at top
speed, with a rising south-westerly wind behind us. By five ten
we had the buoy a-beam to port, it was now pitch dark and we
headed north-west for home, running goosewinged before the
wind.

"Rockall, Malin, Hebrides Southwest 7 to severe gale force 9,
rain and showers," intoned the weather forecaster at five
fifty-five. "Many a slip twixt cup and lip," I thought. We had
120 miles to cover before reaching the shelter of Loch Laxford
and home; we were sailing through a funnel which narrowed at
its neck to only a couple of miles in width after sixty miles, at
the gap between Trodday Island off the north coast of Skye and
Comet Rock the most south-easterly of a chain of rocky islets
strung across the Little Minch towards South Harris.

Rain and showers it was; the visibility was terrible and in the
hour between nine and ten o'clock that evening the glass
dropped three points and the gale blew up to force 9. Running
now before the storm jib alone, we were all too anxious to feel
seasick, and when Staff screamed down through the hatch just
before eleven o'clock that there was a lighthouse dead ahead
and only three miles away, I felt decidedly scared, so I told
everyone to put on their life jackets. Radio beacons were of no
use at this point as the only suitable points were more or less in
line, so we were relying on dead reckoning with the faulty
walker log and an uncertain tidal stream. I judged the light to
be more like six miles off and we identified it as Neist Point on
the most westerly part of Skye.

On and on we rushed, driven before the gale, the surface of
the water showing white in long streaks of spindrift. Past Neist
and round Vaternish Point and so onto the line for Trodday,
twelve miles ahead. It was half past two in the morning of
28th December but no one felt tired as we approached a critical
part of the trip. Every now and then a really big squall would
obliterate everything from sight, but we had had a fleeting
eerie moonlit view of the rugged west coast of Skye, which had
been only two or three miles off to starboard, between the Neist
Point and Vaternish Point lighthouses, but now we had to cross
the broad mouth of Loch Snizort. Dead on the line between
Vaternish lighthouse and Trodday Island lighthouse lay the

unlit rocks of Ant-Iasgair, I reckoned we would be up to them by about five minutes to four—everything depended on our seeing them up ahead and then altering course in time, for I doubted if we'd see the Trodday light at that range because of the thick weather.

It was a wild night, there was no going back against the wind, and no holding still against the tide—it was make or break. Krister was up on watch; I called Jamie, Staff and Marie Christine together for a briefing by the chart table: we were all fully dressed in oilskins, life jackets and harnesses. Rebecca lay asleep in the bunk in her oilskins and life jacket.

"Trodday light is split into three sectors: if you see green we are going to hit Ant-Iasgair or pass inside it and hit the top of Skye, if it shows white we are in the safe sector and we must head straight for the light." I noticed they were all three listening intently, so I went on, "if you see red, we are again in danger—too far west and likely to hit Comet Rock or the islands."

"What if we see nothing?" came Jamie's blunt question.

"That's the most likely thing—until we pass Ant-Iasgair—we must clear those rocks and here's the plan." I could see my wife was literally shaking with fear, the emergency radio slung on her shoulder was swinging to and fro. "Staff, you go up on the bow with the foghorn. When you see the rock give one short blast to let us know, then two blasts means steer to starboard, and one long means head to port—O.K.?"

"Right." Staff took the gas-operated horn and tested it against his palm, it worked.

"Jamie, you'll be on the helm, tell Krister he's looking out for you." I went on, "Marie Christine you stay down here—if we hit trouble I'll grab Rebecca, and Jamie and Krister will throw the liferaft out of the cockpit." There were no questions, Jamie and Staff went up on deck to take up their positions. I looked out into the cockpit and over the side, across a sheet of white-laced sea I could easily make out the dim bulk of Skye. How lucky we had the tide with us until 0530.

"I can see it!" shouted Krister, standing over me. "The rock, it's over there—to port."

We were inside the rock. It was 0340 and five miles more to Trodday.

"Can you alter course to clear it to starboard, Jamie?" I shouted above the shriek of the gale in the rigging.

"Yes, no bother," was his calm reply, and he altered course immediately. Staff hadn't reached the bow when Krister saw the rock so he hadn't sounded his horn; now he moved on up to hang onto the forestay in the pulpit—just in case there were other rocks we hadn't seen.

"It's an island—not a rock," shouted Krister, and I saw a sharp black peak of rock like the prow of a battleship knifing through the water ahead of us. The waves exploded against it sending gouts of brilliant white, high up, and then flying past it on the wind.

Then we were past it, leaving it a couple of hundred yards to starboard. I was worried we might not reach Trodday before the tide turned, this gale against the tide would be dreadful.

"I see the light," came Staff's call from the bow.

"Yep—there it is, it's white," Krister's shout was full of relief as he timed the interval between flashes with the stopwatch.

We spent a nervous hour bowling down towards Trodday, but at last at 0442 we passed to port of it and on into the broader waters of the North Minch, we were fifty-six miles from Loch Laxford. Suddenly we all felt very sleepy, but Krister, with the scent of home in his nostrils, volunteered to stay on watch while the rest of us slept.

It was nine o'clock when I awoke, and Krister was telling me he thought we were further east than he'd hoped, because the wind had veered out to the west and was edging us closer to the mainland.

All morning we pushed on through cold grey seas with ragged clouds and rain, we knew we were only about eight miles from the coast but we couldn't see it until at mid-day we suddenly got a clear view of a rocky headland complete with lighthouse.

"Stoer Head!" said Jamie reassuringly, "I've seen that too often to mistake it."

The last fifteen miles to Laxford seemed to go on for ever, we all knew the area like the backs of our hands, the wind had gone on round to the north-west as the forecast had threatened but it was only force 6–7 and we ploughed along under the No. 2 jib and a heavily reefed mainsail. Rebecca was full of excitement at the thought of seeing Pussy at last, but she couldn't really grasp that the coastline she could see out of the portholes was really home. Marie Christine was feeling as if she had 'flu and lay in the bunk all wrapped up in blankets and sleeping bags; I felt a tremendous sense of relief now that it really looked as if we should get home safe and sound, and a feeling of exhaustion now that the strain was nearly lifted from my shoulders.

We passed close to the gaunt cliffs of Handa Island which I sail around nearly fifty times each summer. A big swell was running in from the open ocean away to the north-west and I was struck by the unaccustomed rawness of the scene which is so familiar to me; the sea looked like liquid green ice and the spray-drenched cliffs were redder and starker than I ever remembered them. The light was already going, and I was in a hurry to get round Red Point and into Laxford before dark lest the wind should suddenly whip up in some unlikely way to drive us away from home at the last minute.

Ben Stack, Arkle and Foinavon were streaked with snow as we turned Red Point and ran down into Laxford, yawing wildly towards the rocky islets, which were only a couple of waves away even though that meant a hundred and fifty yards.

"Isn't it all so small—so enclosed—surely we never tacked in and out of here last summer," said Staff as we turned into Loch à Chadh-fi, with its familiar steep hills running sheer into the water on either side.

"There's Heckie's house!" Rebecca jumped up and down with excitement, convinced she was home at last.

"No sign of a boat on the running mooring—Lance may not be here," commented Jamie, as the sheltered bay opened up before us in the dusk.

"Let's sail on along the front of the wood until we see the blue house up above it, then we'll either see the tilley lamp in the window or smoke from the peat," I said.

"Let's put on all the electric lights and blow the foghorn," suggested the ebullient Krister, and on went the deck flood light, along with masthead, stern and navigation lights.

"They're there!" said Marie Christine, "there's the lamp."

We were all staring up the steep wooded hill at the light in the window—except Rebecca.

"Here comes Lance," she cried, "in the boat from the

school!" and we peered across the dark water under the great bulk of Foinavon; there was no doubt a dinghy was coming down the loch towards us. It was four thirty and Lance would be coming home from his workshop to beat the darkness.

We picked up the mooring at the first run in, and the sails were dropped by the time Lance loomed up at the stern of the yacht, his lean face lit up with the reluctant grin which is the nearest he'll ever admit to pleasure.

"Here comes Heckie too," piped up Rebecca again and another long wooden dinghy slid towards us out of the night, this time with Mona, his faithful sheepdog, perched high on the bow for a figurehead. It was grand to see them come and meet us like this.

Soon we were ashore and Rebecca was hugging Ada, her schoolmistress; we puffed up the hill and found the stove lit and the kitchen freshly painted for a surprise. Then it was along through the wood to the blue house for hot mince-pies fresh from the oven and plenty of tea.

After a while, Lance got up from his chair at the end of the kitchen table by the warm peat stove and went off into the other room to his store-cupboard. We heard the clink of bottles and that was it—it was all a memory.

We were into the home-made beer again.

Appendix

English Rose V

MY AIM was to buy a new boat for the John Ridgway School of Adventure, which could also be used as a floating home on expeditions further afield. The budget was about £15,000—raised mainly by the sale of our previous home in Farnham, Surrey.

I wanted the boat to be heavy displacement with a fin keel, and capable of operating in all weathers at any time of the year and in any part of the world. I decided on a specially built production fibre glass boat which had been in production for a sufficient number of years to be clear of the teething troubles usually encountered in 'one-off' boats.

All things considered, the MK X NICHOLSON 32 appeared to be the boat for me.

Listed below is a modified standard specification for the boat supplied by Camper and Nicholsons Ltd. Also listed are the modifications built into the hull by Halmatic Ltd., and the modifications made to the fit-out done by Camper and Nicholsons Ltd. Finally, I have added some extras either bought separately or transferred from *English Rose IV*, which is laid up ashore during the winter.

I might add that the boat is all I had ever hoped she might be.

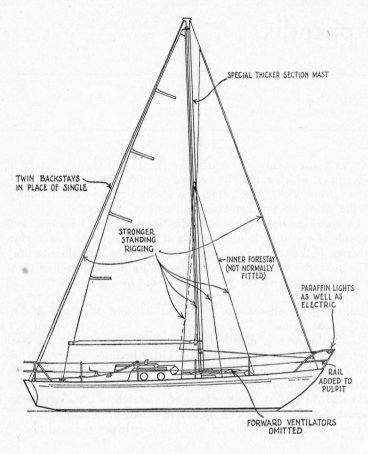

SPECIAL THICKER SECTION MAST

TWIN BACKSTAYS
IN PLACE OF SINGLE

STRONGER
STANDING
RIGGING

INNER FORESTAY
(NOT NORMALLY
FITTED)

PARAFFIN LIGHTS
AS WELL AS
ELECTRIC

RAIL
ADDED TO
PULPIT

FORWARD VENTILATORS
OMITTED

ENGLISH ROSE V: Profile

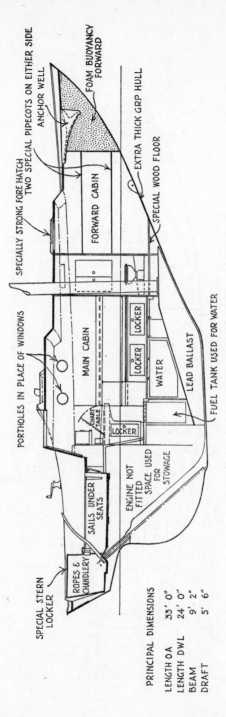

SPECIALLY STRONG FORE HATCH
TWO SPECIAL PIPECOTS ON EITHER SIDE
ANCHOR WELL

FOAM BUOYANCY FORWARD

EXTRA THICK GRP HULL

SPECIAL WOOD FLOOR

FORWARD CABIN

PORTHOLES IN PLACE OF WINDOWS

MAIN CABIN

LOCKER

LOCKER

WATER

LEAD BALLAST

FUEL TANK USED FOR WATER

CHART TABLE

LOCKER

ENGINE NOT FITTED
SPACE USED FOR STOWAGE

SAILS UNDER SEATS

SPECIAL STERN LOCKER

ROPES & CHANDLERY

PRINCIPAL DIMENSIONS

LENGTH OA	33' 0"
LENGTH DWL	24' 0"
BEAM	9' 2"
DRAFT	5' 6"

ENGLISH ROSE V: General arrangement

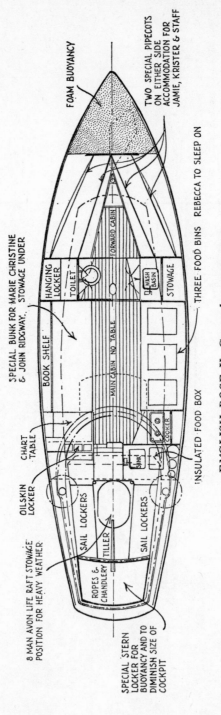

FOAM BUOYANCY

TWO SPECIAL PIPECOTS
ON EITHER SIDE
ACCOMMODATION FOR
JAMIE, KRISTER & STAFF

REBECCA TO SLEEP ON

SPECIAL BUNK FOR MARIE CHRISTINE
& JOHN RIDGWAY. STOWAGE UNDER

HANGING
LOCKER

TOILET

FORWARD CABIN

BOOK SHELF

WASH
BASIN

STOWAGE

MAIN CABIN NO TABLE

THREE FOOD BINS

CHART
TABLE

OILSKIN
LOCKER

COOKER

SINK

INSULATED FOOD BOX

SAIL LOCKERS

TILLER

SAIL LOCKERS

8 MAN AVON LIFE RAFT STOWAGE
POSITION FOR HEAVY WEATHER

ROPES &
CHANDLERY

SPECIAL STERN
LOCKER FOR
BUOYANCY AND TO
DIMINISH SIZE OF
COCKPIT

ENGLISH ROSE V: General arrangement

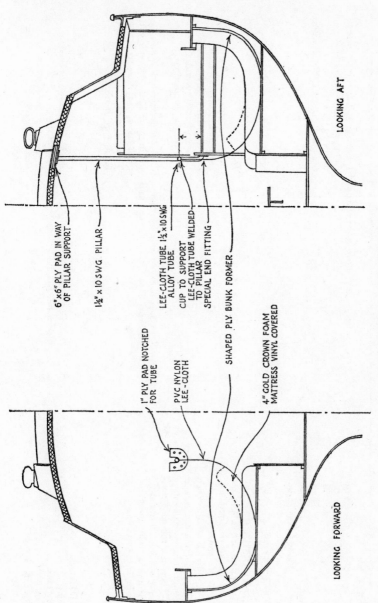

6"×6" PLY PAD IN WAY OF PILLAR SUPPORT

1½"×10 SWG PILLAR

LEE-CLOTH TUBE 1½"×10 SWG ALLOY TUBE

CUP TO SUPPORT LEE-CLOTH TUBE WELDED TO PILLAR

SPECIAL END FITTING

SHAPED PLY BUNK FORMER

4" GOLD CROWN FOAM MATTRESS VINYL COVERED

1" PLY PAD NOTCHED FOR TUBE

PVC NYLON LEE-CLOTH

LOOKING AFT

LOOKING FORWARD

Special bunk in main cabin

NICHOLSON 32 MK 10 SPECIFICATION	MODIFICATIONS	CAMPER & NICHOLSON LTD. —MODIFICATIONS	HALMATIC LTD. —MODIFICATIONS
DIMENSIONS		Fit out to the following standard:	Halmatic to provide the boat to Camper & Nicholson to the following standard: Standard P.A. modified as under:
LOA 33′ 0″ 10.05 m			
LWL 24′ 0″ 7.31 m			
Beam 9′ 3″ 2.81 m			
Draft 5′ 6″ 1.68 m			
Displacement 6.1 Tons 6,200 Kgs.			
Sail Area 594 sq.ft. 55 sq.m.			*Hull*
Thames			(a) 2 oz. extra mat all over.
Measurement 10 Tons			(b) ½ inch closed cell foam covered with 2 × 2 oz. mat, between frames station 2 forward (ice protection).
1. HULL AND DECK			
Both hull and deck are G.R.P. mouldings to Lloyds requirements. A cast lead keel of approximately 3 tons (3,000 kilos) is totally encapsulated. Coachroof, main deck and cockpit sole are of sandwich construction. There is a moulded non-skid deck surface. Four internally moulded scuppers are included to prevent staining of topsides.		*Deck* Special saloon sole, marine ply deck, with access to tanks, and bilge.	*Deck* Transverse deck beam mating with hull transverse with good knees, at station 1.5. Transverse deck beam at station 6.5 at core depth.
STANDARD GRP MOULDINGS		*Rudder* Standard anode, wire to rudder headstack.	*Rudder* Spare head bearing. Special (larger) pintle tail bearing and housing. *Beaching legs* Sockets and bolts fitted.
1. Rudder			
2. Water tank			
3. Engine beds			
4. Cockpit sole hatch			
5. Mast step			

NICHOLSON 32 MK 10 SPECIFICATION	MODIFICATIONS	CAMPER & NICHOLSON LTD. —MODIFICATIONS	HALMATIC LTD.— MODIFICATIONS
6. Cable clench			
7. Toilet compartment			
8. Saloon hatch and cover			
9. Anchor hatch			*Anchor hatch* Special attention to drain spigot, reinforced hose connection, hatch hinged on starboard outboard edge, with one budget lock.
10. Ventilators 2			
11. Battery Box			
12. Ice Box			

2. DECK FITTINGS

a. STEMHEAD FITTING
Fabricated stainless steel electro-polished with tufnol roller.

b. FAIRLEADS
Four—two forward, two aft.

c. MOORING CLEATS
Four—two forward, two aft. 10"

d. MOORING BOLLARD
One on foredeck.

e. RAIL CAPPING
Oiled teak, scarfed and dowelled.

f. HANDRAIL
Oiled teak, through bolted.

g. ANCHOR STOWAGE
Drained well with flush hatch fitted in foredeck.

h. FOREHATCH
Canpa type with Plexiglass top in cast alloy frame. Handles above and below allow the hatch to be opened from on deck.

Standard deck equipment except:
Stemhead fittings Special attention to stemhead bolting.

Forehatch Canpa forehatch specially provided by Camper & Nicholson with thicker perspex and with stainless steel bolts in lieu of standard hinge pins.

i. **MAST APERTURE** Rubber wedging and neoprene mast coat fitted.

j. **PULPITS** 16g. s.s. double rail aft, single rail forward.

k. **CHAINPLATES** Stainless steel 'A' type through stainless steel trunnion bars in GRP webs.

l. **STANCHIONS** 16g. s.s. with nylon ferrules. Sockets polished alloy, through bolted.

m. **GENOA TRACKS** Tee section aluminium alloy with chrome plated sheet sliders.

n. **MAINSHEET TRACK** X section with roller slider and adjustable stops.

o. **SHEET CLEATS** Polished alloy—4 fitted on coamings, one on mainsheet beam. 8"

p. **GENOA WINCHES** 2-speed Lewmar.

q. **TILLER** Laminated ash and mahogany with bronze head fitting allowing tiller to hinge up.

r. **FUEL FILLER** Flush fitting on sidedeck.

Mast aperture Special, thicker section mast.

Pulpits Special double rail pulpit, special bolting.

Chainplates Special chainplates for double backstay.

Stanchions Stanchion bases Lewmar stainless steel.

Mainsheet Mainsheet beam and track deleted. 2 quarter eye plates substituted.

Mast aperture Enlarged to suit special spar section.

NICHOLSON 32 MK 10 SPECIFICATION	MODIFICATIONS	CAMPER & NICHOLSON LTD. – MODIFICATIONS	HALMATIC LTD. – MODIFICATIONS
s. VENTILATION Two water box ventilators fitted for forward cabin and toilet and two cowl water box ventilators fitted over the saloon.			*Ventilation* Ventilators toilet and fo'c'sle omitted.
t. COMPASS Sestrel Minor with black card, 5° markings fitted on bracket on bridge deck with stowage when not in use in heads compartment.			
u. COCKPIT LOCKERS Two large lockers, port and starboard give ample room for sail stowage, and a third locker aft gives stowage for a 4-man liferaft.	8-man Avon liferaft carried in cockpit.		
v. WINDOWS Six windows are fitted in GRP rebates and retained by anodized alloy frames.	Only two fitted.	*Windows* Provide for 6" bronze G.P. circular opening ports with dead-lights, fitted port and starboard sides of coachroof.	*Windows* Mould only toilet window apertures.
3. ACCOMMODATION **a. GENERAL** All joinery is selected hand-rubbed oiled teak and all visible surfaces are lined with washable vinyls. The cabin sole is of teak plydeck. All berths have lee-boards. Teak handrails are fitted to the carlings in the saloon and		Standard for furniture supplied (oiled teak). *Internal handrails* Lifeboat pattern $1\frac{3}{4} \times 1\frac{1}{4}''$ circular grip at deckhead locations, through bolted from on-deck rails, aft only.	

forward cabin port and starboard. All locker doors are flush and have finger rings and internal catches. There is a lockable drinks locker beneath the chart table.			
b. FORWARD CABIN Berths are fitted port and starboard with hinged locker doors below and folding leeboards which stow under the berth cushions. A chain locker and pipe are fitted on the centreline, and a window is fitted at the forward end of the coach roof. Steps up the bulkhead are fitted for easy access to the foredeck through the Canpa forehatch in the deckhead.	Left empty. Fitted our own 4 pipe cots.	*Berths* Special berth to port — forward of chart table with tube-supported leecloth, lockers under, none above. See drawing.	*Forepeak* Watertight bulkhead with area forward station I foam filled.
c. TOILET COMPARTMENT A Blake Lavac W.C. is fitted together with a wash basin and hand freshwater pump. An enlarged clothes locker is fitted outboard of the W.C. and on the starboard side above the basin, sliding mirror doors conceal another cupboard. A paper holder is fitted.	Fitted Baby Blake.	*Toilet* Standard toilet furniture except bulkhead doors. (a) Special forward toilet/fo'c'sle, 'submarine' type watertight door. (b) Submarine aperture only in toilet/saloon bulkhead – no door.	*Bulkhead* Toilet and forepeak right across hull ¾" thickness.
d. SALOON The dinette arrangement on the port-side converts to two single or one double berth, with stowage	Completely different.	*Saloon* Special saloon sole marine ply deck with access to tanks, bilge.	*Beamshelf* 2 oz. extra mat laminating deck to hull and additional 2 oz. extra mat on

NICHOLSON 32 MK 10 SPECIFICATION	MODIFICATIONS	CAMPER & NICHOLSON LTD. —MODIFICATIONS	HALMATIC LTD.— MODIFICATIONS
underneath in two lockers for equipment, stores, etc. On the starboard side a settee berth is fitted with three lockers below, and three lockers above. The cabin table is of teak with two teak melamine surface-hinged leaves.		*Finish* Linings to saloon only, starboard side to window rail, nothing below. *Insulation* of topsides in saloon — ½″ foam covered with 2 × 2 oz. mat from waterline to sheer stations 3.5 to 7.	beamshelf where fitted aft.
e. NAVIGATOR'S SPACE An athwartships chart table is fitted so that the navigator may sit on the port settee and yet have his bookshelf and any navigational instruments within easy reach on the bulkhead aft of it. Chart stowage is fitted beneath the hinged top with two more lockers under this again.		Standard chart table assembly.	
f. THE GALLEY The galley on the starboard side has formica working surfaces, an icebox and a 2-burner Camping Gaz cooker with fiddles fitted in gimbals. A freshwater pump is fitted as standard to the stainless steel sink. Plate and mug stowages are provided and there is ample stowage for food, pans, etc., in lockers over, under and beside the cooker. A large cutlery drawer is fitted under the sideboard forward of the cooker.		Standard galley. *Water supply* and drain with seacock to be provided for galley sink only.	

g. OILSKIN LOCKER
Immediately inside the hatch on the port side, fitted with six hooks.

Standard oilskin locker.

4. PLUMBING
a. FRESH WATER
A GRP tank of approximately 40 gallons under the cabin sole provides fresh water through two feed lines, one to the galley and one to the toilet basins. The tank is filled through a Henderson cover beneath the cabin sole.

Galley only.

Watertank Additional overlamination to ensure it does not come adrift with boat overturned.

b. BILGE
Henderson bilge pump is fitted in the port cockpit locker and discharges through a valve in the yacht's side.

Bilge Standard bilge system but discharge at deck (i.e. just under beamshelf).

c. WATER CLOSET
A Blake Lavac with Blake inlet cock and gate valve outlet is fitted.

Baby Blake fitted.

d. DRAINS
Sink and washbasin both gravity drain via gate valves and there are also drains fitted to the anchor well and icebox.

e. COCKPIT DRAINS
4 cockpit drains are fitted leading to two gate valves.

Two only, fitted in the smaller cockpit.

Cockpit drains Two forward only, to standard seacocks.

NICHOLSON 32 MK 10 SPECIFICATION	MODIFICATIONS	CAMPER & NICHOLSON LTD. —MODIFICATIONS	HALMATIC LTD.— MODIFICATIONS
5. ENGINE INSTALLATION a. A Watermota 4 cylinder Seawolf 29 h.p. petrol engine with 2:1 reduction and reverse gear box is fitted as standard. A Watermota Sea Panther diesel may be fitted at extra cost. All engines have electric starting.	No motor.	Standard engine enclosure and step array.	*Engine hatch* Aperture not moulded. Hatch bonded into rebate.
b. STERN GEAR A 14″ diameter two-bladed propeller is driven by a 1″ diameter manganese bronze shaft. The stern tube is fitted with a white metal bearing outboard and greased gland inboard.	No motor.		
c. EXHAUST SYSTEM Lagged flexible section to Parsons mixer then water-cooled reinforced rubber hose to transom exhaust valve.			
d. FUEL SYSTEM A 15 gallon aluminium alloy fuel tank is filled via deck filler. A calibrated dipstick is supplied. A vent pipe is fitted leading to a swan neck within the cockpit coaming moulding—vented overside. A sediment bowl filter is fitted in the feed line with a small filter at the fuel lift pump.	Used for fresh water. Not fitted.		*Fuel tank* Reinforced installation to ensure retention if boat is inverted.

e. **CONTROLS AND INSTRUMENTS**
A Morse two-lever control for
throttle and gear is fitted and
instruments include ammeter,
warning light and starter switch,
fitted behind hinged perspex
panel at forward end of cockpit.

Not fitted.

6. ELECTRICAL

a. Power is supplied by one 102
amp/hr 12 volt battery, and
provision is made for a second
battery and isolating switch if
required.

Two fitted.
Oil lamps also
fitted.

Electrical system:
Second 12v × 108 amp battery.
Standard Services, i.e. lights,
   booms for 24 volt operation.
   No power generation
   circuitry.
Special bi-colour P.S. light on
   pulpit.

Battery box Fitted with retaining
bars to prevent battery
movement.

b. The engine is fitted with a
40 amp alternator which feeds
the battery through voltage
control equipment.

Not fitted — used
Honda generator.

c. The following lights are fitted as
standard.

1. Saloon deckhead

Oil lamp in main
cabin as reserve.

2. Toilet deckhead
3. Galley deckhead
4. Chart table light
5. Forward cabin bulkheads — two
6. Port and Starboard navigation
7. Stern light
8. Steaming light
9. Compass light with watertight
plug and socket in cockpit.

NICHOLSON 32 MK 10 SPECIFICATION	MODIFICATIONS	CAMPER & NICHOLSON LTD.—MODIFICATIONS	HALMATIC LTD.—MODIFICATIONS
7. MAST AND BOOM Gold anodised mast and boom by Proctor or Sparlight in aluminium alloy, sound deadened and tapered. Track fitted for spinnaker pole. Lewmar type winches for jib and main halliards with handles. Main boom is fitted with enclosed roller reefing gear and an internal clew outhaul. A boom vang eye is fitted as standard on the underside of the boom.		Special larger section mast.	
8. STANDARD RIGGING All standing rigging is in 1 × 19 s.s. wire. Rigging screws and toggles are in stainless steel, locked, and fitted with P.V.C. boots. Cap shrouds and forward lowers are fitted with nylon rollers, and spreader ends have Canpa sail savers to prevent wear on genoa leach.		stronger s.s. wire.	
9. GUARDRAILS Both upper and lower in 1 × 19 s.s. wire with fork ends forward and rigging screws aft. Nylon chafing tubes for mainsheet are fitted.			
10. RUNNING RIGGING Terylene main halliard with key shackle.			

Genoa halliard is wire with a terylene tail and snapshackle. Topping lift in terylene 'D' shackle to boom. Mainsail tack tackle, three part terylene with 2 blocks. Jib track strop s.s. wire with 2 snapshackles. Mainsheet and jib sheets in blue banded superbraid terylene. Burgee halliard terylene. Tiller lashings terylene. 2 halliard elastics.

11. SAILS

By Ratsey & Lapthorn, Cowes.

a. Mainsail 8 oz. Vectis with nylon slides, sail battens and sail bag.

b. Working jib 8 oz. Vectic complete with hanks and sail bag.

c. Mainsail cover—white PVC nylon with hooks and elastic lacings.

Also carried:

a. Spinnaker

b. No. 1 & No. 2 Genoas

c. No. 2 Jib

d. Storm & Spitfire Jibs

e. Trisail

12. PAINTING

a. All teak on deck and below teak oiled.

b. Cabin sole plydeck Bournesealed.

c. Caveta line in gold tape.

d. Antifouling Hard Racing Red.

e. Boot top or style line at extra cost.

Not done.

Finish Standard antifoul (red) taken up to transom aft.

NICHOLSON 32 MK 10 SPECIFICATION	MODIFICATIONS	CAMPER & NICHOLSON LTD.—MODIFICATIONS	HALMATIC LTD.—MODIFICATIONS
13. LOOSE EQUIPMENT			
1 Boathook	Various spare items carried.		
4 Fenders with lanyards			
1 35 lb. CQR anchor			
15 fathoms $\frac{5}{16}''$ chain			
20 fathom $1\frac{3}{4}''$ terylene warp			
2 8 fathom $1\frac{1}{2}''$ terylene warps			
1 Lewmar halliard winch handle			
1 length rubber wedging for mast			
1 butyl rubber mast coat			
1 cabin padlock			
1 forehatch padlock			
1 type 904 Camping Gaz bottle and standard stove			
One complete set of upholstery comprising two cushions forward, two large settee cushions in saloon, two small settee cushions in saloon and two backrest cushions in saloon.	Not fitted.		
1 battery isolating key			
1 ensign staff			
1 roll lavatory paper			
1 Lewmar ratchet handle			
1 Lewmar fixed handle			
1 roller reefing handle			
1 engine starter key and handle			
1 bilge pump handle and one toilet pump handle			
1 set standard sails and cover			
1 set paperwork			

SAILS BY RATSEY & LAPTHORN LTD., MADE FOR
'ENGLISH ROSE V'

a. Mainsail (Three reefs)
b. No. 1 Genoa
c. No. 2 Genoa
d. No. 1 Jib
e. No. 2 Jib
f. Storm Jib
g. Spinnaker

Sails from *English Rose IV*
also Ratsey & Lapthorn Ltd.
1. Spitfire Jib
2. Trisail

EXTRAS CARRIED ON VOYAGE:

a. Handybilly
b. Deck floodlight
c. Brookes & Gatehouse Ltd.
   (1) Homer radio receiver
   (2) Homer short wave converter
   (3) Heron radio direction finder
d. Callbuoy emergency transmitter
e. Fire extinguisher (dry powder) and asbestos blanket
f. Harness lifelines port and starboard and in cockpit
g. 17 steps on main mast
h. Spare Lewmar tracksliders
i. Spare winch handles
j. Hasler self-steering gear
k. Storm boards in three pieces, bottom two perspex, top two teak.
l. Food stowage lockers on starboard side of saloon with three compartments, each having a hinged lid, locker top fitted with 4" fiddle in teak-faced ply, oiled on outside and inside coated with anti-mildew emulsion white paint.
m. After end of cockpit blanked off to top of coaming, and forward to mainsheet track beam, watertight hatch in top in marine ply, polyurethane painted to match deck
n. Heavy section booming out pole (chocked on deck)
o. Twin backstays
p. Inner forestay
q. Walker log.
r. Honda generator
s. Sprayhood
t. Sidescreens (dodgers)

u. Camping Gaz cooker—perfectly adequate
v. Avon Redseal dinghy
w. Seagull silver century
x. Avon 8 main liferaft (in cockpit in bad weather)